THE COMPLETE MANUSCRIPT PREPARATION STYLE GUIDE

CAROLYN J. MULLINS

A SPECTRUM BOOK

Prentice-Hall, Inc., Englewood Cliffs, New Jersey 07632

Library of Congress Cataloging in Publication Data

Mullins, Carolyn J.
   The complete manuscript preparation style guide.

   "A Spectrum Book."
   Bibliography: p.
   Includes index.
    1. Manuscript preparation (Authorship)
2. Authorship—Style manuals.   3. Typewriting.
I. Title.
PN160.M8   808'.02   82-517
ISBN 0-13-162180-7   AACR2
ISBN 0-13-162172-6 (pbk.)

This Spectrum Book is available to businesses and organizations at a special discount when ordered in large quantities. For information, contact Prentice-Hall, Inc., General Publishing Division, Special Sales, Englewood Cliffs, N.J. 07632.

1   2   3   4   5   6   7   8   9   10

Editorial/production supervision by Kimberly Mazur
Cover design by Jeannette Jacobs
Manufacturing buyer: Barbara A. Frick

Permission to reprint the following is gratefully acknowledged:
Robert B. Chickering and Susan Hartman, *How To Register a Copyright and Protect Your Creative Work.* Copyright © Robert B. Chickering and Susan Hartman (New York: Charles Scribner's Sons, 1980). Adapted with the permission of Charles Scribner's Sons.

ISBN 0-13-162180-7
ISBN 0-13-162172-6 {PBK.}

Prentice-Hall International, Inc., *London*
Prentice-Hall of Australia Pty. Limited, *Sydney*
Prentice-Hall Canada Inc., *Toronto*
Prentice-Hall of India Private Limited, *New Delhi*
Prentice-Hall of Japan, Inc., *Tokyo*
Prentice-Hall of Southeast Asia Pte. Ltd., *Singapore*
Whitehall Books Limited, *Wellington, New Zealand*

For Joyce, who made it possible,

For Peg, who made it better,

and

For Jill, who gave it meaning.

Contents

LIST OF TABLES AND ILLUSTRATIONS

Preface

This book presents the first complete collection ever of information and examples of all major manuscript preparation styles. Here you have systematic information on all the major styles and examples of typed pages that show headings, titles, figures, tables, lists of references, and all other manuscript features that differ from style to style. In some cases you have more information than a style sheet gives because publishers have responded to my questions about ambiguities.

You have systematic style sheets and sample manuscripts that show the requirements of major styles. You have tips on how to handle minor styles, including a blank form for analyzing style requirements, and a summary of copyright and permission requirements. For free-lance typists, one chapter contains business tips. Throughout the book are pointers to show how word processing automates typing.

Writers, editors, and typists will benefit from the lack of clutter on shelves. With few exceptions, no longer will you need a different book, booklet, or sheet for each style. This book has it all--sample text pages, title pages, tables, illustrations, reference lists, bibliographies, headings, subheadings, equations, and formats for books, articles, plays, poems, greeting cards, and instructions. You also get a Greek alphabet (for technical typing) and summaries of rules for use of capital letters, hyphenation, punctuation, and numbers--details omitted from many style sheets. To help you find information quickly, cross-references are to numbered paragraphs, and each chapter begins with a two-level outline of the chapter's contents.

Teachers and students, who use a variety of styles throughout their careers--you will benefit from having the needed variety of styles on hand all the time in the same resource. Indeed, Part II was planned especially for you.

Business organizations and research institutes will also benefit from Part II, which shows a variety of ways to format data and text. Simply choose the model that best suits your situation.

Everyone will benefit, too, from practical demonstrations of how word processing takes the hassle out of typing. You get more than general explanations. When you see **WP advantage,** you'll know that what follows is a simple explanation of how word processing solves a common typing problem.

This book is unique in covering all major styles. It is unique in tying word processing and photocomposition to all aspects of manuscript preparation. It is also unique in tying these features to business tips that will help free-lance typists run more efficient, more profitable businesses.

This book's purpose is to make writing, editing, and typing time more productive and more profitable. Toward that end it contains information on styles in easy-to-use form and integrates that information with tips on the use of word processing.

Several organizations helped in the preparation of this book. The American Sociological Association gave permission for me to reproduce portions of their style guidelines in Chapter 8. The Writer, Inc. gave permission for the use in Chapter 4 of summaries based on information in Udia G. Olsen's <u>Preparing the Manuscript,</u> 9th edition, copyright (c) 1978. The University of Chicago Press gave permission for the use in Chapter 7 of summaries based on Kate L. Turabian's <u>A Manual for Writers of Term Papers, Theses and Dissertations,</u> 4th edition, copyright (c) 1973. Charles Scribner's Sons gave permission for use in Chapter 9 of summaries based on Robert B. Chickering and Susan Hartman, <u>How to Register a Copyright and Protect Your Creative Work,</u> copyright (c) 1980. All organizations were asked to comment on my style sheets and sample manuscripts to ensure accuracy. For helpful responses I want especially to cially to thank Rosemary Horstman, Managing Editor, Technical Journals, American Society for Testing and Materials; Ellen E. Swanson, Director, Editorial Services, American Mathematical Society; Marianne Brogan, Associate Head, Books and Journals Division, Journals Department, American Chemical Society; and Ann I. Mahoney, Managing Editor, APA Publications, American Psychological Association.

For helpful criticism I want to thank Peg Clarke, Irene Abaganale, Betty Horton, and Amy Jackson, all present or past administrative officers of different schools within the Institute for Advanced Studies, Princeton, N. J.; Elizabeth Fink, Assistant Director of the Institute for Social Research, University of North Carolina, whose typists tested an early draft of the manuscript; Beverly Clinkingbeard, who suggested the form in Figure 2.1 and also offered other ideas; and Sue Hall, former Administrative Secretary of the Institute of Social Research, Indiana University. Joyce Swango's loving care of my children gave me the time to write.

I welcome comments on usability and suggestions for revision. Write to me in care of Prentice-Hall, Inc.

Carolyn J. Mullins

Bloomington, Indiana

chapter 1

Introduction
and
Basic Principles

1.1 Manuscript preparation style, also known as "editorial style," refers to rules for mechanical details such as spacing lines; typing title pages, tables of contents, references, citations, and headings; and presenting tables, equations, and illustrations. The following list shows the most common styles and the abbreviations used in this book. Complete information on each style is in documents listed in the bibliography. The documents are coded with the bracketed number listed with each style.

American Chemical Society [1]   AChemS
American Institute of Physics [9]   AIP
American Mathematical Society [2]   AMathS
American Medical Association [3]   AMA
American Psychological Association [4]   APA

American Society for Testing and Materials [5]   ASTM
American Sociological Association [6]   ASA
Council of Biology Editors [7]   CBE
American Institute of Industrial Engineers [8]   AIIE
Manual of Style, Humanities [13]   MSH

Manual of Style, Natural Science [13]   MSN
Modern Language Association [10]   MLA
Turabian [11]   Turabian
U. S. Government Printing Office [12]   GPO

Three minor styles frequently mentioned are:

Journal of the American Statistical Association   JASA
Sage journal style   Sage
Suggestions to Authors   SA

1.2 In addition to these styles are several styles for specialized text forms such as plays, television scripts, poems, greeting card verse, and instructions in manuals. Some magazines and journals routinely print style sheets in each issue, often inside the front or back cover or on the back cover, and book publishers routinely give their authors a copy of the house style guide, usually at the time a book contract is signed. Many magazines and organizations write their own style guides and supply them on request, often for a small fee. When you request a style guide:

** Send a stamped, self-addressed large manila envelope (hereafter called SASE). Even when the guide is free, many magazines won't supply the guidelines unless you supply the envelope and postage.

1.3 One apparent omission may puzzle some readers. Some publishers follow the requirements of guides such as The New York Times Manual of Style and Usage, which is one of several whose purpose is to "assure consistency of spelling, capitalization, punctuation and abbreviation in printing the written word" and "safeguard the language from debasement."[1] These books contain no rules for matters of editorial style and format, the main topic of this book, so I have excluded them. However, the bibliography lists several of these books as reference works. For the same reason, and to prevent excessive bulk, Chapter 3 lists only the most common rules of capitalization and punctuation, and Chapters 6 through 9 do not contain the vocabulary lists that a few style books provide. Lists of abbreviations of journal names are also omitted.

1.4 To learn stylistic details most efficiently:

** Get your own copy of a style guide when you receive your first manuscript that must follow it. When the style is a major one, you'll find a typing guide in this book.

** Use the typing job to learn the details of the style.

1.5 Although many styles are similar and each style has many versions, until now no one has written a detailed guide to manuscript preparation for typists, writers, and editors. Most existing guides are little more than brief asides in sheets, pamphlets, and books addressed solely to writers. One exception: the APA's Publication Manual, which devotes Chapter 4 to typing rules.[2]

1.6   To make matters worse, most writers are inconsistent in their treatment of headings, subheadings, documentation, tables, and other details. Typists of technical documents, especially those for publication in scholarly journals or as scholarly books, must follow exceptionally detailed guidelines. Yet many typists, especially free-lancers, rarely use the same style for every manuscript, and across all styles only a few rules are universal. For all other aspects of typing each manuscript, every typist must eventually answer many specific questions about typing style.

BASIC PRINCIPLES

1.7   Ideally, all styles and "formats" (page layout) and writers' use of them should conform to four general principles that can be summarized as:

** Emphasis.

** Simplicity.

** Consistency.

** Distinctiveness.

For example, the leading asterisks and listed display above emphasize the four principles by making them stand out more than anything else in Section 1.7. Simplicity requires choosing the simplest option. Therefore, I didn't boldface or underline the items in the list. Neither would have made the principles any more obvious than they already were. Consistency requires identical treatment for identical texts. Therefore, I always use asterisks before displayed items; I don't use, say, asterisks one time, plus signs a second, and dashes on yet a third time. Distinctiveness means making sure readers won't confuse one feature of style with another. For instance, if an article style required capital letters for both the title and major (first-level) headings, capitalized typing at the top of a page wouldn't automatically signal whether it made up a title or a heading. Carefully planned styles avoid such confusion.

1.8   For manuscript typists the important rule is: following these principles of style and format enhances readability. Writers who want more detailed information on these principles will find it in Sections 11.19 through 11.33 in Mullins's <u>The Complete Writing Guide</u>.[3]

A ROADMAP THROUGH THE BOOK

1.9   This guide is addressed to typists, editors, and writers, including teachers and students everywhere. For every part of a manuscript this manual:

** Tells what rules are universal.

** Points out potential traps and ways to avoid getting caught in them.

** Lists the most common solutions to common problems.

** Gives typed examples that show exactly where to type each character and how many spaces to leave above, below, and between characters.

** Recommends procedures to follow in the absence of specific style requirements.

** Tells how word processing can make tasks easier.

Throughout the book, the code **"WP Advantage:"** points out features and techniques of word processing that make typing easier.

1.10   Readers who are using a major style will probably want to skim the chapters, paying special attention to Chapters 2 and 3, and then concentrate their attention on one or more of the sample manuscripts and style descriptions in Chapters 6 through 8. For users of a minor style, which are too numerous to include even in a large book, I suggest the following procedure:

** Read Chapters 2-5 to find out which details to watch for.

** Fill in a copy of Form 2.1 as completely as possible.

** Compare that form with the forms for major styles (Appendix A) until you find the style whose specifications are most like those on your form.

** Find the sample manuscript for that style and use it as a typing guide.

** Save the form for future use.

** Whatever your special area or type of document, add your voice to the many others that plead for less diversity in the mechanical aspects of style.[4]

Good reasons exist for at least three major forms of documentation--author (date), sometimes called "Harvard style"; ordinary footnotes (or endnotes); and citation by document number. Specialized systems, such as that for legal documents, also can be justified. But I have never been able to justify the more than 40 identifiably, though microscopically, different forms of author (date) citation in, for instance, the social science field alone. Possibly it's so editors can quickly spot manuscripts previously rejected by competitors?

1.11   As if the variety weren't bad enough, styles change frequently, sometimes with a change of editors or deans. However, this book provides all the basic models to help you cope with the changes.

1.12   Chapter 2 discusses the basic tools of manuscript typing, tells how to use and care for them, and provides a basic form for recording details of style. Chapter 3 describes the basic rules for typing ordinary text, while Chapter 4 describes the rules for typing specialized text such as script forms, poetry, and instructions in manuals. Chapter 5, which many typists and writers will never need, explains the basic rules for typing documentation, notes, tables, illustrations, and "front and back matter" (respectively, everything that comes before the main text and everything that comes after it). Chapters 6 through 8, primarily focused on scholarly and other technical manuscripts, summarize style rules and show sample manuscripts in different styles, pointing out some of the differences and omissions in instructions. Chapter 9 describes details of copyright law and permission requirements, and Chapter 10 tells how to wrap and mail manuscripts. Chapter 11, especially for free-lance typists, contains business tips on typing rates, record keeping, and relations with clients. Appendix A contains a completed copy of the form for each major style.

A WORD ABOUT THIS BOOK

1.13   With few exceptions, this book, prepared from word-processed copy, follows the requirement of <u>A Manual of Style</u>,[5] which is the most nearly universal style for books. The chapter notes are in the <u>Manual</u>'s humanities style (MSH) while the bibliography is in natural science style (MSN). Exceptions to the style are the printed portions such as the title page and the chapter openings, the depth from top of page to chapter openings (which the <u>Manual</u> requires to be at least three inches), the extra horizontal spacing and boldface on headings, the placement of page numbers after the running head (instead of flush with the right margin as the <u>Manual</u> requires), and the use of space-and-a-half and single-spacing instead of double-spacing for the main text. The reason for the lack of double-spacing is the need to conserve space on the printed page. The reason for the spacing and boldface on headings is to make them stand out on typed pages. One additional exception is the documentation in Chapter 8, which is done in MSN style.

1.14   In Chapters 6 through 8, some style guidelines use technical terms (such as "determinant" in AMathS style) that will be unfamiliar to readers whose work is not in that field. For the most part, these terms are not defined because they are not needed to explain the style requirements. Defining them would only lengthen the manuscript to no purpose.

1.15   The three-hole punch in the paperback edition is for the convenience of readers who break the binding to make the pages lie flat on a desk and who therefore need to store the pages in a notebook to keep them together.

NOTES TO CHAPTER 1

1. Lewis Jordan, ed., <u>The New York Times Manual of Style and Usage</u>, Rev. ed. (New York: Times Books, 1976), p. vii.

2. American Psychological Association, <u>Publication Manual of the American Psychological Association</u>, 2d ed. (Washington, D. C.: American Psychological Association, 1974).

3. Carolyn J. Mullins, <u>The Complete Writing Guide to Preparing Reports, Proposals, Memos, Etc.</u> (Englewood Cliffs, N. J.: Prentice-Hall, 1980).

4. Eugene Garfield, "Style in Cited References," <u>Current Contents</u>, 13 March 1978, p. 7, points out that even the American National Standards Institute, <u>American National Standard for Bibliographic References</u> (New York: American National Standards Institute, 1977) offers two formats!

5. University of Chicago Press, <u>A Manual of Style</u>, 12th ed. (Chicago: University of Chicago Press, 1969).

part I
MANUSCRIPT BASICS

chapter 2

Basic Tools

2.1   Typing requires many tools--style guidelines, paper, correction fluids, pencils, storage media, dictionaries, and so forth. This chapter deals with those tools and explains how to use them efficiently.

GENERAL OFFICE SUPPLIES

2.2   Stock up on pens and pencils (in various colors), erasers, paper clips, note pads, carbon paper, and typing paper. Editorial Experts, Inc.[1] also suggests:

** Rub-on letters and numbers, such as Quik Stik Set #697 (Math Symbols) and Quik Stik Set #694 (Form Preparation Symbols).

** Nonphoto-blue pencils--Col-Erase 1298, for writing on paper that is camera-ready copy.

** Fine-line black ballpoint pen.

** Ultra Fine Flair felt-tip pen for filling bullets.

** OCR (Optical Character Recognition) type element if you type documents to be read by an optical scanner.

** Optional (for locating margins): a backing sheet with margins drawn on it.

** Optional (for making corrections): light table, clear 8 X 6 triangle, X-Acto knife and #11 blades, and drafting tape and white cellophane tape (1/4 and 3/8 inch sizes).

WP Advantage: you'll need the optional equipment only if you frequently type camera-ready final copy and you don't use a word processor.

STYLE GUIDELINES AND STYLE SHEET

2.3   Before you begin typing the next manuscript:

** Get a copy of the most recent guidelines on the style required (recency is important because styles change frequently). Sources of information are in Section 1.1 and the bibliography. Chapters 3 and 6 through 8 contain sample manuscripts.

** Get sample pages--preferably typed, but printed pages will give a general idea of style.

** Read the general instructions in Chapters 2 and 3 and in the style guide. Look through the forms in Appendix A and the sample manuscripts. Then read the first 12 pages of the manuscript and write down any questions you have.

** Get answers before beginning to type. To help keep answers straight, use a style sheet like the one in Figure 2.1, which is at the end of this chapter.   (Some of the abbreviations may make sense only after you have read Chapters 2, 3, and 5.)

Figure 2.1 lists most possible points of style. On no manuscript should you be able to specify all items. Indeed, some, such as chapter vs. article title, are mutually exclusive for the same document.

2.4   As you type, other questions will probably occur to you. Keep a list of questions and answers with the completed manuscript. Sometimes you will find no answers to questions. In such cases:

** Look through the appropriate section of this book for alternatives.

** As a general rule, make the simplest choice. For example, if the choice is to underline or not, don't underline.

** Record the choices on the style sheet.

** Having made a choice, follow it consistently.

2.5   A special word to typists: when style instructions are ambiguous or absent, chances are the writer will be of little help in deciding how to type something. Your knowledge of the basic principles of style will be your best guide in making decisions. In fact, some writers gratefully leave all such decisions to their typists and employ them for their judgment as well as their typing skill. However, because some writers complain about the results any time they haven't been consulted:

** Ask clients whether they want to be consulted and record the answer on the style sheet.

If a writer declines and later proves to be a complainer, note that fact in your records to warn you before you accept his or her next job. The same advice holds for use of editing skill. Many writers are grateful for typists who can correct punctuation and spelling and even reword an occasional awkward sentence. Others want absolutely no changes. Find out in advance what the client wants and keep records for future jobs. Remember that many writers happily pay higher rates for typists with editorial skills.

2.6 When you write comments and questions on a manuscript, make checking easier by using a different color from any other used for handwritten notes. Don't use red. I recommend another color, such as green, because many people associate red with being graded!

TYPING PAPER

Original ("Ribbon") Copy

2.7 Never use an "erasable" bond or other highly glazed paper. The type is easily smudged by readers' and editors' fingers. Instead:

** Use white paper of appropriate quality. Sixteen-pound bond is the minimum acceptable. Of the major styles, <u>JASA</u> and MLA require twenty-pound bond. Turabian requires twenty-pound with 50% rag content. AChemS simply says "heavy duty" paper. For jobs that require camera-ready copy, you'll need photocopy paper with no watermark.

** Check requirements for rag content. The most common requirement is for 25% rag, but Turabian requires 50%. Illustrations, in contrast, must usually be done on paper with no rag content.

** In general, when asked to type on masters, don't use spirit types, such as "ditto." The copies are unacceptable to many publishers.

** Use paper of appropriate size. The American standard is 8 1/2 x 11 inches (22 x 28 centimeters). The British standard is ISO-size A4, 210 x 297 millimeter paper (approximately 8.2 x 11.6 inches).

** Type on only one side of every page.

Nonoriginal Copies

2.8 Many publishers will not accept either carbon or spirit-master copies. Mimeograph, multilith, and xerographic copies are usually acceptable.

TYPEWRITER RIBBON AND PITCH

Rules for All Manuscripts

2.9 On all manuscripts:

** Clean the typeface. Follow the typewriter manufacturer's instructions, or ask a serviceman for instructions.

** Check "pitch", or type spacing, and use the same pitch throughout the manuscript. "Pica" type has 10 spaces/characters per inch. "Elite" has 12. None of the major styles requires one or the other although MSN and MSH express a preference for pica because it is larger.

** Use a type style that has both upper- and lowercase letters. Styles with either all caps or large and small caps are not acceptable. (EXCEPTION: speeches are often typed in large and small caps for easy reading.)

If you use a dual-pitch typewriter, make certain the pitch setting matches the pitch on the typing element. A pica element requires 10-pitch spacing; an elite element requires 12-pitch.

2.10 Pica and elite styles allow the same amount of space for each letter on the element. For instance, a capital "W" and a lowercase "i" will print in the same amount of space, even though the "W" will use most of the space and the "i" will have lots of space between it and the letters on either side. "Proportional type," long available on typewriters such as the IBM Executive, vary the space allowed for each letter, giving more to letters such as "W" and less to an "i" or an "l." Proportional type looks almost printed, but corrections can be very difficult. For instance, without retyping an entire page, how would you correct a typing error that required you to squeeze a "W" into the space allowed for an "i" you typed by mistake?

2.11 **WP Advantages:** most word processors allow typists to choose pitch--pica, elite, or proportional--and to change from one pitch to another without retyping. Thus, a paper that is too long in pica type could be easily changed to elite for a 20 percent savings in length. Furthermore, with typesetting costs rising steadily, and many writers and publishers using proportionally typed copy in place of typeset printing, typists who offer proportional print often gain a substantial advantage over competitors.

Manuscripts Typed on Bond

2.12 For manuscripts typed on bond, use a new black ribbon. Some publishers, such as GPO, require a black carbon ribbon. On camera-ready copy, negotiable instruments, and legal documents, <u>don't</u> use a self-correcting ribbon combination. The reasons, respectively, are:

** The carbon ribbon has some tendency to spatter on the paper.

** The type can be lifted off and changed after the typing has been finished.

2.13   **WP Advantage:** boldface, achieved by overstriking the same character one or more times, emphasizes selected words and phrases and enables special stylistic effects. Although cumbersome on a typewriter because of the constant backspacing involved, many word processors create this effect at the touch of a key or the insertion of a command. Boldface is especially useful on manuscripts to be printed directly from typed copy. One example of boldface is the **"WP Advantage"** that I use to call readers' attention to the special benefits of word processing. Some processors allow choice of emphasis by letting typists decide how many overstrikes they want.

Manuscripts Typed on Masters

2.14   For manuscripts typed on mimeograph stencils:

** Shift the typewriter ribbon out of printing position.

** Clean the typeface. Then put paper in the typewriter and print each key once or twice to be sure you have removed excess ink.

** Set the paper position lever at 1, or A (depending on the brand and model of the typewriter).

** On a selectric typewriter, set the gear on the type ball at 5. Also check the manufacturer's instructions on use of different type styles. Some styles are better suited than others for typing mimeograph stencils.

2.15   For manuscripts typed on multilith offset masters:

** Read the instructions that come with the masters. They may require a special kind of ribbon (usually carbon) and may suggest specific type styles.

** Type with a light or medium pressure. A heavy touch creates hollow images.

** Be very careful not to touch the typing surface. Fingerprints will reproduce along with the type. Simply grasp the master by the extreme edges.

** Charge an additional fee for the xeroxes you'll have to make so the writer can check the work without damaging the masters.

STORAGE MEDIA

2.16   For manuscripts typed on word processors, make sure you have an adequate supply of the storage medium--magnetic cards, cassettes, diskettes, tapes, or whatever. If you type for many different writers, simplify categorization and storage by starting large jobs on a new unit of the medium. You'll have a difficult time organizing if half a diskette contains part of Smith's article and the rest contains two chapters of Jones's report.

2.17   Set up a system that will enable easy retrieval of the storage medium for each job. You'll need boxes, notebooks, or storage wheels, and a master list of the storage units, the contents of each unit, and the contents of each medium. If the processor has a hard disk and centralized catalogue and file maintenance, learn how to name documents sensibly, how to use them, and how to get back old files that have been "purged," or taken off, the system.

CORRECTIONS DURING TYPING

Corrections on Bond

2.18   Errors are easiest to correct when a page is still in the typewriter. If you are typing on paper and don't have a correcting typewriter:

** Use a correction fluid such as Liquid Paper or correction tape.   Tape works well when the original is only to be copied and not mailed out.

** Type the correction as soon as the fluid is dry.

The fluid comes in white and several pastel colors such as cream, yellow, pink, and blue. When properly applied, the fluid dries quickly, completely covers errors, and is invisible. Also, the fluid does not damage the surface of the paper as erasing often does. Keep the fluid thin for best results. More elaborate correction techniques are described in Sections 2.27-2.29.

Corrections on Masters

2.19   When correcting mimeograph stencils:

** Rub gently over the error with a paper clip.

** Paint a very small amount of correction fluid on top.

** Then type the correct letters or words.

This technique minimizes the waxy build-up that can cause blurred corrections.

2.20   On multilith masters, read the instructions first. In general:

** Use a multilith or other smooth, nonoily eraser.

** Erase gently so as not to damage the surface of the plate.

** Type the correct character with a normal touch.

** Clean the eraser frequently.

Word-Processing Corrections

2.21   On word processing equipment that records on disk or tape, usually backspacing and typing over an error instantly corrects it. On a CRT (cathode ray tube paperless terminal), the correction usually replaces the error on the screen in front of you. On paper, as might be the case with a mag card or an electronic typewriter, the error and the strikeover will continue to show even though the error is no longer in memory. The corrected version will show only when you "play out," or print, a fresh copy on the typewriter. To find out more about word processing, read Chapter 4 in Mullins's The Complete Writing Guide, McCabe and Popham's Word Processing, and Waterford's Word Processing.[2]

PROOFREADING AND CORRECTING FINISHED TYPING

Instructions for Handling

2.22   After you have finished typing, proofread the manuscript. When you have typed on bond, <u>don't</u> mark on the copy. Instead, write corrections on separate paper, identified by page, paragraph, and line number. The reason is that preventing marks on the original helps to make neat corrections more likely. Also, later, the list can be checked with the corrected manuscript to verify that corrections have been made properly.

2.23   When you have typed a manuscript on mimeograph masters:

** Use the technique described in the previous section

** Keep your fingers off the typing and the masters away from the heat. Warmth can soften the wax and blur the typing.

** If someone else handles them, warn them to keep fingers off the typing.

2.24   When you have typed a manuscript on multilith masters, mark corrections on a xerographic copy of each master. If anyone but you must handle the masters, caution them to place their fingers at the extreme edges so that their fingerprints don't spot the masters.

2.25   When you have typed the document on word processing equipment:

** Mark corrections on a paper copy.

** Don't cut, paste, and move things around physically, and don't let anyone else do so. If you do, you may have a hard time locating the sections in your electronic copy of the document.

With people who are unfamiliar with word processors, you also may need to explain that a freshly typed copy will have no new errors. Without an explanation, many people still dismiss the idea of word processing as just so much black magic that makes no difference in the way <u>they</u> work!

Proofreader's Marks

2.26   Proofreading is best done by two people, one of whom reads the original manuscript out loud, including all punctuation, while the other reads the clean copy and notes the errors. (For instructions on this technique, see Peggy Smith's <u>Simplified Proofreading</u>.[3]) When proofreading, use the following standard symbols to indicate corrections:

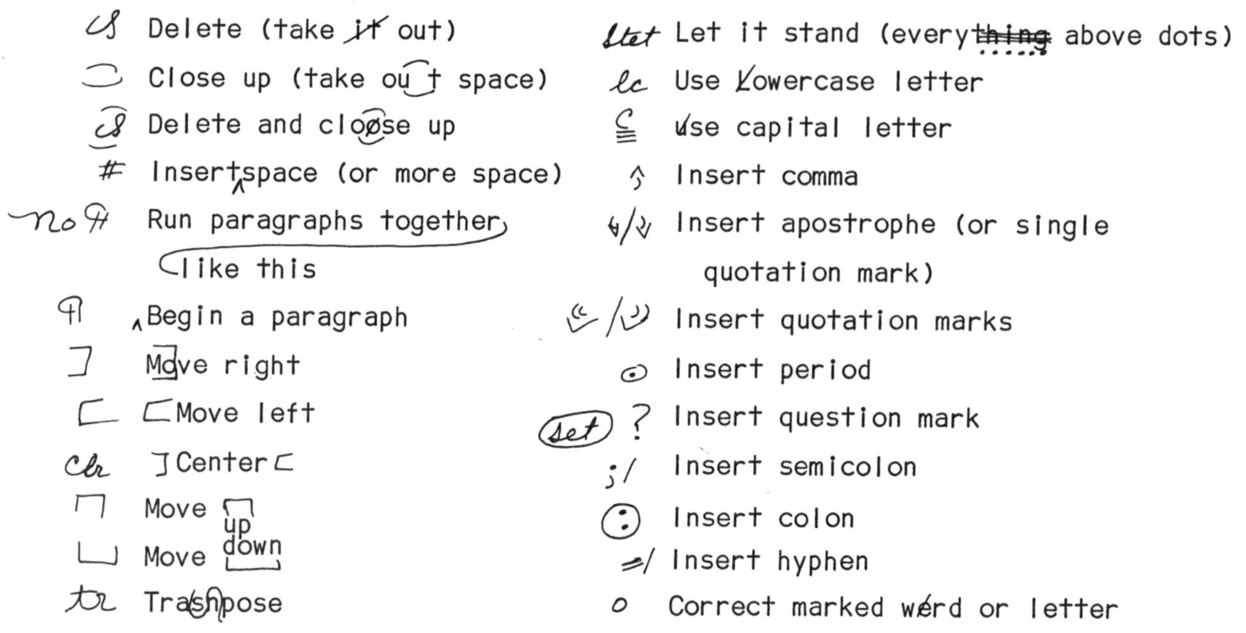

ℰ	Delete (take ~~it~~ out)	Let	Let it stand (every~~thing~~ above dots)
⌒	Close up (take ou⌒t space)	lc	Use ~~L~~owercase letter
ℰ̶	Delete and clo⌀se up	≡	~~U~~se capital letter
#	Insert‸space (or more space)	⌃	Insert comma
no ¶	Run paragraphs together⌒like this	⅋/ℓ	Insert apostrophe (or single quotation mark)
¶	‸Begin a paragraph	ℰ/ℓ	Insert quotation marks
⏋	M�^ove right	⊙	Insert period
⊏	⊏Move left	(set) ?	Insert question mark
Ctr ⏌Center⊏	;/	Insert semicolon
⊓	Move up	⊙̈	Insert colon
⊔	Move down	⸗/	Insert hyphen
tr	Tra⸈nⓈpose	○	Correct marked w⸍ord or letter

When writers use other marks that are unfamiliar, look them up in <u>Webster's Dictionary</u> or in the <u>Manual of Style</u>.[4]

Corrections on Finished Typing

2.27 Whether you are correcting bond, stencils, or masters, <u>always type corrections</u>. Never handwrite them. There are three ways to insert words on a completely typed page. One way, which is always suitable, is to retype the page, but that requires re-proofreading. The other two methods avoid a complete recheck. Unless the manuscript is to be camera-ready, most publishers will accept a very few of either type of correction. However, both types are usually forbidden on theses, dissertations, and many business reports.

2.28 One of these methods is to type the correction above the affected line and use a caret mark (an upside-down "v") to indicate position. The second, sometimes suitable with a lengthy insert, is to type the entire insert on a separate page and assign it an "a" number (for example, page 21a would contain an insert for page 21; a caret on page 21 would show where the insert goes). When in doubt about the acceptability of either type of correction, retype the page. **WP Advantage:** word processing eventually will make both methods obsolete because it makes retyping automatic and doesn't introduce new errors.

2.29   When the original pages are to be copied and not distributed, try "cut-ins," which replace part of a typed page with a new part and require use of the optional equipment listed in Section 2.2. Because the purpose is to avoid retyping (and thus re-proofing) correct sections, the technique is valuable primarily to typists without word processors. If you need these techniques and don't know them, seek instruction either informally from a printer, artist, or typing production supervisor, or formally through a class in drafting, illustrating, or printing.

WORD COUNTS

2.30   Many manuscripts intended for publication must contain a statement of the estimated number of words they contain. To get this estimate:

1.   Count the number of lines on a full page. Write down the number.

2.   Count the number of words in each of four full lines and write down those numbers.

3.   Find the average number of words per line by adding the four numbers (to get the total number of words) and dividing by four (to find the average per line).

4.   Multiply the average per line by the total number of lines on a full page.

5.   Multiply the number of words per page times the number of pages. The result is the approximate total number of words.

6.   Type the number in the upper right-hand corner of the first page of the document.

Two general principles are (1) count every word, even those of a single letter, and (2) count every line, even partial ones.

2.31   Another method is:

1.   Count the total number of words on each of three full pages.

2. Write down and add those numbers.

3. Divide by three to find the average number of words per page.

4. Multiply the average number per page by the total number of pages.

2.32   WP Advantage: some word processors automatically count and report the number of words. Lacking such a counter, typists with word processors, especially microcomputers and computer-based text processors, can write simple programs to do word-counting arithmetic for them. Then all they have to do each time is to put into the program the numbers of (1) words per line, (2) lines per page, and (3) pages in the manuscript. The computer will do the arithmetic and give back the correct numbers.

READABILITY ANALYSIS

2.33   Some writers, especially of textbooks and instructions, need to meet specific readability standards. Readability measures, as the name implies, help writers find out how easily their intended audience will be able to read their writing. Probably the simplest measure is the SMOG index,[5] which works best on long documents and is calculated as follows:

1. Take ten sentences from the beginning, ten from the middle, and ten from the end of the document--a total of 30 sentences.

2. Count the total number of words with more than two syllables in all 30 sentences. Don't include proper nouns (capitalized).

3. Take the square root and add 3.

The number you get is, roughly, the number of years of formal education a person must have had before he or she can understand the document without difficulty. Thus, if the number is 10, people with less than a tenth grade education will have trouble reading it. Interestingly, most textbook publishers require that books for freshman in college have a readability level of 10--an implication that reading skills lag behind grade levels.

2.34   Ralph John, writing for accountants, recommends a more elaborate way to assess readability.[6] The first steps analyze the difficulty of words:

1. Count the total number of words in a sample of text. One long paragraph or a few short ones will do nicely.

2. Count the number of words with more than two syllables. Don't include verbs made into two syllables by adding "ed," "ing," or "es," and omit proper nouns (capitalized) and compound words made up of easy elements (for example, bookkeeper, dishwasher).

3. Divide the number of words with more than two syllables by the total number of words.

When the result is .3 or higher, more than 55% of American managers won't understand the writing. Anyone with less education will have even more trouble.

2.35   The next steps, which involve analyzing sentences, are:

1. Count the number of sentences in the sample.

2. Divide the total number of words by the number of sentences.

When the result--the average length of sentences--is more than 13, many managers will have trouble understanding the writing. This fact doesn't mean that only short sentences are good. However, it _does_ mean writers need to use short sentences whenever possible and save the longer ones for ideas they can't express any other way.

2.36   A note to writers: John points out that simple sentences, with no dependent clauses, are the easiest to understand. Compound sentences, which have at least two independent clauses, and complex sentences, which have at least one independent and one dependent clause, make writing harder to read. John recommends that in any given document, no more than 20% of the sentences be compound sentences, and no more than 40% be complex.

2.37   **WP Advantage:** at least one measure, based on the readability tests of Rudolph Flesch, has been computerized as program S.T.A.R., written in BASIC, and is available free from General Motors.[7] Typists who can install this program on their word processors will be able to offer a valuable service at little extra cost to themselves.

GREEK ALPHABET

2.38 The following list, of special use for technical typing, shows upper-case Greek letters first, italic second, and Roman third.

FORMS			NAMES	FORMS			NAMES
	Italic	Roman			*Italic*	Roman	
A	α	α	alpha	N	ν	ν	nu
B	$б\ \beta$	β	beta	Ξ	ξ	ξ	xi
Γ	γ	γ	gamma	O	o	o	omicron
Δ	δ	δ	delta	Π	π	π	pi
E	ϵ	ϵ	epsilon	P	ρ	ρ	rho
Z	ζ	ζ	zeta	Σ	σ	$\sigma\ \varsigma$	sigma
H	η	η	eta	T	τ	τ	tau
Θ	θ	θ	theta	Y	υ	υ	upsilon
I	ι	ι	iota	Φ	ϕ	φ	phi
K	κ	κ	kappa	X	χ	χ	chi
Λ	λ	λ	lambda	Ψ	ψ	ψ	psi
M	μ	μ	mu	Ω	ω	ω	omega

WAYS TO IMPROVE TYPING

2.39 To improve your typing on future manuscripts:

** List the errors you make over and over again. In the future, concentrate on eliminating those errors.

** Keep copies of finished manuscripts to use as models.

NOTES TO CHAPTER 2

1. Editorial Experts, Inc. Typing Manual (Alexandria, Va: Editorial Experts, Inc., 1979), p. iii.

2. Carolyn J. Mullins, The Complete Writing Guide to Preparing Reports, Proposals, Memos, Etc. (Englewood Cliffs, N. J.: Prentice-Hall, 1980); Helen M. McCabe and Estelle L. Popham, Word Processing: A Systems Approach to the Office (New York: Harcourt Brace Jovanovich, Inc., 1977); Shirley A. Waterhouse, Word Processing Fundamentals (New York: Harper & Row, 1979).

3. Margherita S. Smith, Simplified Proofreading (Arlington, Virginia: National Composition Association, 1980).

4. University of Chicago Press, Manual of Style, 12th ed. (Chicago: University of Chicago Press, 1969), Figure 3.1.

5. G. H. McGlaughlin, "SMOG Grading--A New Readability Formula," Journal of Reading 12 (1969): 639-46.

6. Ralph C. John, "Improve Your Technical Writing," Management Accounting, September 1976, pp. 49-52.

7. General Motors, S.T.A.R. (Detroit: GM Public Relations Staff, n.d.). To get a copy, write to 3044 W. Grand Boulevard, Detroit, MI, 48202.

STYLE SHEET

Name _____ Address _____

Phones _____ Color of handwriting is: _____

Consultation desired? Y/N   Edit check: Spelling, Y/N   Punctuation, Y/N

Comma rules: Serial? Y/N   After short intro clauses? Y/N

Type of ms. _____ Style _____ Draft/Final copy/Camera-Ready/OCR

Corrections: Eraser/Fluid/Tape/Cut-ins/Strikeovers   Hyphenation: Y/N

Paper wt., qual./Master (type) _____ Size: Ltr/Legl/ISO

Ribbon: Carbon/Cloth/None   Self-corr OK? Y/N   Color: Black/Other: _____

Margins: Left _____ Right _____ Top _____ Bottom _____

Pitch: Pica/Elite/Proport. Style _____ Tabs _____ Boldface: Y/N

Underline: Words/Solid; For'n wrds? Y/N Spelling: Webster/Oxford/Other ____

Spacing of text: Triple/Double/Single/One and a half/Other _____

Chp/Artcl title All caps/Up-Low/Init cap   Centered left to right/flush left

   Chapter # Arabic/Roman/None   With/Above ttl/NA __ empty lines

   Word "Chapter" before number? _____ Caps/Up-Low/NA/Other _____

   Spaces: Top to # _____ # to title _____ Title to text _____

Running Hds: Lt/Rt/Alt/NA   Top/Bottom   Title pgs? Y/N Spaces to RH _____

Text page #s Lt/Rt/Alt/Ctr   Top/Bottom   Title pgs? Y/N Ident wrds? Y/N

Prelim. #s   Lt/Rt/Alt/Ctr   Top/Bottom   Title pgs? Y/N Ident wrds? Y/N

Part	Exist?	Seq. #?	Separate? Y/N	Counted? Y/N	Pg. # Typed On? Y/N
Frontispiece	Y/N	Y/N	Y/N	Y/N	Y/N; Rom/Ara.
Title page	Y/N	Y/N	Y/N	Y/N	Y/N; Rom/Ara.
Half-title	Y/N	Y/N	Y/N	Y/N	Y/N; Rom/Ara.
Dedication	Y/N	Y/N	Y/N	Y/N	Y/N; Rom/Ara.
Epigraph	Y/N	Y/N	Y/N	Y/N	Y/N; Rom/Ara.

Tbl of Cnts	Y/N	Y/N	Y/N	Y/N	Y/N; Rom/Ara.
List of Ill	Y/N	Y/N	Y/N	Y/N	Y/N; Rom/Ara.
List of Tbls	Y/N	Y/N	Y/N	Y/N	Y/N; Rom/Ara.
Foreword	Y/N	Y/N	Y/N	Y/N	Y/N; Rom/Ara.
Preface	Y/N	Y/N	Y/N	Y/N	Y/N; Rom/Ara.
Acknowl	Y/N	Y/N	Y/N	Y/N	Y/N; Rom/Ara.
Biography	Y/N	Y/N	Y/N	Y/N	Y/N; Rom/Ara.
Abstract	Y/N	Y/N	Y/N	Y/N	Y/N; Rom/Ara.
Classif schem	Y/N	Y/N	Y/N	Y/N	Y/N; Rom/Ara.
Part ttl pg	Y/N	Y/N	Y/N	Y/N	Y/N; Rom/Ara.
Text	Y/N	Y/N	Y/N	Y/N	Y/N; Rom/Ara.
Chp ttl pgs	Y/N	Y/N	Y/N	Y/N	Y/N; Rom/Ara.
Each table	Y/N	Y/N	Y/N	Y/N	Y/N; Rom/Ara.
Each illus	Y/N	Y/N	Y/N	Y/N	Y/N; Rom/Ara.
Caption list	Y/N	Y/N	Y/N	Y/N	Y/N; Rom/Ara.
Notes	Y/N	Y/N	Y/N	Y/N	Y/N; Rom/Ara.
Chp notes	Y/N	Y/N	Y/N	Y/N	Y/N; Rom/Ara.
Ref notes	Y/N	Y/N	Y/N	Y/N	Y/N; Rom/Ara.
Ident refs	Y/N	Y/N	Y/N	Y/N	Y/N; Rom/Ara.
List of refs	Y/N	Y/N	Y/N	Y/N	Y/N; Rom/Ara.
Bibliography	Y/N	Y/N	Y/N	Y/N	Y/N; Rom/Ara.
Appendix	Y/N	Y/N	Y/N	Y/N	Y/N; Rom/Ara.
Budget	Y/N	Y/N	Y/N	Y/N	Y/N; Rom/Ara.
Glossary	Y/N	Y/N	Y/N	Y/N	Y/N; Rom/Ara.
List of abbr	Y/N	Y/N	Y/N	Y/N	Y/N; Rom/Ara.
Index	Y/N	Y/N	Y/N	Y/N	Y/N; Rom/Ara.
Supplem Text	Y/N	Y/N	Y/N	Y/N	Y/N; Rom/Ara.

Text: empty lines, running head/pg. # to text __ Par. ind. __ Just. Y/N

Documentation: Author (date)/[#] (#) #/superscript: *,**,#/#s/a,b,c

Notes typed: Footnotes/End of subunit/Collected, end of doc./Not allowed

Designate by: *,#/1,2/a,b Superscript? Y/N Spaces after? ___

First line: Flush left/Para. ind. Period after #? Y/N

Turnovers: Flush left/Block, hang under first letter

Symbols: Handwritten/Type only/Rub-on   Accents: Handwritten/Type/Rub-on

Rules for numbers in text: Hum./Tech./Other: _____ Percent/% _____

Headings: Empty lines above __ below ____   Turnovers: Block/Indent 1 space

    1-level   Caps/U-L/Init. cap/#ed   Underline Y/N C/L/Para. leader

    2-level   Caps/U-L/Init. cap/#ed   Underline Y/N C/L/Para. leader

    3-level   Caps/U-L/Init. cap/#ed   Underline Y/N C/L/Para. leader

    4-level   Caps/U-L/Init. cap/#ed   Underline Y/N C/L/Para. leader

Quotations: Brit/Amer   Block 5/7/10 L/R/Both Indnt 1st line 0/3/5 sp.

    Empty lines: Above ___ Below ___   Spacing: Dbl/Sngl/Other _____

    Emphasis: []ed inside quotes/() at end/In note

    Comments:

Tables: Models? Y/N   #ed? Y/N, Rom/Ara.   #, ttl: Fl. Left/Cntr/U-Line

    Number: W/"table"? Y/N Caps/U-L/Init   Per. after? Y/N   Spcs to ttl __

    Title: Caps/U-L/Init   On line with number? Y/N   Per. at end? Y/N

        Turnovers: Flush left/Centered/Hanging ind. ____ spaces.

    Bars: Above #? Y/N   Below: ttl (1 or 2 lines)/Col. hds./body/notes

    Cl. hds: Caps/U-L/Init   Ctr/Lft   Turnovers: Ctr/Lft

    Stubs: Caps/U-L/Init; Turnovers: Flush/Indent __ spaces

    Substb: Caps/U-L/Init   Indent __ spaces   Turnovers: Ind. __ more sp.

    Notes: Which comes first: Source __   General __   Specific __

        "SOURCE" and "NOTE" as labels? Y/N Caps/Initial cap only

        Specific: *,#/1,2/a,b   Superscript? Y/N Spaces after? ___

        First line: Flush left/Indent ___ spaces

    Turnovers: Flush left/Ind. __ sp./Ind. to first letter of note

    Tables in text: __ spaces above and below

Comments, examples:

Figures: Models? Y/N   #ed? Y/N, Rom/Ara.   #, capt: L/Ctr/Ind __ /U-Line

   Number: With "Figure" or "Fig."? Y/N Caps/Init Top/Btm Per. after? Y/N

   Caption: Caps/U-L/Init Top/Btm   On line w/#? Y/N   Per. after? Y/N

          First line: Flush left/Indent ___ spaces

          Turnovers: Flush left/Centered/Hanging ind. ____ spaces.

   Comments, examples:

Displayed equations: Centered/Indented ___ spaces from left margin

Equation Numbers: L/R/None/NA; in Brackets/Parens/Open

     Comments:

Readability analyses? Y/N   Word count? Y/N; Typed where? _____

Key words: Y/N   Total # of copies, including original: 1/2/3/4/5/6

Treatment of uncertain bibliographic data:

Other comments:

_____

Fig. 2.1. Form for recording stylistic details.

chapter 3

Text Typing

3.1   This chapter describes the basic rules of manuscript typing such as width of margins, spacing requirements, treatment of quotations, and so forth. The style sheets in Appendix A specify the rules for each of the major styles. The two sample manuscripts at the end of the chapter, one double-spaced and the other partly single-spaced, are labeled to show examples of features such as line length, margin width, spacing, and headings. Both samples are in MLA style, a popular style for documents in the humanities and languages.

LINE LENGTHS AND MARGINS

General Rules

3.2   The minimum margin allowed is 1 inch on each side. When a document is to be bound, 1 inch is essential, and bound pages look better when the left margin is at least 1 1/2 inches. Some publishers require a left margin of 1 1/2 inches. Some, such as AIIE, require 1 1/2 inches on all sides. Some, such as AMathS, specify 1 1/4 inches on the left and the right. Other publishers specify line length. For instance, ASA requires 6-inch lines. Sage requires 160 millimeter lines. If you are not typing on a word processor:

** Guided by a backing sheet, lightly mark margins with nonphoto-blue pencil.

WP Advantages: margins are automatic. You can change them whenever you wish, either temporarily, as for a quotation, or permanently, as when you change a document from one style to another. You can also get "justified" (even) left and right margins, like the ones in this book. Caution: some styles, such as AMA, forbid justification.

3.3   In general, type the same number of lines on each page. However, when observing this rule would force you to type a heading or first line of text on the bottom line of a page, leave a short page and begin the next page with the heading or the first line at the top. Similarly, don't begin a page with the last line of a paragraph. Instead, carry over at least two lines to the top of the page. **WP advantage:** many word processors automatically prevent such "widow" lines or allow typists to choose where to break a page.

Hyphenation and Margins

3.4   To make pages look neat when hyphenation is allowed:

** Try to keep every line as long as possible within the specified limits.

** Try to keep ends of lines as even as possible, but don't let more than three consecutive lines end with hyphenated words.

** Try not to have a difference of more than six pica letters or eight elite between the shortest and longest lines on a page. Most of the time the difference should be no more than two or three spaces.

WP Advantage: some word processors hyphenate automatically as needed.

3.5   When hyphenation is forbidden, as it sometimes is when a manuscript is being prepared for copy editing:

** Don't hyphenate under any circumstances.

** When the length of a final word on a line forces a choice between a short line and a line that would extend into the margin, choose the short line.

This procedure yields very ragged right margins, but it saves copy editors the effort of specially marking each instance of hyphenation.

SPACING

Vertical Spacing

3.6   For documents that are to be published, such as articles, books, and plays, the general rule is:

** **Double-space** (leave one empty line) between all lines of all title pages, biographies, dedications, epigraphs, abstracts, prefaces, tables of contents, lists of tables and illustrations, text pages, quotations, equations, notes, tables, illustrations, captions and legends, appendixes, bibliographies, lists of references, glossaries, and indexes.

** **Single-space** only when and what a writer or publisher tells you to.

3.7   On reports, dissertations, prospectuses, unpublished documents, and proposals, single-spacing, especially of quotations, notes, tables, and bibliographies, is more likely. Examples are in the sample documents at the end of this chapter.

3.8   Regardless of whether a document is mostly single- or double-spaced, in some places you'll need to leave a bit of additional space to set off certain special parts, such as headings, quotations, and the like. For example, common exceptions to double spacing are:

** **Single-space** (leave no empty lines) between the lines of headings and table and figure titles broken across two or more lines.

** **Triple-space** (leave two empty lines) between the text and the beginning and end of a blocked, indented quotation.

** **Triple-space** above first-level headings.

** **Triple-space** above second-level headings unless there is no text between the second-level heading and the immediately prior first-level heading. In such cases, double-space.

** On short documents with no separate title page, **leave 2 inches** between the top of the page and the titles on the abstract page and first page of text.

** On all documents **leave 2 inches** between the top of the page and the titles "Biography," "Notes," "Reference Notes," "Identifying References," "Acknowledgements," "References," "Bibliography," and "Appendix" when the manuscript includes those sections. **Quadruple-space** (leave three empty lines) between the titles and the next typed line.

** On longer documents, for MSH and MSN, **leave at least 3 inches** between the top of the page and the first line of typing on the first page of the half-title page, title page, dedication, epigraph, table of contents, lists of tables and illustrations, preface, foreword, part-title pages, each chapter, notes to each chapter, bibliography, appendixes, glossary, and index. **Quadruple-space** (leave three empty lines) between titles and the next line of typing on the title page, table of contents, preface, foreword, each chapter, notes to each chapter, bibliography, glossary, and index.

The parts of this book, which were produced from typed pages, provide many examples, as do the sample manuscripts in Chapters 6 and 7. **WP Advantage:** spacing is easy to change within a document and between revisions. For instance, typists can double-space drafts (to make corrections easy to mark) and single-space final copies simply by changing the spacing command.

Horizontal Spacing

3.9   From left to right:

** Indent the first line of a paragraph five spaces (eight for Turabian style).

** **Single-space** after words, commas, semicolons, colons, and periods; and question marks and exclamation marks when they are within, and do not mark the end of, a sentence. For example:

Wow! shows surprise.

** **Double-space** after periods, question marks, and exclamation marks that end sentences. For example:

Wow! She was impressed enough to reply at once.

** **Leave no spaces** between the letters of words, or between dashes and the words preceding and following the dashes. For example:

Decision-making process

His goal--to finish the report--seemed unattainable.

3.10   In outlines and numbered lists, line up the periods after the numerals (or letters). Line up the numerals (or letters) for subsections beneath the text of the previous section. Leave <u>two</u> spaces between the periods and the beginning of text in outlines and lists. Examples are on the next page.

I. Words

    A. Words

        1. Words

        2. Words

           a. Words
           b. Words

              (1) Words
              (2) Words

                (a) Words
                (b) Words

    B. Words

II. Words

III. Words

IV. Words

1. Words

2. Words

3. Words

4. Words

5. Words

6. Words

7. Words

8. Words

    a. Words
    b. Words

9. Words

10. Words

112. Words

MANUSCRIPT PARTS AND PAGE NUMBERS

Separate Pages

3.11   In all documents certain parts, listed at the top of the next page, often begin on separate pages. Form 2.1 contains space for marking which parts exist and whether they begin on separate pages. Don't assume that the form in a rough draft is the correct form. For example, rough drafts of scholarly books and articles often have footnotes and tables typed onto pages of text simply because the writers had to type their class papers and theses that way. They never learned that requirements for publication are different. Filling out Form 2.1 with an experienced typist not only prevents misunderstanding but also educates writers on publication requirements.

Short Documents	Longer Documents
	Front Matter
Title, by-line	
Biography	Frontispiece
Abstract	Half-title page
First page of text	Title page
Each table	Blank page
Each illustration	Dedication
List of captions	Epigraph
Notes	Table of contents
Reference notes	List of illustrations
Identifying references	List of tables
Acknowledgments	Foreward
List of references	Preface
Bibliography	Acknowledgments
Each appendix	
Budget	Body
Supplementary material	
	Part-title pages
	Each chapter
	Notes to each chapter
	Back Matter
	Each appendix
	Bibliography or list of references
	Glossary
	List of abbreviations
	Index
	Budget

WP Advantage: mispaging is easy to correct because new page commands can be added or removed as easily as words.

Order of Parts, Page Numbers, and Running Titles

3.12   **Short documents.** Form 2.1 contains space for writers to indicate the order of manuscript parts, whether to count the parts in the page numbering scheme, whether the page number is typed on that part, and whether in

Roman or Arabic numerals. The organization of a manuscript does not always reflect what the writer wants. For example, many writers will interleave text pages with pages of tables and illustrations and even number those pages in sequence with text pages, but they will be very unhappy if typists do likewise. There are many different ways to count and number pages. For example, APA style requires the procedure below:

Part of Manuscript	Page Number Counted and Typed
Title Page	Not counted
Abstract	Page 1, but not typed
First page of text	Page 2, typed
Subsequent pages	Counted and typed
Reference notes	Counted and typed
List of references	Counted and typed
Notes	Counted and typed
Tables	Counted and typed
Illustrations	Not counted
Captions	Counted and typed
Appendixes	Counted and typed
Running head (foot)	Top or bottom of every page

3.13   All pages are numbered in sequence from 1 (the abstract) through the last page of the last appendix. Page numbers are typed in the upper right-hand corner of the page. In ASA style, otherwise very similar to that of the APA, notes occur before the list of references, and neither the tables nor the illustrations receive page numbers. Appendixes, if any, are numbered in sequence after the list of references. To find the numbering scheme for your style, look at the page specifications on the form in Appendix A. Regardless of style, the general rules are:

** Type page numbers just inside the right-hand margin, about 3/4 of an inch from the top of the page.

** Type them in the same spot on each page.

** Unless explicitly told not to, type a word or two from the title just above the page number for identification. Then, if pages of the manuscript accidentally blow off a desk, you or someone else will have an easy way to tell which pages go together in what order.

** Check whether to type a "running head"--a shortened title--at the top of all or most pages, often on a line with the page numbers and even with the opposite margin. Manuscripts by free-lance writers often have a running head that consists of the title (sometimes abbreviated) and the author's last name.

** If you are not typing the final page numbers, handwrite the number lightly with a nonphoto-blue pencil.

WP Advantage: most word processors automatically count page numbers and type them in the same place on each page. They also store and repeat running heads (or feet) and short titles. Typists can specify placement and change it at will. For instance, you might want page numbers in the upper right-hand corner of each page except for title pages, when you might want either to skip the number or to type it in the center of the bottom margin.

3.14   Long documents. For long documents, the common order of parts is the order shown in the right-hand list in Section 3.11. The most common variation: some publishers prefer that the notes to each chapter be collected as a unit and numbered with the back matter, usually following the last chapter (when a book has no appendixes) or after the appendixes and before the bibliography or list of references. General instructions are the same as those in Section 3.13. In addition:

** Number the front matter with lowercase roman numerals. The first typed page number usually is on the second page of either the preface or the table of contents.

** Type no page numbers on tables and illustrations.

** Number the body and back matter with sequential arabic numerals.

Some styles specify no page number on the first page of chapters, appendixes, and other sections that are separate parts, but type numbers on all other pages. When numbers are required on first pages, normally they are typed in the center of the bottom margin.

HEADINGS AND SUBHEADINGS

3.15   Nonfiction writers often use first-order, second-order, and third-order headings and subheadings. As the examples on page 38 show, the variation in stylistic treatment is substantial. For headings at each order of importance, crucial features of style are:

** Capitalization, underlining, and placement on the page.

The sample documents at the end of this chapter and in Chapters 6 and 7 show headings and subheadings in each major style. In general, writers using a style with no requirements for headings and subheadings are also doing a kind of writing, such as fiction, in which headings are rare. However, if you are using such a style and still need headings and subheadings, use APA style. It is the simplest one that also makes the headings stand out on typed pages.

3.16   General rules for typing headings and subheadings are:

** **Single-space** any two-line heading regardless of the spacing of the document. EXCEPTION: double-space APA-style headings.

** When headings and subheadings are too long for one line, break them by sense and good looks. No line should be much shorter or much longer than the others. For instance, in the examples on page 38, breaking <u>JASA</u> subheading 1.1 after "under" would be wrong because the first line would end with a lowercased word and the second line would be very short.

** Don't divide words in centered headings.

** On each page make sure each heading has at least two lines of text following it. If necessary, leave a page a few lines short and start the next page with the heading.

** In general, when headings are either centered or flush left, leave two empty lines above and two below. EXCEPTIONS: For AIP and APA styles, leave one empty lines above and one below. GPO style requires three empty lines above and two below.

TREATMENT OF NUMBERED SUBPARAGRAPHS

3.17   Numbered subparagraphs can be treated in one of three ways, depending on length. **WP Advantage:** some word processors have "counters" that automatically number and renumber lists, outlines, paragraphs, and so forth. For instance, in this book I didn't type the paragraph and note numbers. Instead, I used a counter code. When I printed a chapter, the processor numbered the items in sequence. When I revised, I could insert or delete paragraphs and notes easily because renumbering was automatic.

AIP

                  I.   FIRST-ORDER HEADING

              A.   Second-order heading

          <u>1. Third-order heading</u>

     <u>a. Fourth-order heading</u>. Followed immediately, on same line, by text of paragraph. The numbers aren't always required.

APA

                 <u>First-Order Heading</u>

<u>Second-Order Heading</u>

     <u>Third-order heading</u>. Followed immediately . . .

ASA

                FIRST-ORDER HEADING

<u>Second-Order Heading</u>

     <u>Third-order heading</u>. Followed immediately . . .

<u>JASA</u>

            1.   FIRST FIRST-ORDER HEADING

1.1 First Second-Order Heading
    under First Heading

Sage

FIRST-ORDER HEADING

Second-Order Heading

<u>Third-Order Heading</u>

Long Subparagraphs

3.18   When most of the subparagraphs take up six or more typed lines:

** Indent the first line as you would an ordinary paragraph.

** Type subsequent--"turnover" or "runover"--lines flush with the left margin.

** Leave an extra empty vertical line between subparagraphs.

** Space the subparagraphs themselves just like all other paragraphs.

** Optional: when requirements don't forbid it, leave two or three empty vertical spaces above the beginning and below the end of subparagraphs.

This procedure doesn't display the numbers as obviously as the style described in the next paragraph, but it has the virtue of conserving paper.

Short Subparagraphs

3.19   Short numbered paragraphs lend themselves nicely to "flush-and-hang" style in which the first line begins with the number, typed flush left, and the text is blocked to "hang" beneath the first letter of the first word of text, as in the asterisked sentences below. When most subparagraphs take up five or fewer typed lines, follow the instructions for long subparagraphs with these exceptions:

** When the number of paragraphs is 10 or greater, indent a space from the margin on paragraphs 1-9 to make the periods after the numbers line up (for instance, see Section 3.10).

** Don't return turnover lines to the left margin. Instead, line them up beneath the first character after the period that follows the number.

** Line up the first line of subsubparagraphs directly beneath the turnover lines for the previous level. Line up their turnover lines beneath the first character after the period that follows the second-order number.

This procedure is the same as that for typing outlines (for help, see Section 3.10). The text looks rather like a stairway turned upside-down. **WP Advantage:** most word processors automatically line up turnover lines.

3.20   Treat short numbered lists the same way. EXCEPTION: In GPO style, because the entries are one line or shorter, single-space between them.

TREATMENT OF QUOTATIONS

Integrated Quotations

3.21   For quotations that are integrated into the text:

** Use quotation marks at the beginning and at the end.

** For **American publishers,** use double marks. Place periods and commas in-side the quotation marks, and question and exclamation marks outside. Place question and exclamation marks inside only when they are part of a quotation. Use single marks for quotations inside a quotation.

** For **British publishers,** use single marks around quotations and double marks for quotes within quotes. Place all punctuation outside the quota-tion.

For example, "Americans treat integrated 'quotes' this way." British publish-ers 'Treat integrated "quotes" this way.' When needed, alter capitalization of initial word to make sense in the sentence. For more detailed rules on punctuation with quotation marks, consult any good grammar book.[1]

Blocked Quotations

3.22   Quotations that exceed seven typed lines (five in MLA style) are usu-ally indented and blocked this way:

** Block the entire quotation four (Turabian), five (APA style), seven (most styles), or ten (MLA style) spaces from the left margin. Check for inden-tation on the right.

** Leave one (APA, Turabian) or two empty lines (most other styles) above and below the quotation to separate it from the surrounding text. EXCEPTION: in Turabian style leave no extra line above or below blocked quotes in footnotes.

** Check internal spacing (see Section 3.6-3.8).

** Use no quotation marks at the beginning or the end. When writers have used quotation marks internally, type double marks for American publishers and single for British.

** Use paragraph indentation only on second and subsequent paragraphs in a blocked quotation. For example, in the quotation below, the first line of the first paragraphs is not indented; the first line of the second paragraph is. EXAMPLE:

> This paper bridges the gap between [sociological and psychological models of voting behavior] (1) by specifying a causal model of voting behavior, . . . (2) by providing quantitative measurement of causal relationships among variables, . . . and (3) by comparing parameters of the model over time.[2]
>
> Indent the first line of the second paragraph five spaces as is done here. . . . Block the remaining lines <u>with the lines of the prior</u> paragraph, again as is done here. (Emphasis added.)

EXCEPTION: In Turabian style, indent any paragraph beginning four spaces. When quoting from poems, follow the instructions in Section 4.9 except when the lines are too long to center. In such cases, indent all lines four spaces from the left margin. Indent turnover lines an additional four spaces. In MLA style, indent second and subsequent paragraphs only three spaces. Indent first paragraphs three spaces only when they are paragraph beginnings in the texts from which they are taken. **WP Advantage:** most word processors automatically center and indent.

Omissions, Changes, and Emphasis

3.23   An **ellipsis**, three periods with a space between each pair, shows that the writer omitted words <u>within</u> a quotation. Treat omissions in all languages alike. Common practice is not to use ellipses at the beginnings and ends of quotations. The assumption is that in the original, any quote has something that precedes and something that follows it. Nevertheless, some writers still prefer to use ellipses when a quote does not begin at the beginning of a sentence or end at the end of a sentence. Whatever a writer's preference, always put punctuation before the ellipsis. For example, when omitting the last words in a sentence, type the period followed by the ellipsis, as in the quotation in Section 3.22. Turabian recommends use of a full line of ellipsis points when a writer omits (1) a line or more of poetry or (2) one or more full points in a numbered list.

3.24   **Brackets** show changes that writers have made in the wording of a quotation, or words they have added.   **Underlining** (italics in print) emphasizes certain words. At the end of quotations with underlining, writers should indicate the source of emphasis either in text or in a footnote. The quotation in Section 3.22 shows examples of brackets, emphasis, and statement of source of emphasis. Be consistent in how you designate the source of emphasis. The most common designations are:

          (Emphasis added.)   (Smith's emphasis.)

          (Emphasis in original.)   (Smith's italics.)

Brackets used with [sic] indicate errors in an original. Don't overdo the use of [sic], especially in obviously archaic or illiterate writing.

SYMBOLS, ACCENTS, AND EQUATIONS

General Principles

3.25   To prevent misinterpretation, don't try to fake symbols and accents. The best procedure is to use a typing element (ball, thimble, daisywheel, etc.) with special characters. When using such an element, change it every time you reach a spot that requires a symbol or accent. Don't store up the changes to do together at the end of a page. Either you'll forget or some of the characters won't align correctly. In the absence of an appropriate element, use "rub-on" characters (such as ArType), which are available in stationery and art stores. Sometimes handwriting is acceptable if you use India ink or a fine-point black pen. Form 2.1 has a place for writers to indicate a preference. When a document to be printed contains many symbols, make a list to help the printer. **WP Advantage:** word processors with twin-track (dual-element) printers switch back and forth between elements automatically and at high speed, saving considerable time.

3.26   Punctuate equations according to their function in a sentence. Underline symbols that can have a numerical value. Always check the rules for use of "percent" and "%" in text. Many styles permit and even require "%," not "percent," when writers give percentages in text. Others, such as ASTM, require "percent." Section 5.26 discusses the use of "%" and "percentage" in tables. When two units of measure are followed by a symbol, repeat the symbol. Thus: 4°-8°, 3" x 5". If possible, avoid using the letter "l" for the number "1." Clarify symbols with encircled marginal notes. ASTM style requires writing and circling the word "times" and "zero" over the "X" (times sign) and "0" respectively. Also beware of possible confusion between Greek and English letters such as Greek epsilon and "e," Greek eta and "n," and so forth. The first time a Greek letter appears, write and circle, say, "Gk epsilon," "Gk alpha," and so forth above the letter.

Formats

3.27   When an expression is short and simple, leave it in the line of text unless it must be numbered for later reference. Use a solidus (slash--/), not a horizontal line, for fractions and use parentheses (and sometimes brackets and curly brackets) liberally to group appropriate mathematical units. When you type equations into text that is single-spaced:

** Leave an additional half space above lines that contain superscript numbers and an additional half space below lines that contain subscripts.

** When you have to break an equation over two or more lines, try to break it before an operational sign.

Use sparingly subsubscripts, sub- to superscripts, and other second-order notation. To avoid confusion in hand-written copy, write and circle "l.c." over lowercase letters such as "c," "o," and "p." Underline capital letters three times. Use carets and inverted carets to mark sub- and superscripts. Don't use third-order notation.

3.28   Display any expression that is nearly half a line or longer. Otherwise, typesetting may break the equation between two lines, making it hard to read. Also display any equation that is at least 1 1/2 inches long and has no convenient breaking point. When you set off equations from text:

** Leave two empty lines above and below the equation.

** In manuscripts with lots of equations, indent each at least seven spaces from the left margin; GPO requires 10 spaces. With only one or a few equations, consider centering each one between the left and right margins.

** Break very long equations before an operational sign.

** When possible, line up equal (=) signs.

** Check whether to number equations and, if so, how. Some styles, such as AMathS, restrict numbering to important equations that are referenced later in the manuscript.

** Type any identifying numbers, usually within parentheses or brackets, flush with the right (more commonly) or left margin. For example:

(9)

[10]

If you do a great deal of technical typing, get specialized help from the STC's Typing Guide for Mathematical Expressions.[3]

SPELLING AND DIVISION OF WORDS

General Spelling Principles

3.29   Check dictionary preference. Common American choices include the American College Dictionary, American Heritage Dictionary of the English Language, and Webster's New Collegiate Dictionary. The British preference is for The Oxford English Dictionary. GPO provides a lengthy section on spelling and word division. Among the GPO spellings that might surprise typists are:

aline (not align)	marihuana (not marijuana)
canceled, cancellation	moneys (not monies)
diagramed, diagraming, diagrammatic	programed, programing, programmatic
gage (not guage)	subpena (not subpoena)
insure (not ensure)	toward (not towards)

For use of apostrophe in the spelling of plurals, see Section 3.35. **WP Advantage:** many word processors come with a "dictionary" that automatically checks spelling. In most such systems, users can add to the dictionary.

Word Division (Hyphenation)

3.30   When word division can't be avoided, American practice is to divide words according to pronunciation (e.g., rep-re-sent. In contrast, British practice is to divide according to word derivation (e.g., re-pre-sent). As the Modern Language Association points out,[4] other languages have their own rules. For instance, French usually divides on a vowel. Follow these general rules for American usage:[5]

** Never divide the last word in headings and titles.

** Never hyphenate the last word in a paragraph or on a page.

** Never end more than three consecutive lines with a hyphen.

** Try not to separate words in close association, such as the parts of a date or name or groups of initials. (If you must divide a date or name, the year and the last name, respectively, can go on the second line.)

** Don't divide contractions, abbreviations, one-syllable words, words with fewer than five letters, or words that leave a two-letter ending.[6]

** Don't divide a word between two letters pronounced as one:

        Use laud- able, not la- udable.

        Use plain- tive, not pla- intive.

** Don't make one-letter divisions such as u- nite.

** Don't divide suffixes such as able, ible, cious, geous, gion, tion.

** Don't divide final double consonants in verbs:

        Use process- ing, not proces- sing.

        Use stuff- ing, not stuf- fing.

** Spell solid those words that have the prefixes anti, bi, extra, infra, inter, intra, multi, non, over, post, pre, pro, pseudo, re, semi, sub, super, supra, sub, ultra, un, under. You may hyphenate these prefixes at the ends of lines. Exceptions to the solid spelling (with reasons) are:

        anti-inflation (solid spelling would produce a double vowel) anti-Semitic, non-Federal (prefix with proper noun)

re-sort re-treat (meaning to <u>sort</u> or <u>treat</u> again)

** Divide hyphenated compounds, like the above, only where the hyphen occurs. Thus, <u>anti- inflation</u>. <u>Anti-in- flation</u> is incorrect.

** Use a hyphen to connect:

Compound numerals and compound words indicating fractional parts: <u>thirty-four</u>, <u>two-thirds</u>, <u>fifty-odd</u>.

A capital letter to a word used as a compound adjective: <u>X-ray techni-cian</u>.

Two different nouns of equal importance: <u>writer-consultant</u>.

The words in a compound adjective: <u>well-to-do</u>, <u>sickly-looking boy</u>. (EXCEPTION: spell open when there is a modifier (<u>very sickly looking boy</u>) or when the term is a predicate adjective (<u>he is sickly looking</u>).

The words in a compound noun: <u>father-in-law</u>, <u>fathers-in-law</u>, <u>jack-o'-lantern</u>, <u>jack-o'-lanterns</u>.

The words in compounds with <u>ex</u>, <u>self</u>, <u>quasi</u>, <u>vice</u>, <u>well</u>.

** Don't hyphenate:

Noun forms such as <u>decision making</u>, <u>food preparing</u>.

Chemical terms such as <u>boric acid ointment</u>.

Compound adjectives indicating color (<u>gray green</u>, <u>ruby red</u>) except when followed by a noun.

** When dividing words at the ends of lines, hyphenate:

After a prefix, as in <u>dis- taste</u>.

Before a suffix, as in <u>success- ful</u>.

Between vowels pronounced as separate syllables, as in <u>peri- odic</u>.

Between two consonants when they result from doubling of a final conso-nant, as in <u>glad- den</u>, <u>swim- ming</u>.

WP Advantage: many word processors have a hyphenation dictionary built into them. Most of these allow users to add to the dictionary. See also Sections 3.4 through 3.5.

CAPITALIZATION

Headings and Titles

3.31   For headings and titles of books, chapters, articles, and other manu-scripts, the general rule is:

** Capitalize the first word, the last word, and the first word after a colon; all nouns, pronouns, verbs, adjectives, and adverbs; and all prepositions that contain more than four letters.

EXCEPTIONS: (1) reference lists and bibliographies in certain styles (discussed in sections 5.2 through 5.21 below and in Chapters 6 through 8); (2) GPO style, which capitalizes any preposition four or more letters long, as well as infinitives and short verbs, such at <u>To Be</u> and <u>To Go</u>; (3) use of lowercase in long titles of works published in earlier centuries; and (4) titles of foreign works.

References to Titles

3.32   In general, capitalize references to specific chapters, appendixes, tables, figures, and the like, as this book does. For instance: Chapter 3, Appendix A, Table 5.1. EXCEPTION: In GPO style, use the initial cap only when the title follows. Thus: <u>chapter 3</u> but <u>Chapter 3: Basic Rules</u>. Turabian prefers <u>chap. 3</u>, <u>bk. 2</u>, <u>fig. 2.1</u> and so forth. She counsels against abbreviation of <u>act</u>, <u>line</u>, and <u>table</u>.

In Text

3.33   This section lists some of the basic rules on capitalization. The most important rule is: when in doubt, don't! Too many writers sprinkle their writing with caps, sometimes solely for emphasis. The result is usually confusing and sloppy, and rapidly loses impact on the reader. Specific rules on use of caps include:

** When referring to administrative bodies by their full and proper title, use
   initial caps; otherwise, use lowercase letters. Thus:

   Department of Sanitation   the sanitation department

** Don't capitalize <u>Federal,</u> <u>State</u> and other such terms unless the words are
   in proper titles.

** Don't capitalize <u>northern,</u> <u>southern,</u> <u>northeastern,</u> and other such terms
   when they refer to geographical areas.

** DO capitalize <u>North,</u> <u>South,</u> <u>Northeast,</u> and other such terms when they are
   directions.

** Don't capitalize positions or job titles unless they are part of a formal
   title. Thus:

   the dispatcher   Dispatcher Brown

   the governor   Governor Bowen

   EXCEPTION: The president of the United States can be referred to as either
   "the President" or "President _____."

** Capitalize all proper nouns.

WP Advantage: most word processors have an automatic search procedure that
makes it easy to check for errors in capitalization.

ABBREVIATIONS IN TEXT

3.34   Following a few simple rules ensures consistent use of abreviations:

** With few exceptions, don't use periods in abbreviations. Thus: <u>GPO</u> (not
   <u>G.P.O.</u>); <u>AFL-CIO</u> (not <u>A.F.L.-C.I.O.</u>).

** Use periods with these exceptions: <u>A.D.</u>, <u>B.C.</u>, <u>a.m.</u>, <u>p.m.</u>, <u>B.A.</u>, <u>B.S.</u>,
   <u>e.g.</u>, <u>F.R.</u> (Federal Register), <u>i.e.</u>, <u>Ph.D.</u>, <u>r.p.m.</u>, <u>A & M.</u> (as in <u>Florida</u>
   <u>A. & M.</u>), <u>U.N.</u>, <u>U.S.C.</u> (U.S. Code).

** Use abbreviations for scholastic degrees: <u>B.A.</u>, <u>M.S.</u>, <u>Ph.D.</u>

** Leave a single space between individuals' initials. Thus: <u>D. L. J.</u>, <u>L. L. Bean</u>.

** DON'T abbreviate addresses; always spell out <u>Street</u>, <u>Avenue</u>, <u>Boulevard</u>, and other such designations.

** See also Section 3.32.

WP Advantage: most word processors have an automatic search procedure that makes it easy to check for errors in abbreviation.

PUNCTUATION RULES

Apostrophe

3. 35   This section and those that follow list some of the most common punctuation rules. Use apostrophes to mark the omission of figures (as in <u>Class of '56</u>) and the omission of letters in dialect (as in <u>she's a-goin'</u>). Use "'s" to form the plural of all small letters (<u>a's</u>, <u>b's</u>) and of all capital letters that could be misread without the apostrophe. Thus: <u>A's</u>, <u>Ss</u>. Also use apostrophes in certain colloquial expressions (a <u>month's work</u>, an <u>hour's drive</u>), in contractions (<u>can't</u>, <u>didn't</u>; rarely acceptable in scholarly writing) and in possessives. In most cases, form the possessive by simply adding <u>'s</u> to the noun or pronoun. When a proper name ends in <u>s</u>, <u>z</u>, <u>sh</u>, <u>zh</u>, <u>ch</u>, or <u>j</u>:
** To names of one syllable and names with a silent final s, add <u>'s</u>: <u>Jones's</u> book, <u>Vais's</u> book. EXCEPTION: Names in classical literature (e.g., <u>Mars' wish</u>).

** To names of more than one syllable, add only an apostrophe: <u>Maris' book</u>.

With certain common nouns (e.g., conscience, appearance, righteousness), a regard for euphony dictates forming the possessive solely with the apostrophe. Thus: <u>conscience'</u> sake. Don't use apostrophes with possessive pronouns; <u>her's</u>, <u>his'</u>, and <u>it's</u> are wrong. Note, though, that <u>it's</u> as a contraction of <u>it is</u> is correct. Never use an apostrophe as a substitute for grave or an acute mark in a foreign word.

Bullet

3.36   Bullets are small filled circles used to emphasize points or items in
lists.   Word processors sometimes have a bullet command or key.   On word processors that don't and on ordinary typewriters, use a small "o", typed on the
line with text and filled in with a fine-line magic marker.   Bullets are used
in much the same way I use double asterisks in this book.   The style requirements are:

** Leave one or two spaces between the bullet and the first word of text (GPO
   style requires two spaces).

** Either use no punctuation or punctuate consistently.   End the last item in
   a list with a period.

** Double-space between bulleted items.

** Single-space the turnover lines of a single bulleted item, following the
   style in this item, unless a publisher has required double-spacing for all
   lines in a manuscript.

Colon

3.37   Use colons to show that what follows is an example, explanation, or
elaboration of what has just been said.   Skip a space after a colon.   Colons
often introduce quotations.   For use of colons in documentation and bibliographies, see descriptions of styles in Chapters 6 and 7.

Comma

3.38   General rules about use of commas are:

** Decide whether to use a serial comma before <u>and</u> and <u>or</u> in a series such as
   <u>boys</u>, <u>girls</u>, and <u>parents</u>. Mark your choice on the style sheet. GPO style
   requires it; most styles leave the choice to the writer or typist. Whichever you choose, be consistent.

** Decide whether to use commas after short introductory clauses. Mark your
   choice on the style sheet.   The only set rule is: be consistent.   For
   example:

In the early 1980s[,] she . . .

By storytime[,] he was tired.

** Use a comma between coordinate adjectives (a large, mean dog) and before coordinating conjunctions that join independent clauses (e.g., Do this, and then go).

** Set off parenthetical words and phrases with commas:

In that event, then, . . .

The rules in Part I, Chapter 3, say that . . .

John Smith, President of the Soccer Club, . . .

John Smith, the internist, . . .

** Use a comma after fairly long phrases or clauses that precede the main clause in a sentence. For example, see the last sentence in Section 3.37.

** Use a comma after a series of adjectives: a large, strong, red dog.

** Use commas to separate identical or nearly identical words:

They walked in, in turn.

** Use a comma after these expressions: i.e., e.g., etc.

** Use a comma in numbers with four or more digits: 1,000, 2,560. EXCEPTIONS: addresses, telephone numbers, common decimal fractions, serial numbers, and astronomical or military time.

** Use no comma between the month and the year. For example: June 1982. DO use one after the year in complete dates: June 21, 1962, is the date.

** Use a comma before and after a state name that is combined with a city name in text; for example: Tampa, Florida, and Bloomington, Indiana.

** Use a comma followed by a space after Jr., Sr., Esq., and Inc.

** Use a comma as a substitute for a cedilla in a foreign word.

Dashes

3.39   An "en dash," used to replace the word to when it denotes a period of time or sequence of numbers, is typed as a hyphen. Thus: <u>1950-1960</u>, <u>September-June</u>, <u>Sections 3.4-3.7</u>. An "em dash," used to set off parts of a sentence, is typed as two dashes with no space around them. The basic uses, with examples, are:

** To set off an element that breaks the flow of thought:

      John--he had tired of babysitting--tried lawnmowing.

** To set off a summarizing conclusion:

      John left--too tired to stay any longer.

** To show breaks in speech:

      "It's hard--but going is--I just don't know."

You can end a line with one or two dashes (don't split double dashes), but don't begin a line with a dash unless it begins an item in a list.

Exclamation Mark

3.40   Exclamation marks express surprise. They are rarely used in scholarly and technical writing and should be sparingly used in other kinds of writing. Too many dilutes the effect of all exclamation marks.

Parentheses

3.41   Parentheses are used to enclose parenthetical remarks (somewhat like a pair of double dashes) and to enclose some items in documentation (more details are in the discussions of styles in Chapters 6 through 8).

Period

3.42   Use periods to end sentences, notes, and complete blocks of information. Place a period after a parenthesis at the end of a sentence unless the entire sentence is inside parentheses and thus independent, in which case the period goes before the parenthesis. Turabian recommends no period at the end of items in short numbered lists. See also Section 3.23 for the use of periods with an ellipsis. Place periods inside closing quotation marks unless a parenthetical or bracketed reference intervenes. For instance:

John's work was "complete."

John's work was "complete" (or so he said).

Quotation Marks

3.43   Use quotation marks to enclose words misused or used in a special sense (see example just above), words referred to as words, and parenthetical English translations of words and phrases from another language. DON'T use quotation marks with words used as examples of language; instead, underline them (See Section 3.47). Quotation marks are also acceptable as a substitute for an umlaut in foreign words. Sections 5.9, 5.16, and 5.18 and Chapters 6 through 8 treat the use of quotation marks in documentation styles.

Semicolon

3.44   Use semicolons:

** To separate items in a series when some of the items require internal commas (e.g., dogs, cats, and horses; birds, fish, and worms).

** To separate independent clauses not joined by a coordinating conjunction (e.g, next-to-last sentence, previous paragraph).

** To separate independent clauses joined by a coordinating conjunction _if_ one of the clauses contains several internal commas.

Slash (Virgule)

3.45   Use a slash to separate lines of poetry (as when quoted in text), elements of dates, and (occasionally) alternative words; for instance: and/or. Also use slashes to enclose phonemic transcriptions.

Square Brackets

3.46   Use square brackets to enclose parenthetical expressions within parentheses, to enclose changes in quotations (see Sections 3.23 and 3.24), missing data in documentation (see discussions of styles in Chapters 6 and 7), and phonetic transcription.

Underline (Italics)

3.47   Except for the required underlining of headings and subheadings in some styles, as a general rule avoid underlining, even for emphasis. A little goes a long way; too much, especially in text prepared for publication, destroys the effect and clutters pages.   The special conventions are:

** Underline words and phrases used as examples and proper names of art works, long musical works, ships, and aircraft.

** Underline only the most obscure foreign words and phrases. EXCEPTION: Legal documents, which require underlining of terms such as <u>et al.</u>, <u>ibid.</u>, and <u>op. cit</u>.

** Don't underline foreign proper names and titles.

WP Advantage: some word processors automatically underline as needed. The typist touches the underline key at the beginning and the end of a passage to turn the underlining on and off.

FIGURES OR WORDS?

General Rules

3.48   Two different sets of rules govern the use of figures versus words to express numerals in text. Rules for **nontechnical writing** most often apply to nonscholarly manuscripts and to manuscripts in the humanities, languages, history, and nonquantitative social sciences because such manuscripts have few numbers in them. Also, book publishers are more likely than journal editors to prefer these rules. Rules for **technical writing** most often apply to manuscripts in mathematics, natural and physical sciences, engineering, behavioral sciences, and quantitative social sciences. GPO style follows rules for technical writing. For rules on punctuation of numbers, see Section 3.38. For rules on treatment of continued numbers, such as pages and years, see the rules for pages in Section 5.16. For treatment of outline numbers and numbered lists, see Sections 3.10 and 3.17 through 3.20 respectively.

3.49   Some rules apply to both conventions. For instance, always use figures for:

** Parts of a book or article: p. 6, Part 4, Table 7.1.

** Decimals, ratios, fractions, arithmetic percentages, units of time, years, eras (such as 48 B.C., 77 A.D.), time expressed with A.M. or P.M. (including noontime, which is expressed as 12:00 M), monarchs and popes (such as Wilhelm VI, John Paul II), family names (such as William E. Smith III), exact amounts of money, scores and points on scales, numbers mentioned as numerals, page numbers, series of four or more, and numbers of lodges and unions when the number follows the name (e.g., Secretarial Union No. 16).

3.50   Other general rules are:

** Use words for numbers that begin a sentence, fractions that stand by themselves (without a whole number), and numbers that precede the name of churches, lodges, and unions (e.g., Seventh Day Adventists).

** Use both figures and numbers to express very large round numbers: 4.3 billion, $4 million, $6.5 billion.

** In American styles, use commas between third and fourth numbers from the right, the sixth and seventh, and so forth. In British styles, use a decimal instead of a comma. EXCEPTIONS in both styles: page and line numbers, years, and addresses.

** Don't use a capital 1 (I) in place of an arabic 1.

Nontechnical Writing

3.51   In nontechnical text matter:[7]

** Spell exact numbers that are less than 100.

** Use figures for numbers 100 or above.

** Use figures for numbers grouped within a sentence or several sentences in a sequence when <u>any</u> of the numbers is 100 or more.

** Use figures for round numbers when several occur in the same sentence or paragraph.

** In MLA and Turabian styles, use numbers for any numeric value, including percentages and amounts of money, that cannot be written out in one or two words. For example: <u>two</u>, <u>fifty</u>, <u>two pounds</u>, <u>one hundred</u>, <u>one thousand</u>, <u>one million</u>; <u>3 1/4</u>, <u>203</u>, <u>357</u>.[8]

3.52   Use words for:

** Round numbers in the hundreds, thousands, and millions.

** Centuries and decades (twentieth century, forties). EXCEPTION: Use <u>1950s</u> (MSH, MSN) or <u>1950's</u> (GPO), NOT <u>nineteen fifties</u>.

** Governments, political divisions, military units: Third Reich, Ninety-eighth Congress; Fifth Ward, Third Precinct; Sixth Army.

Technical and Statistical Writing

3.53   In technical and statistical writing, where numbers are frequently used, stylistic conventions permit a more liberal use of numerals to save space. For cardinal numbers (1, 2, 3, 4; one, two, three, four) and ordinal numbers (1st, 2nd, 3rd, 4th; first, second, third, fourth):

** Use words for the numbers zero through nine, except as specified below.

3.54   Express in figures:

** Numbers 10 or greater.

** Numbers that refer to the same unit and are grouped within a sentence or several sentences in a sequence <u>when any</u> number is 10 or more.

** All percentiles and quartiles: 4th (not fourth) percentile.

3.55   In general, use arabic numerals unless roman numerals are part of an established term, such as Type I and Type II errors.[9]

NOTES TO CHAPTER 3

1. For instance, try Porter G. Perrin, <u>Writer's Guide and Index to English</u>, 5th ed. (Glenview, Ill.: Scott, Foresman, 1972), p. 550 and 684-86.

2. David Knoke, "A Causal Synthesis of Sociological and Psychological Models of American Voting Behavior," <u>Social Forces</u> 53 (1974): 93.

3. Society for Technical Communication, <u>Typing Guide for Mathematical Expressions,</u> (Washington, D. C.: STC, 1976).

4. <u>MLA Handbook for Writers of Research Papers, Theses, and Dissertations</u> (New York: Modern Language Association, 1980).

5. Barbara Hughes, <u>Typing Manual,</u> 3rd ed. (Alexandria, Va: Editorial Experts, Inc., 1979), p. 8; Udia G. Olsen, 9th ed. <u>Preparing the Manuscript</u> (Boston: The Writer, 1978), pp. 92-96; Kate L. Turabian, <u>A Manual for Writers of Term Papers, Theses, and Dissertations</u> 4th ed. (Chicago: University of Chicago Press, 1973).

6. Olsen, <u>Preparing,</u> p. 94.

7. University of Chicago Press, <u>A Manual of Style,</u> 10th ed. (Chicago: University of Chicago Press, 1969), pp. 196-204.

8. MLA, <u>MLA Handbook,</u> p. 13-15.

9. American Psychological Association, <u>Publication Manual of the American Psychological Association,</u> 2d ed. (Washington, D.C.: American Psychological Association., pp. 41-43.

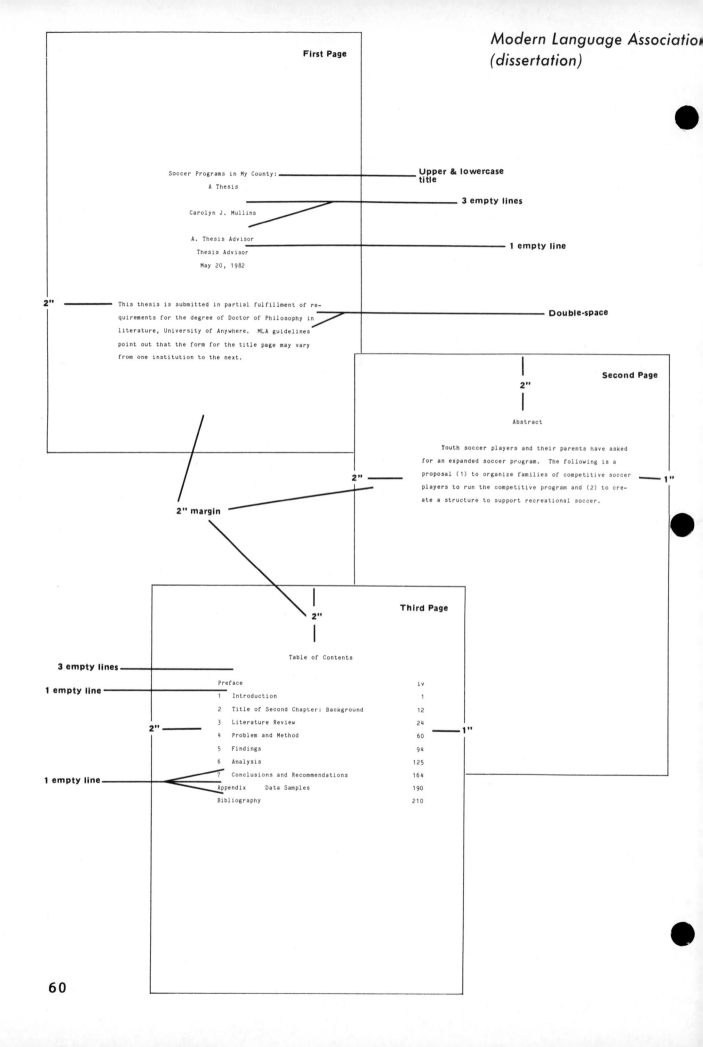

First Page

Soccer Programs in My County: **Upper & lowercase title**
A Thesis

                                                 3 empty lines
Carolyn J. Mullins

A. Thesis Advisor   **1 empty line**
Thesis Advisor
May 20, 1982

2"   This thesis is submitted in partial fulfillment of re-   **Double-space**
quirements for the degree of Doctor of Philosophy in
literature, University of Anywhere. MLA guidelines
point out that the form for the title page may vary
from one institution to the next.

Second Page

2"

Abstract

        Youth soccer players and their parents have asked
for an expanded soccer program. The following is a
proposal (1) to organize families of competitive soccer   **1"**
players to run the competitive program and (2) to create a structure to support recreational soccer.

2"

2" margin

Third Page

2"

Table of Contents

3 empty lines

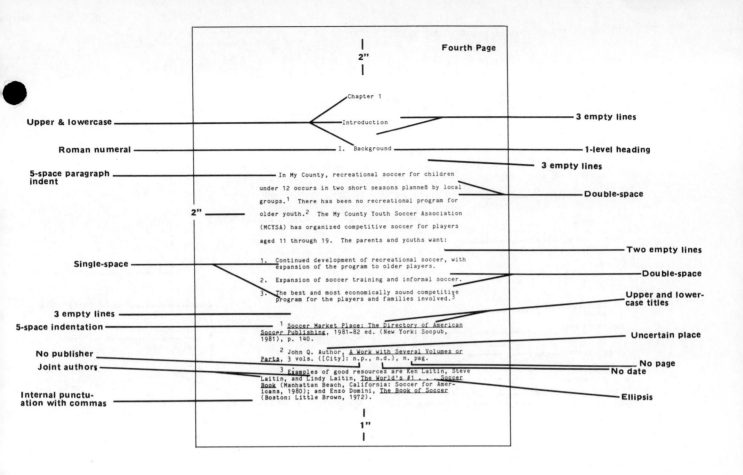

Fourth Page

2"

Chapter 1

Upper & lowercase —— Introduction —————————— 3 empty lines

Roman numeral —— I. Background ———————————— 1-level heading

———————————— 3 empty lines

5-space paragraph indent —— In My County, recreational soccer for children

under 12 occurs in two short seasons planned by local ——— Double-space

groups.[1] There has been no recreational program for

2" —— older youth.[2] The My County Youth Soccer Association

(MCYSA) has organized competitive soccer for players

aged 11 through 19. The parents and youths want:

———————— Two empty lines

Single-space —— 1. Continued development of recreational soccer, with
    expansion of the program to older players.

2. Expansion of soccer training and informal soccer. ——— Double-space

3. The best and most economically sound competitive
    program for the players and families involved.[3]

———————— Upper and lower-case titles

3 empty lines ——
5-space indentation ——   [1] Soccer Market Place: The Directory of American
Soccer Publishing, 1981-82 ed. (New York: Socpub, ——— Uncertain place
1981), p. 140.

No publisher ——   [2] John Q. Author, A Work with Several Volumes or
Joint authors —— Parts, 3 vols. ([City]: n.p., n.d.), n. pag. ——— No page / No date

   [3] Examples of good resources are Ken Laitin, Steve
Internal punctu- —— Laitin, and Lindy Laitin, The World's #1 . . . Soccer
ation with commas —— Book (Manhattan Beach, California: Soccer for Americans, 1980); and Enzo Domini, The Book of Soccer ——— Ellipsis
(Boston: Little Brown, 1972).

1"

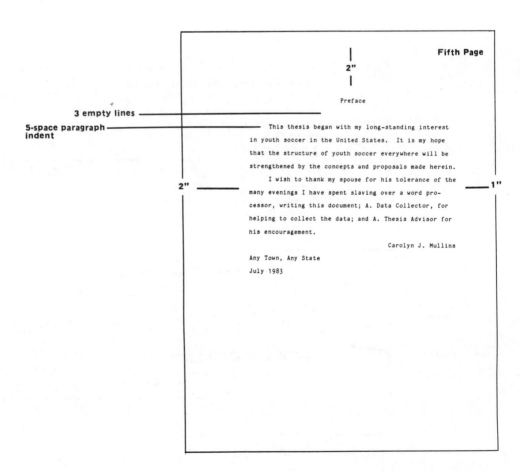

Fifth Page

2"

Preface

3 empty lines ——

5-space paragraph —— This thesis began with my long-standing interest
indent
in youth soccer in the United States. It is my hope

that the structure of youth soccer everywhere will be

strengthened by the concepts and proposals made herein.

2" —— I wish to thank my spouse for his tolerance of the —— 1"

many evenings I have spent slaving over a word pro-

cessor, writing this document; A. Data Collector, for

helping to collect the data; and A. Thesis Advisor for

his encouragement.

Carolyn J. Mullins

Any Town, Any State

July 1983

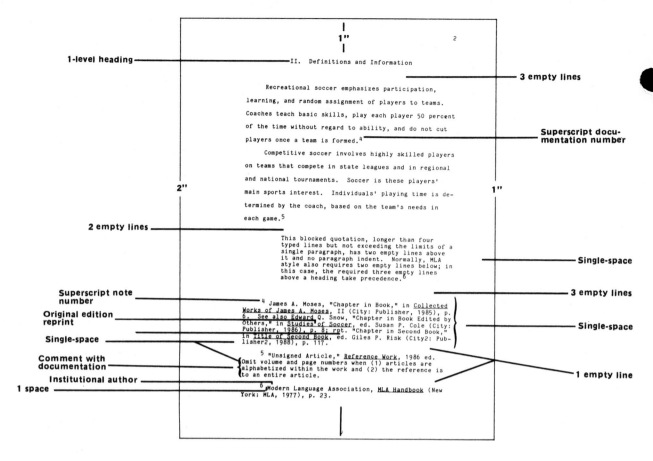

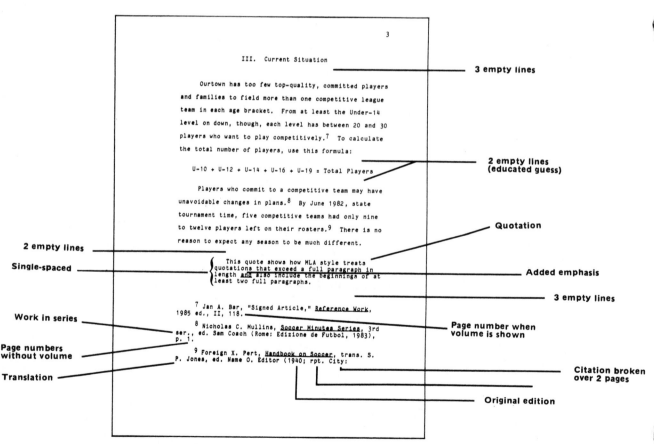

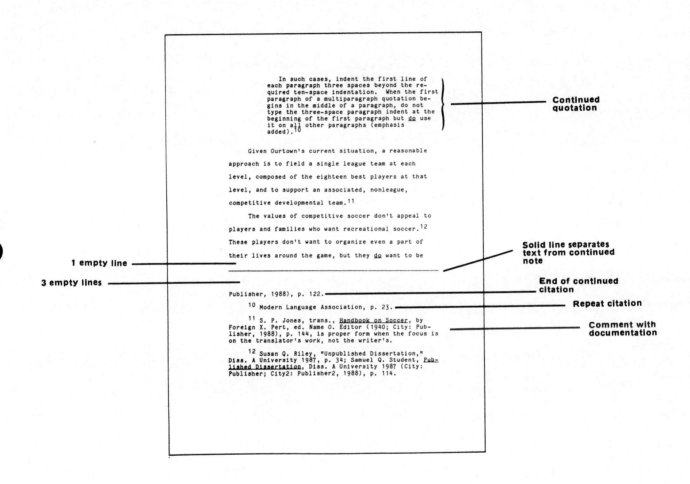

In such cases, indent the first line of each paragraph three spaces beyond the required ten-space indentation. When the first paragraph of a multiparagraph quotation begins in the middle of a paragraph, do not type the three-space paragraph indent at the beginning of the first paragraph but _do_ use it on all other paragraphs (emphasis added).[10]

Continued quotation

Given Ourtown's current situation, a reasonable approach is to field a single league team at each level, composed of the eighteen best players at that level, and to support an associated, nonleague, competitive developmental team.[11]

The values of competitive soccer don't appeal to players and families who want recreational soccer.[12] These players don't want to organize even a part of their lives around the game, but they _do_ want to be

Solid line separates text from continued note

1 empty line

3 empty lines

End of continued citation

Publisher, 1988), p. 122.

[10] Modern Language Association, p. 23.

Repeat citation

[11] S. P. Jones, trans., _Handbook on Soccer_, by Foreign X. Pert, ed. Name O. Editor (1940; City: Publisher, 1988), p. 144, is proper form when the focus is on the translator's work, not the writer's.

Comment with documentation

[12] Susan Q. Riley, "Unpublished Dissertation," Diss. A University 1987, p. 34; Samuel Q. Student, _Published Dissertation_, Diss. A University 1987 (City: Publisher; City2: Publisher2, 1988), p. 114.

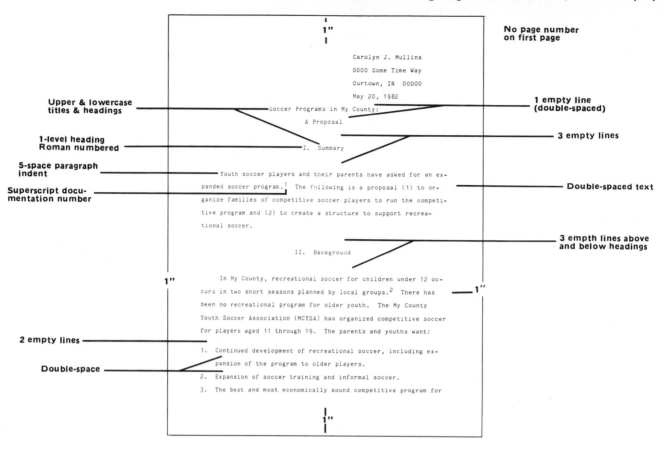

No page number on first page

Upper & lowercase titles & headings

1-level heading Roman numbered

5-space paragraph indent

Superscript documentation number

1"

2 empty lines

Double-space

1 empty line (double-spaced)

3 empty lines

Double-spaced text

3 empth lines above and below headings

1"

Carolyn J. Mullins
0000 Some Time Way
Ourtown, IN 00000
May 20, 1982

Soccer Programs in My County:

A Proposal

I. Summary

Youth soccer players and their parents have asked for an expanded soccer program.[1] The following is a proposal (1) to organize families of competitive soccer players to run the competitive program and (2) to create a structure to support recreational soccer.

II. Background

In My County, recreational soccer for children under 12 occurs in two short seasons planned by local groups.[2] There has been no recreational program for older youth. The My County Youth Soccer Association (MCYSA) has organized competitive soccer for players aged 11 through 19. The parents and youths want:

1. Continued development of recreational soccer, including expansion of the program to older players.
2. Expansion of soccer training and informal soccer.
3. The best and most economically sound competitive program for

1"

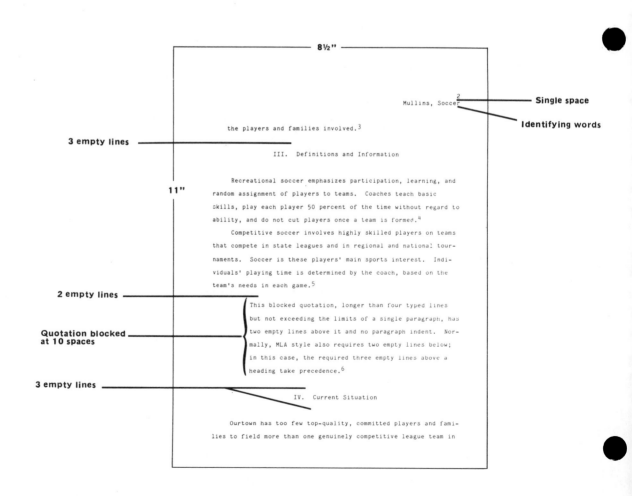

8½"

11"

3 empty lines

2 empty lines

Quotation blocked at 10 spaces

3 empty lines

Single space

Identifying words

Mullins, Soccer [2]

the players and families involved.[3]

III. Definitions and Information

Recreational soccer emphasizes participation, learning, and random assignment of players to teams. Coaches teach basic skills, play each player 50 percent of the time without regard to ability, and do not cut players once a team is formed.[4]

Competitive soccer involves highly skilled players on teams that compete in state leagues and in regional and national tournaments. Soccer is these players' main sports interest. Individuals' playing time is determined by the coach, based on the team's needs in each game.[5]

This blocked quotation, longer than four typed lines but not exceeding the limits of a single paragraph, has two empty lines above it and no paragraph indent. Normally, MLA style also requires two empty lines below; in this case, the required three empty lines above a heading take precedence.[6]

IV. Current Situation

Ourtown has too few top-quality, committed players and families to field more than one genuinely competitive league team in

each age bracket. From at least the Under-14 level on down,
though, each level has between 20 and 30 players who want to play
competitively.[7] To calculate the total number of players, use
this formula:

2 empty lines (educated guess)

$$U-10 + U-12 + U-14 + U-16 + U-19 = Total Players$$

Players who commit to a competitive team may have unavoidable changes in plans.[8] By June 1982, state tournament time,
five competitive teams had only nine to twelve players left on
their rosters.[9] There is no reason to expect any season to be
much different.

2 empty lines

3-space indent

This quote shows how MLA style treats quotations
that exceed a full paragraph in length _and_ also include
the beginnings of at least two full paragraphs.

Added emphasis

3 space indent

In such cases, indent the first line of each paragraph three spaces beyond the required ten-space indentation. When the first paragraph of a multiparagraph
quotation begins in the middle of a paragraph, do not
type the three-space paragraph indent at the beginning
of the first paragraph but _do_ use it on all other paragraphs (emphasis added).[10]

2-paragraph quotation

Double-space

Superscript documentation number

2 empty lines

Given Ourtown's current situation, a reasonable approach is
to field a single league team at each level, composed of the
eighteen best players at that level, and to support an associated, nonleague, competitive developmental team.[11]

The values of competitive soccer don't appeal to players and
families who want recreational soccer.[12] These players don't
want to organize even a part of their lives around the game, but
they _do_ want to be able to play it strictly for fun. Players between the ages of 12 and 19 have special needs in this regard.

V. Proposed Plan

Organized soccer requires players, coaches, fields, referees, teams, and parent support (Jones, p. 145). MCYSA has
players, fields, referees, and teams for both programs.[13] It
also has coaches and parent support for most competitive teams[14]
but none for a recreational program. However, MCYSA could, as
Figure 1 shows, provide the structure to support one.

In-text reference

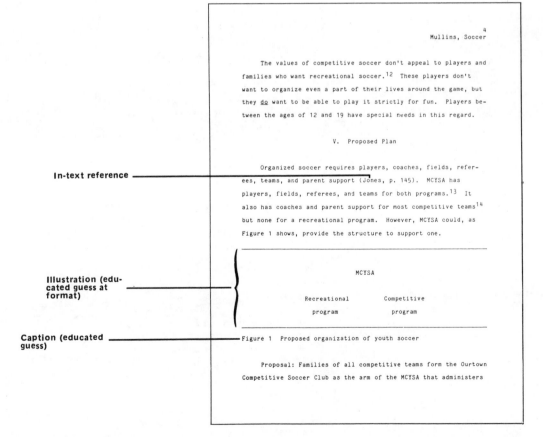

MCYSA

Recreational   Competitive
program   program

Illustration (educated guess at format)

Caption (educated guess)

Figure 1 Proposed organization of youth soccer

Proposal: Families of all competitive teams form the Ourtown
Competitive Soccer Club as the arm of the MCYSA that administers

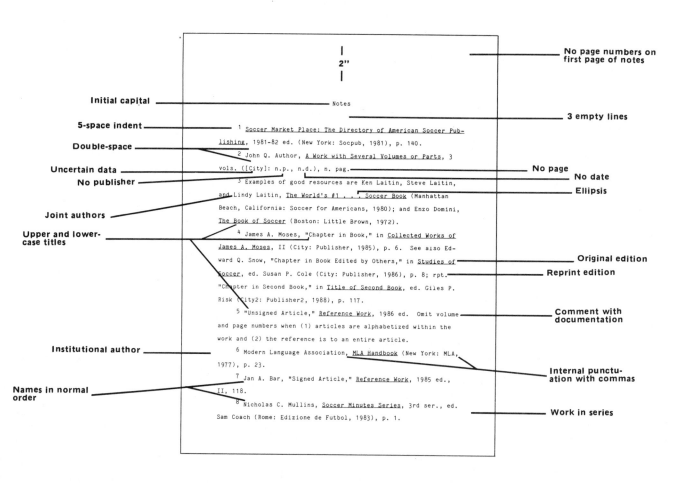

Translated work ⟶ 9 Foreign X. Pert, <u>Handbook on Soccer</u>, trans. S. P. Jones, ed. Name O. Editor (1940; rpt. City: Publisher, 1988), p. 122.

Repeat citation ⟶ 10 Modern Language Association, p. 23.

Reprint ⟶ 11 S. P. Jones, trans., <u>Handbook on Soccer</u>, by Foreign X.

Original edition ⟶ Pert, ed. Name O. Editor (1940; City: Publisher, 1988), p. 144, is proper form when the focus is on the translator's work, not the writer's.

12 Susan Q. Riley, "Unpublished Dissertation," Diss. A University 1987, p. 34; Samuel Q. Student, <u>Published Dissertation</u>, Diss. A University 1987 (City: Publisher; City2: Publisher2, 1988), p. 114. ⟵ **Specific page cited**

13 Frederick P. Lake, "Conference Paper," <u>Conference on Soccer</u>, Proc. of a Conference on American Soccer, 4-5 Nov. 1986 ⟵ **Months abbreviated** (City: Publisher, 1987), p. 118.

14 My County Youth Soccer Association, <u>By-Laws</u>, rev. ed. (Ourtown, Indiana: MCYSA, 1980), p. 6.

15 <u>Cong. Rec.</u>, 12 Mar. 1977, pp. 3821-41; E. B. Walsh, <u>Soccer Riots in South America</u>, U.S. 208th Cong., 3rd sess., H. Rept. 106 (1977; rpt. New York: Publisher, 1980); New York City, Smith Commission, <u>Smith Commission Report</u> (New York: Arno, [1973?]), pp. 23-24; Great Britain, Ministry for Women, <u>Document Title</u> (London, HMSO, 1987), IV, 135. ⟵ **Several citations; one note**

Book volumes in capital Roman numerals ⟶ 16 Jane R. Ramsey, "Article in Journal with Continuous Pagination Through Annual Volume," <u>Journal Name</u>, 21 (1987), 15.

⟵ **"p." or "pp." not needed because volume number is given**

17 Jane R. Ramsey, "Article from Journal that Pages Each Issue Separately," <u>Journal Name</u>, 20, No. 5 (1988), 4-6. ⟵ **Journal volumes in Arabic numerals**

Underline journal name ⟶ 18 Francis M. Ludlow, "Article from Journal with More than

---

New series ⟶ One Series," <u>Journal Name</u>, NS 1 (1987), 67.

19 Mary P. Pugh, "Article in Weekly Magazine or Newspaper," <u>Newspaper</u>, 22 Sept. 1988, p. 1, col. 2.

20 "Anonymous Article in Monthly Magazine," <u>Name of Magazine</u>, Oct. 1985, p. 91.

21 Vera R. Tanner, "Article in Daily Newspaper," <u>Newspaper Name</u>, Late City Ed., 12 Oct. 1985, Sec. 1, p. 36, col. 2.

22 Daniel P. Sheets, "Editorial Title," Editorial, <u>Name of Newspaper</u>, 26 July 1986, Sec. A, p. 22, cols. 1-3.

23 Daniel P. Sheets, Letter to Editor, <u>Publication Name</u>, 21 (1987), 15.

24 David C. White, rev. of <u>Soccer Coaching</u>, by John M. Coach, <u>Magazine or Journal Name</u>, 13 (1986), 76-77.

Book review ⟶ 25 "Unsigned Review," rev. of <u>Soccer and Coaching</u>, ed. John M. Coach, <u>Weekly Newsmagazine</u>, 13 Sept. 1986, pp. 76-77.

26 "Review of James G. Thomas' 'Title,'" <u>Journal</u>, 1 (1974), 220-21.

27 Susan W. Student, "Article from Dissertation Abstracts," <u>DA</u>, 29 (1967), 3026A (University Name).

Typescript ⟶ 28 Notebook 34, TS, p. 44. This and all other notebooks cited are in the Soccer Hall of Fame, City, State.

Convention paper ⟶ 29 Mary Lecturer, "Title of Paper," Section 7, Lecturers' Convention, City, 24 May 1975.

Movie ⟶ 30 Movie Director, dir., <u>Title of Movie</u>, with Name O. Star, Movie Company, 1985.

Play ⟶ 31 Play Director, dir., <u>Title of Play</u>, by Name O. Playright, with Name O. Starr, Theatre Name, City, 5 Mar. 1985.

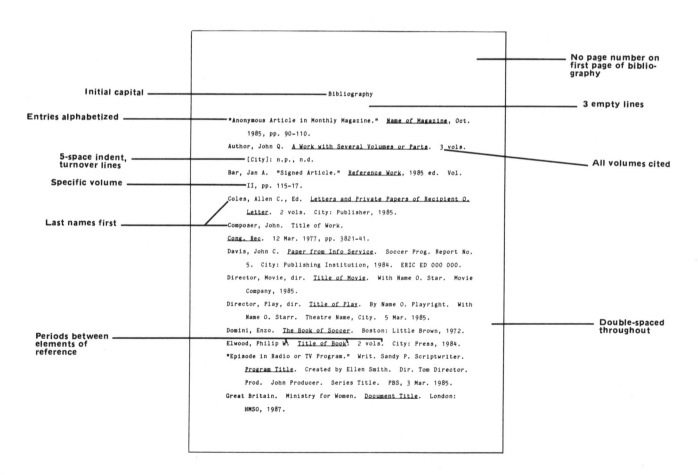

Musical work — 32 John Composer, Title of Work.

Radio or TV program — 33 "Episode in Radio or TV Program," writ. Sandy P. Scriptwriter, Program Title, created by Ellen Smith, dir. Tom Director, prod. John Producer, Series Title, PBS, 3 Mar. 1985.

Song catalogue number — 34 Star Singer, "Title of Song," Title of Album, Recording Company, 12345, 1985.

35 "To Recipient O. Letter," 6 May 1948, Letter 452, Letters and Private Papers of Recipient O. Letter, ed. Allen C. Coles (City: Publisher, 1985), II, 322-23.

Correspondence — 36 Letter Writer, Letter to John C. Recipient, 25 May 1985, John C. Recipient Papers, Southwest Library, Ourtown, Indiana.

Correspondence with author — 37 Letter received from David W. Hains, 24 June 1985.

38 Personal interview with Sue C. Low, 27 July 1984.

39 John C. Davis, Paper from Info Service, Soccer Prog. Report No. 5 (City: Publishing Institution, 1984), p. 22 (ERIC ED 000 000).

Indirect source — 40 James P. Edge, 14 Dec. 1934, as quoted in Philip W. Elwood, Title of Book, II (City: Press, 1984), 450.

Interview

No page number on first page of bibliography

Initial capital — Bibliography

3 empty lines

Entries alphabetized — "Anonymous Article in Monthly Magazine." Name of Magazine, Oct. 1985, pp. 90-110.

Author, John Q. A Work with Several Volumes or Parts. 3 vols.

5-space indent, turnover lines — [City]: n.p., n.d.

All volumes cited

Bar, Jan A. "Signed Article." Reference Work, 1985 ed. Vol.

Specific volume — II, pp. 115-17.

Coles, Allen C., Ed. Letters and Private Papers of Recipient O. Letter. 2 vols. City: Publisher, 1985.

Last names first — Composer, John. Title of Work.

Cong. Rec. 12 Mar. 1977, pp. 3821-41.

Davis, John C. Paper from Info Service. Soccer Prog. Report No. 5. City: Publishing Institution, 1984. ERIC ED 000 000.

Director, Movie, dir. Title of Movie. With Name O. Star. Movie Company, 1985.

Director, Play, dir. Title of Play. By Name O. Playright. With Name O. Starr. Theatre Name, City. 5 Mar. 1985.

Domini, Enzo. The Book of Soccer. Boston: Little Brown, 1972.

Double-spaced throughout

Periods between elements of reference — Elwood, Philip W. Title of Book. 2 vols. City: Press, 1984.

"Episode in Radio or TV Program." Writ. Sandy P. Scriptwriter. Program Title. Created by Ellen Smith. Dir. Tom Director. Prod. John Producer. Series Title. PBS, 3 Mar. 1985.

Great Britain. Ministry for Women. Document Title. London: HMSO, 1987.

Hains, David W. Letter to author. 24 June 1985.

Jones, S. P., trans. Handbook on Soccer. By Foreign X. Pert.
    Ed. Name O. Editor. 1940; City: Publisher, 1988.

Joint authors' names reversed for first author only

Laitin, Ken, Steve Laitin, and Lindy Laitin. The World's #1
    Best-Selling Soccer Book. Manhattan Beach, California:
    Soccer for Americans, 1980.

Names not reversed

Lake, Frederick P. "Conference Paper." Conference on Soccer.
    Proc. of a Conference on American Soccer. 4-5 Nov. 1986.
    City: Publisher, 1987.

Lecturer, Mary. "Title of Paper." Section 7, Lecturers' Conven-
    tion. City. 24 May 1975.

Low, Sue C. Personal interview. 27 July 1984.

Ludlow, Francis M. "Article from Journal with More than One Ser-
    ies." Journal Name, NS 1 (1987), 65-101.

Inclusive page numbers

MLA Handbook for Writers of Research Papers, Theses, and Disser-
    tations. By the Modern Language Association. New York:
    MLA, 1977.

Modern Language Association. MLA Handbook for Writers of Re-
    search Papers, Theses, and Dissertations. New York: MLA,
    1977.

Specific book volume used

Moses, James A. "Chapter in Book." In Collected Works of James
    A. Moses. Vol. II. City: Publisher, 1985.

Mullins, Nicholas C. Soccer Minutes Series. 3rd ser. Ed. Sam
    Coach. Rome: Edizione de Futbol, 1983.

My County Youth Soccer Association. By-Laws. Rev. ed. Ourtown
    Indiana: MCYSA, 1980.

New York City. Smith Commission. Smith Commission Report. New

Student, Susan W. "Article from Dissertation Abstracts." DA, 29
    (1967), 3026A (University Name).

Tanner, Vera R. "Article in Daily Newspaper." Newspaper Name,
    Late City Ed., 12 Oct. 1985, Sec. 1, p. 36, col. 2.

Section

Column

"Unsigned Article." Reference Work. 1986 ed.

"Unsigned Review." Rev. of Soccer and Coaching, ed. John M.
    Coach. Weekly Newsmagazine, 13 Sept. 1986, pp. 76-77.

Reprint

Walsh, E. B. Soccer Riots in South America. U.S. 208th Cong.,
    3rd sess. H. Rept. 106. 1977; rpt. New York: Publisher,
    1980.

White, David C. Rev. of Soccer Coaching, by John M. Coach. Mag-
    azine or Journal Name, 13 (1986), 76-77.

Writer, Letter. Letter to John C. Recipient. 25 May 1985. John
    C. Recipient Papers. Southwest Library, Ourtown, Indiana.

Uncertain date

York: Arno, [1973?].

Notebook 34, TS, p. 44. Soccer Hall of Fame, City, State.

Pert, Foreign X. Handbook on Soccer. Trans. S. P. Jones. Ed.
    Name O. Editor. 1940; rpt. City: Publisher, 1988.

Pugh, Mary P. "Article in Weekly Magazine or Newspaper." News-
    paper, 22 Sept. 1988, p. 1, cols. 2-3; p. 21, cols. 1-2.

Ramsey, Jane R. "Article in Journal with Continuous Pagination
    Through Annual Volume." Journal Name, 21 (1987), 14-20.

----------. "Article from Journal that Pages Each Issue Separ-
    ately." Journal Name, 20, No. 5 (1988), 2-8.

"Review of James G. Thomas' 'Title.'" Journal, 1 (1974), 220-21.

Riley, Susan Q. "Unpublished Dissertation." Diss. A University
    1987.

Same author as previous entry—ten dashes

Sheets, Daniel P. "Editorial Title." Editorial. Name of News-
    paper, 26 July 1986, Sec. A, p. 22, cols. 1-3.

----------. Letter to Editor. Publication Name, 21 (1987), 15.

Soccer Market Place: The Directory of American Soccer Publishing.
    1981-82 ed. New York: Socpub, 1981.

Singer, Star. "Title of Song." Title of Album. Recording Com-
    pany, 12345, 1985.

Snow, Edward Q. "Chapter in Book Edited by Others." In Studies
    of Soccer. Ed. Susan P. Cole. City: Publisher, 1986, pp.

Inclusive pages

    4-13. Rpt. "Chapter in Second Book." In Title of Second
    Book. Ed. Giles P. Risk. City2: Publisher2, 1988, pp.
    110-21.

Student, Samuel Q. Published Dissertation. Diss. A University
    1987. City: Publisher; City2: Publisher2, 1988.

69

Scripts, Poetry, Fillers, and Manuals

4.1   This chapter describes the basic rules for typing text forms such as scripts, poetry, and instructions.   Each forms has its own rules for line length and margins, vertical spacing, organization of parts, and underlining. This chapter describes the rules and shows how to apply them.   Illustrations are at the end of the chapter.

TREATMENT OF SCRIPT FORMS

General Rules

4.2   Most parts of plays--the title page, for example--can be typed following the patterns that govern parallel parts of other documents. Even parts that sound as esoteric as "character plot" and "lighting plot" can follow the rules for text typing described in Chapter 3. However, typing dialogue requires following strict, specialized rules so that readers can visually separate characters from dialogue and both from stage directions. The following sections, which describe these rules, summarize information given by Udia G. Olsen in <u>Preparing the Manuscript</u>.[1]

4.3   Play, television, and other scripts have parts quite different from other manuscripts. Furthermore, the treatment of parts depends on length as much as on style. For example, the first page of a one-act play may bear the title, author's name, list of characters, description of scenes, identification of time and place, and even the beginning of the play. In contrast, a full-length play might take a full page for the title and author's name and a page each for the list of characters, descriptions of acts and scenes, and synopsis. Play writers must decide what approach best suits their manuscript. In general, though, take into account the following elements:

** **Title page** with title of script and author's name and address.

** **Copyright** information.

** **Dedication.**

** **Story** of the play.

** **Cast of characters,** listed in order of appearance.

** **Synopsis** of **acts and scenes,** together with statements of **time and place.**

** **Plots of scenes,** including complete description of state setting with diagram.

** The **play.**

** **Plot of characters and wardrobes**--brief descriptions of characters and the clothes they wear.

** **Lighting plot**--special effects for each scene and act.

** **Property plot**--list of all props to be used on stage and off, organized by act and scene.

WP Advantage: many word processors make it easy to set up "forms" or "models" for, say, title pages that typists can copy over and over as needed. The forms save the time required for individual formating.

American Play Style

4.4   American style, illustrated in Figure 4.1, Part A, is one of two ways to prepare the body of a play. In this style:

** Center the character names on the page and type them completely in capital letters.

** Double-space the dialogue directly under the character's name, with the first line indented 5 spaces from the left margin.

** Type "turnover" (second and subsequent) lines "flush" (not indented).

** Single-space stage directions under the dialogue; indent all lines 5 spaces from the left margin, underline them, and enclose them in parentheses.

** If brief stage directions must be inserted in dialogue, always enclose them in parentheses and underline them.

WP Advantage: centering keys or commands and automatic indentation make this kind of typing easier and faster.

English Play Style

4.5   In the English style, shown in Figure 4.1, Part B:

** Type character names all in caps, flush with the left margin, with a colon following each name.

** When possible, begin the first line of dialogue on the same line as the character name, one or two spaces after the colon.

** Indent turnover lines of dialogue 5 spaces from the left margin to make a "hanging indentation" (the first line "hangs" over the following lines).

** Double-space the dialogue.

** Indent all lines of stage directions 10 spaces from the left margin, single-space and underline them, and enclose them in parentheses.

** If brief stage directions are essential in dialogue, underline them and enclose them in parentheses.

Television Script Style

4.6   Television scripts, illustrated in Figure 4.1, Part C, normally follow a two-column form with one column (about half the page) left blank so that the director has space to make notes on camera shots, lights, positions, and the like. For extremely long scripts, editors occasionally use a single, wide column placed in the middle of the page, with dialogue, stage directions, and camera directions included in the column. This form is used only when using the narrow side column would make the script too bulky to handle easily. **WP Advantage:** word processors allow typists to change margins at will. Thus, changing from a narrow side column to a wide center column, or vice versa, is an easy matter of two or three commands or keystrokes.

4.7   With the double-column format, editors are about evenly divided on whether to leave the left or the right blank, so it's wise to check with the potential purchaser before typing. **WP Advantage:** changing from one side to the other is a simple matter of two or three commands or keystrokes. The formating instructions are:

** Completely capitalize names of characters, underline them, and center them over the dialogue.

** Type all lines of directions capitalized and flush with the left margin.

** Indent all lines of dialogue 4 or 5 spaces from the left margin.

** Preface the script with a list of characters, descriptions of them, the number of sets in the script, and brief descriptions of sets.

** Complete a release form (get one from the program for which you are writing) to submit with the script.

TREATMENT OF VERSE FORMS

4.8   Poems and greeting card verses also follow specialized rules for text preparation. This discussion is summarized from Olsen's <u>Preparing the Manuscript</u>.[2]

Poems

4.9   When typing a poem:

** Center it vertically and horizontally on a full sheet of paper.

** Type it on a separate sheet of paper.

** Double-space between the lines of verse.

** Triple-space between stanzas.

** Center the longest line so that its ends are equally distant from the left and right margins.

If one line is so long as to throw the whole poem out of balance on the page, type a part of the line on the next line, indented 5 spaces (4 in Turabian style), with single spacing between the two lines. Then double-space and continue with the next line. **WP Advantage:** even if you guess wrong about vertical centering, word processing makes it easy to add or remove spaces at the top or bottom as needed to center a poem exactly. Similarly, when you start out not knowing which line is longest, word processing makes it easy to center all lines to find out. Then you can respace the shorter ones to line up with the beginning of the longest.

Greeting Card Verses

4.10   If poems are paper-spenders, greeting card verses are paper-savers. Type each on a separate sheet of paper; however, half-sheets, 3 x 5 cards, and 4 x 6 cards are all acceptable. Double-space unless the verse is long, in which case single-spacing is acceptable. Suggestions for illustrations should be made either on the page with the verse or on a separate page, attached to the verse page with a clip. Typing requirements are:

** Type the name and address on each page in the upper left-hand corner of the sheet.

** If the verses are numbered, type the number in the upper right-hand corner of the sheet, opposite the name.

** Center the heading for the verse and type it in capital letters. Skip a few spaces before beginning the verse.

** Type the name on each page even when several verses are to be sent in a single envelope. Don't count on the pages to stay together.

FILLERS

4.11   When typing fillers and other short pieces, always use a full-size sheet for each item. Type the name, address, and a word or two from the title on each page, even when two or more such pieces will be submitted in the same envelope. Treat prose pieces according to the rules in Chapter 3.

MANUALS

4.12   As with script forms, ordinary text follows the rules in Chapter 3. However, specific instructions and directions often are best suited to other forms of presentation such as playscripts, task outlines, information mapping, flow charts, pictures, and combinations of pictures and text. The following sections deal with the typed portions of these forms of presentation. Information comes from the works of Horn, Matthies, and Van Duyn.[3]

Playscripts

4.13   Playscripts present tasks in order of occurrence in a two-column format. They are particularly useful when more than one "actor" (person or office) in an organization participate in a procedure. The right column lists steps and substeps in order. The left column lists the person or office that does the steps and is blank except for the names. "Turnover" (second and subsequent) lines in the steps and substeps are indented according to the rules in Sections 3.10 and 3.19. For instance:

Actor

Actor 1

Actor 2

Action

1. Do . . .

2. Do second step . . . .

3. Do third step in procedure, which

<table>
<tbody>
<tr><td></td><td>brings someone different into the action.</td></tr>
<tr><td></td><td>4. Do fourth step . . .</td></tr>
<tr><td></td><td>5. Do fifth step . . .</td></tr>
<tr><td>Actor 3</td><td>6. Do final step in procedure, which has two possible ends.</td></tr>
<tr><td></td><td>a. If this, do . . .</td></tr>
<tr><td></td><td>b. If that, do . . .</td></tr>
</tbody>
</table>

Task Outlines

4.14   Like playscripts, task outlines list steps in procedures in time order. Unlike them, they involve only a single actor or office. Often, playscripts refer to one or more task outlines. At least two formats exist. One is exactly like playscript format except that the left side lists groups of items such as categories of work, sets of forms, kinds of mail, or sets of tools. For instance:

<u>Group of Items</u>	<u>Steps</u>
Letters	1. Do . . .
	2. Do . . .
Bills	3. Do . . .
	4. Do . . .

4.15   The second form is much like the task outlines I give in this book and can usually be typed in the same way. One major difference: instead of leading asterisks, some firms might use bullets, dashes, or numbers. For a good example, see the list of instructions on mimeograph stencils in Section 2.19.

4.16   The same principles govern both formats:

** Make the steps as clear and separate as possible.

** Make the actor as clear as possible.

** Make the beginning and the end obvious.

Information Mapping

4.17   Information mapping presents information in horizontal blocks separated by a horizontal line. In simplified form, an information-mapped page might look like this:

Introduction	The introduction block begins at the top of the page and continues in blocked paragraph form.
Definition	The definition block follows the introduction and continues in blocked paragraph form.
Example	The example block comes next. It is usually the longest section. It will continue as long as is needed to make the procedure clear. The hope is to keep the length of each map to a page or less.

4.18   The general rules for typing information maps are:

** Keep the information in blocks and draw lines between blocks.

** Type all lines even with the left margin (use no paragraph indentation).

** Never put more than one map on a page, even when you have several to type and each occupies only part of a page. (The separate pages make updating easier.)

Flowcharts

4.19   Flowcharts consist of instructions typed inside variously shaped symbols such as circles, squares, rectangles, triangles, trapezoids, cylinders,

and the like. These symbols stand for business and computer elements and operations such as magnetic tape, auxiliary operations, processing, merging
(combining two or more sets of items into one set), manual operations, magnetic disks, and so forth. Connecting arrows depict the flow of work.

4.20   As you might expect, brevity is absolutely necessary because the
words have to fit inside the symbols. Editors, writers, and typists with a
flair for scrapping useless words can be extremely valuable to the producers
of flowcharts. The general typing rules are:

** Single-space the lines.

** Type all lines even with the left margin of symbols that have a vertical
   left side. Don't indent first lines of paragraphs.

** In other symbols (circles, ovals, trapezoids, etc.), center each typed line
   between the left and right margins.

** After decision blocks, type the "Yes" and "No" above the shaft of horizontal arrows and to the right of the shaft of vertical arrows. For example:

Yes   No

Text-Type Procedures

4.21   Text-type procedures, the style favored by the military, closely resemble the instructions in this book. The general typing instructions are:

** List steps in order of occurrence.

** Pay careful attention to numbering procedures; they differ from one organization to the next and are required by the military.

** Single-space the steps.

** Double-space between steps.

** Use arabic numerals (1, 2, 3) for major steps. Use letters (a, b, c) for substeps.

** Put periods and two spaces after the numbers of letters. Line up the periods according to the instructions in Section 3.10.

** Indent turnover lines of text according to the instructions for numbered short subparagraphs in Sections 3.19 and 3.20.

** Type "START OF PROCEDURE" at the beginning and "END OF PROCEDURE" at the end. For instance:

START OF PROCEDURE

1. Step 1 . . .

2. Step 2 . . .

10. Step 10 (omitting the intermediate steps) . . .

END OF PROCEDURE

Text-Flowchart Procedures

4.22   Text-flowchart procedures, as the name implies, combine text and flowchart techniques. Pages are divided into two parts, as in a playscript procedure. In simple formats, the work flowchart keeps step with the written instructions. In sophisticated formats, the flowchart shows an immediate action, the output from the action, and the destination of the outputs.

4.23   The basic typing instructions are:

** Divide the page. Put the flowchart portion on the left.

** Number the flowchart symbols to correspond to the text numbers.

** Single-space the text. Leave an extra space around headings and between items.

** Draw arrows to connect the symbols.

A simple example would look like this:

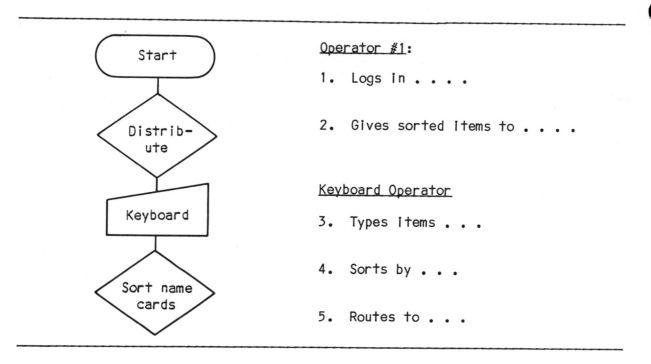

Operator #1:

1. Logs in . . . .

2. Gives sorted items to . . . .

Keyboard Operator

3. Types items . . .

4. Sorts by . . .

5. Routes to . . .

Picture and Picture-Text Procedures

4.24   From the typing perspective, picture and picture-text procedures are like flowchart and text-flowchart procedures. One difference is the shape of the pictures in contrast to the flowchart symbols. Often the picture is of an actual form such as a travel voucher. Another difference is the location of the typing, which may be over, beside, or beneath the picture. Because the format can vary with the elements pictured:

** Get a model that shows what the final product should look like. (The draft you get won't necessarily be in the proper form!)

NOTES TO CHAPTER 4

1. Summaries based on information published in pages 15-19 of <u>Preparing the Manuscript</u>, 9th ed., by Udia G. Olsen. The Writer, Inc. (Boston), publishers. Copyright (c) 1978. The form of this note differs from that of other notes because it was specified by The Writer, Inc. as a condition of permission to use the summaries.

2. Summaries based on information published in pages 14-15 of <u>Preparing the Manuscript</u>, 9th ed., by Udia G. Olsen. The Writer, Inc. (Boston), publishers. Copyright (c) 1978. The form of this note differs from that of other notes for the reason given in Note 1.

3. Robert E. Horn, "Information Mapping," <u>Datamation</u>, January 1975, pp. 85-88; Leslie H. Matthies, "The Task Outline," <u>The Technical Writing Teacher</u> 4, no. 3 (1977): 107-9, and "Preparing a Playscript Procedure," <u>The Systemation Newsletter</u>, no. 115 (Colorado Springs: Systemation, Inc., 1963); Julia Van Duyn, <u>Practical Systems and Procedures Manual</u> (Reston, Virginia: Reston, 1975).

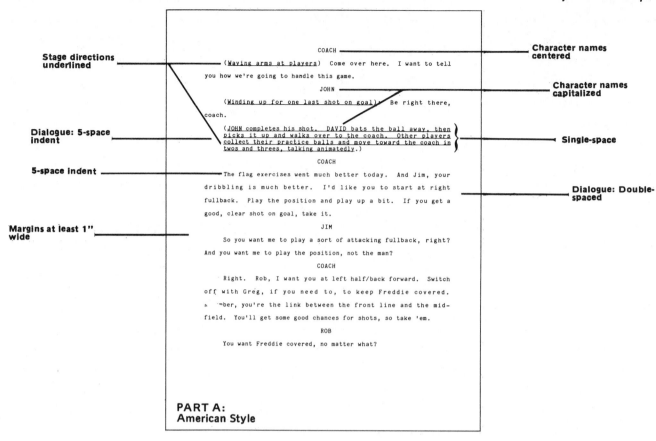

Stage directions underlined

Character names centered

COACH

(<u>Waving arms at players</u>) Come over here. I want to tell you how we're going to handle this game.

JOHN

Character names capitalized

(<u>Winding up for one last shot on goal</u>) Be right there, coach.

Dialogue: 5-space indent

(<u>JOHN completes his shot. DAVID bats the ball away, then picks it up and walks over to the coach. Other players collect their practice balls and move toward the coach in twos and threes, talking animatedly.</u>)

Single-space

COACH

5-space indent

The flag exercises went much better today. And Jim, your dribbling is much better. I'd like you to start at right fullback. Play the position and play up a bit. If you get a good, clear shot on goal, take it.

Dialogue: Double-spaced

JIM

Margins at least 1" wide

So you want me to play a sort of attacking fullback, right? And you want me to play the position, not the man?

COACH

Right. Rob, I want you at left half/back forward. Switch off with Greg, if you need to, to keep Freddie covered. Remember, you're the link between the front line and the mid-field. You'll get some good chances for shots, so take 'em.

ROB

You want Freddie covered, no matter what?

PART A:
American Style

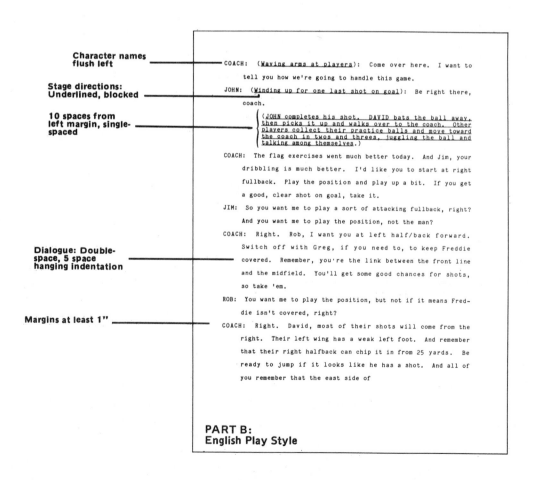

Character names flush left

COACH: (<u>Waving arms at players</u>): Come over here. I want to tell you how we're going to handle this game.

JOHN: (<u>Winding up for one last shot on goal</u>): Be right there, coach.

Stage directions: Underlined, blocked

10 spaces from left margin, single-spaced

(<u>JOHN completes his shot. DAVID bats the ball away, then picks it up and walks over to the coach. Other players collect their practice balls and move toward the coach in twos and threes, juggling the ball and talking among themselves.</u>)

COACH: The flag exercises went much better today. And Jim, your dribbling is much better. I'd like you to start at right fullback. Play the position and play up a bit. If you get a good, clear shot on goal, take it.

JIM: So you want me to play a sort of attacking fullback, right? And you want me to play the position, not the man?

COACH: Right. Rob, I want you at left half/back forward. Switch off with Greg, if you need to, to keep Freddie covered. Remember, you're the link between the front line and the midfield. You'll get some good chances for shots, so take 'em.

Dialogue: Double-space, 5 space hanging indentation

ROB: You want me to play the position, but not if it means Freddie isn't covered, right?

Margins at least 1"

COACH: Right. David, most of their shots will come from the right. Their left wing has a weak left foot. And remember that their right halfback can chip it in from 25 yards. Be ready to jump if it looks like he has a shot. And all of you remember that the east side of

PART B:
English Play Style

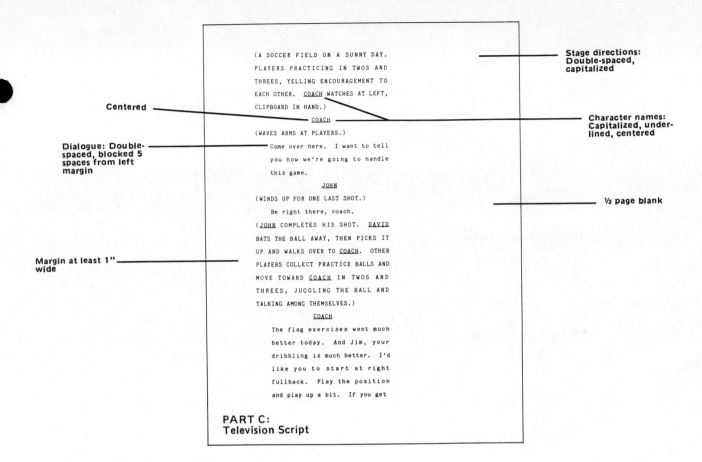

Centered

Dialogue: Double-spaced, blocked 5 spaces from left margin

Margin at least 1" wide

Stage directions: Double-spaced, capitalized

Character names: Capitalized, underlined, centered

½ page blank

(A SOCCER FIELD ON A SUNNY DAY. PLAYERS PRACTICING IN TWOS AND THREES, YELLING ENCOURAGEMENT TO EACH OTHER. COACH WATCHES AT LEFT, CLIPBOARD IN HAND.)

COACH

(WAVES ARMS AT PLAYERS.)

Come over here. I want to tell you how we're going to handle this game.

JOHN

(WINDS UP FOR ONE LAST SHOT.)

Be right there, coach.

(JOHN COMPLETES HIS SHOT. DAVID BATS THE BALL AWAY, THEN PICKS IT UP AND WALKS OVER TO COACH. OTHER PLAYERS COLLECT PRACTICE BALLS AND MOVE TOWARD COACH IN TWOS AND THREES, JUGGLING THE BALL AND TALKING AMONG THEMSELVES.)

COACH

The flag exercises went much better today. And Jim, your dribbling is much better. I'd like you to start at right fullback. Play the position and play up a bit. If you get

**PART C:
Television Script**

83

chapter 5

Typing Documentation, Notes, Tables, Illustrations, and Front and Back Matter

5.1   Documentation, tables, illustrations, and many elements of front and back matter don't exist in many documents, so many editors, writers, and typists will never need this chapter. Others may need only the information on title pages. Those who do read it, however, will need to pay considerable attention to details, because requirements vary quite a bit from style to style. This chapter discusses the features that vary. Examples are mostly in Chapters 6 through 8.

DOCUMENTATION

5.2   Documentation lends credibility and authority to a work and enables readers to locate sources easily. Documentation is indicated by in-text notes and symbols that list or point to lists of the authorities a writer cites to substantiate assertions. Take information from the title page of books and from the cover page and article pages of periodicals. In general, use the most recent edition of a work. When several documents are cited to support a single point consolidate them into one note to prevent a large number of short ones. Don't let scholarly mechanics get in the way of readability. Be as brief as possible while giving the reader necessary data. For instance, page numbers normally aren't needed for references to articles in reference works that arrange articles alphabetically. Several quotes from the same source can be taken care of with a single note, followed by a statement such as "I follow Bay's account throughout. Documentation is most common in academic and other kinds of technical writing. Differences in the form of documentation are distinctive features of style.[1]

Author (Date) Documentation

5.3   Author (date) documentation, sometimes called "Harvard style," is particularly common in technical and scientific manuscripts. Examples are APA, ASA, some forms of AChemS and CBE, JASA, Linguistic Society of America, SA, and Sage. The typing requirements have to do with the following elements:

** **Punctuation between name and date** when both elements are inside parentheses. For example:

    (Mullins, 1977)   APA, ASA, SA, Sage

    (Mullins 1980)   CBE, JASA, MSN

** **Punctuation between date and page number.** Variations are:

    Mullins (1980:3)   ASA, SA, Sage

    Olson (1982, p. 30)   APA, JASA, MSN

** **Use of and or & between names:**

    Lang and Long (1982)   APA, ASA, JASA, Sage

    Lang & Long (1982)   SA

    Lang and Long (1982:6)   ASA, Sage

    (Lang and Long 1982:6)   Linguistic Society of America

    (Lang & Long, 1982:6)   APA, SA

** **Use of brackets** when part of all of a citation is enclosed within parentheses along with a short comment. Variations:

    Lang (1982; one . . .)   APA, SA, Sage

    Lang ([1982]; one . . .)   ASA

    (Lang, 1982; one . . .)   APA, SA, Sage

    (Lang 1982; one . . .)   MSN

(Lang [1982]; one . . .)   Not common

** Within parentheses, **use of comma to separate dates** for two or more documents by the same author, and a semicolon to separate the bibliographic data on documents by different authors. For example:

(Lang, 1975, 1976)   APA, ASA, SA, Sage

(Lang 1975, 1978)   JASA, MSN

(Lang, 1975; Long, 1978) APA, ASA, SA, Sage

(Lang 1975; Long 1978)   JASA, MSN

** **Use of "et al." (ASA), "et al" (AMA), or "et al." (SA)** to replace the names of second and subsequent authors in references to documents written by more than two authors. For example, ASA requires use of first author's last name and "et al." in place of all other names for <u>all</u> references to a document with more than two authors. MSN permits "et al." only for citation of documents with more than <u>three</u> authors and only for second and subsequent citations. For example:

Lang et al. (1982)

Lang, Long, and Low (1982); and Lang et al. (1982)

Lang, Long, Low, and Lowe (1982); and Lang et al. (1982)

(Lang et al., 1982)

(Lang et al. 1982)

5.4   Don't use "et al." when doing so would produce identical abbreviations of citations of two or more documents. For example, in the second and third examples just above, "Lang et al. (1982)" is used to abbreviate the citation of two different documents. To prevent confusion, use all names each time.

5.5   In general, punctuate citations within the sentences to which they are attached. For example:

That finding is clear (Jones 1974).

"That finding is clear" (Jones 1974).

        NOT

That finding is clear. (Jones 1974)

"That finding is clear." (Jones 1974)

Citation of Document by Number

5.6   A few styles--notably AMathS, AMA, and ASTM--require writers to show documentation by inserting a bracketed, parenthesized, or superscripted number in the text. A few minor styles mimic this style by using one of the endnote styles with the number bracketed or parenthesized in text.

5.7   Different styles determine the number in different ways. For example, ASTM and AMA use the number established by the order in which the writer first cites a document. Thus, if the second and tenth citations were of a paper given by Jones, both citations would be: [2]. In contrast, AMathS cites the number established by the document's position in a bibliography whose entries are (1) alphabetized by author's last name and (2) subsequently numbered in that order. The important typing requirements are:

** Except for superscript numbers, punctuate documentation within the sentences involved.

** Type the citations as in the following examples. Bracketed references are first; parenthesized, second; and superscripted, third. For example:

Jones [2] found it.

See Jones [2, p. 5].

Jones (2) found it.

See Jones (2, p. 5).

Jones found it.[2]

See Jones[2] (p. 5).

Superscripts, Endnotes, and Footnotes

5.8   AIP, MLA, MSH, Turabian, and many specialized systems of documenta-

tion--for example, of congressional and legal documents--require documentation
in the form of superscript numbers (occasionally asterisks; see Section 5.12)
and either endnotes (collected at the end of a paper, chapter, or book) or
footnotes (at the bottom of a page of text). Usually the superscript number
is typed a bit above the line, after any punctuation, and looks exactly like
the number 2 in the example just above. EXCEPTION: a few styles require that
the number in text not be superscripted but instead be typed on a line with
text, inside brackets or parentheses. In such cases, type the brackets or
parentheses with the number outside the period at the end of a sentence.
Don't type the number next to a mathematical symbol (lest the number be taken
as part of a mathematical expression). Type the number at the end of a sentence or syntactic unit that is as near as possible to the material quoted or
referred to. The note itself resembles the notes to chapters in this book,
which are in MSH style. Notes to the papers at the end of Chapter 3 are in
MLA style.

5.9   Check aspects of the documentation for consistency. Most commonly,
the general characteristics of this style of documentation are:

** Complete information on first references with abbreviations allowed on second and subsequent.

** Numbers in sequence, according to position in manuscript, by chapter, section, or document.

** Names in normal order.

** Article titles placed within quotation marks, and book titles italicized.
Capitalization follows rules in Section 3.31.

** Date near the end of each reference.

** Commas, not periods, between the elements in the reference.

** Page numbers preceded by "p." or "pp."

** Abbreviation of journal names by a standard list, such as the American National Standard for Abbreviation of Titles of Periodicals. Some manuals,
such as that by the AIP, include the list.

Check where to type notes--at the end of documents, parts, or chapters ("endnotes") or on the bottom of pages of text ("footnotes").

5.10   Endnotes. Most styles require endnotes. The general typing requirements for endnotes are:

** Begin on a separate page, entitled <u>Notes</u>. Use the same margins as for text. Type <u>Notes</u> 2 inches from the top of the page and leave three empty lines before typing the first line of the first note. Some styles, such as MLA, omit the page number on the first page.

** Type the author's name in normal order. First name, middle initial, and last name is the usually preferred order.

** Check internal spacing. Some styles require double spacing of all lines.

** Leave at least one empty line between notes. EXCEPTION: some styles require two empty lines <u>between notes.</u>

<u>Never</u> single-space any note or type it at the foot of the page on which it occurs unless explicitly told to do so. Documents that sometimes require single-spacing are research proposals, project reports, class papers, theses, dissertations, convention papers, and manuscripts to be printed directly from camera-ready copy.

5.11   When manuscripts have several chapters (as books, theses, and long reports and proposals do), many styles require that notes be typed at the ends of chapters or the end of the document. General style requirements are:

** Find out whether to group and number notes by chapter or as a whole at the end of the document.

** In the absence of instructions, group notes at the ends of chapters.

** Type them on a page entitled, say, <u>Notes to Chapter 4</u>, as I do in this book, or <u>Notes</u> (if you group at the end of a shorter document).

** Number pages in sequence after chapters or at the end of the book (usually after the last page of the Appendix).

** In MLA style, use brackets around missing or incomplete data. For example, if a date were missing you might use [   ] or, say, [1981?], depending on whether you could make a reasonable guess about the date.

5.12   Footnotes. When footnotes are required, unless you have a word processor you'll have to do careful measuring and counting of lines to ensure that you leave enough space at the bottom of a page to type the footnotes that go with superscripts on that page. General rules are:

** Check whether to use sequential numbers or asterisks (one for the first note on a page, two for the second, etc.) as the superscript. If the numbers are sequential, check whether by page, chapter, section, or document.

** Check whether to type an inch or two of underline or a full line of underline from left margin to right to separate the text from the notes.

** Skip a space below the underline.

** Check whether to single- or double-space. Often the requirement is to single-space the notes and double-space between them.

** Check turnover requirements. Styles usually require that turnover lines line up either flush with the left margin or directly under the first character of the first word in the note.

** Check rules for carrying the end of one note to the next page.

** Type the superscript number (or, occasionally, single or double asterisk), sometimes followed by a space, and the note.

When a note occur near the end of a page, leaving too little space at the bottom for the complete note, continue the note at the bottom of the next page ahead of any notes that occur on it.

5.13   **WP Advantages:** some word processors have "counters," which let typists use a code instead a number for footnote numbers. When the document is printed, the system automatically reads the code and numbers the superscripts and the notes in order. The codes stay in the electronic version of text, so if revision moves the notes around or deletes or adds notes, the superscripts and notes will automatically be renumbered. Some text formatters allow the code to contain not only the counter code but a formatting code that lines up and indents the turnover lines. Many word processors offer "floating footnotes" that electronically tie a superscript to a block of note text. Whatever page the superscript is typed on, the note will automatically print at the bottom of the page. (The system automatically adjusts the length of the main text to accommodate the note!). A few processors tie the superscript and the note text and allow typists to choose whether they want notes on the bottom of the pages or at the end. These systems make page formatting automatic.

They also make changes, even from one style to another, easy and almost automatic.

LISTS OF REFERENCES

5.14 Lists of references, sometimes called "Sources Cited," give full bibliographic data for the items mentioned in either author-date or numbered-document citations. Formats and requirements vary greatly from one style to the next.

5.15 Begin typing a list of references on a separate page:

** Title the first page <u>References</u> (whatever the style requires), 2 inches from the top of the page (MSH style requires 3 inches).

** Quadruple-space before beginning the first line of the first reference.

** Double-space thereafter. EXCEPTION: some styles, such as MSN, require a triple space <u>between</u> references.

A Typical Example

5.16 The references for this book (the collected list at the end of the book) are typed in MSN style. The basic characteristics of this style are:

** Names reversed, initials only, followed by a period.

** Order alphabetical, by author's last name.

** Date follows name, followed by a period.

** Article and chapter titles have no quotation marks; only the first word and the first after a colon are capitalized.

** Page numbers have minimal abbreviation. When the first number is less than 100 or is 100 or a multiple, use all digits. For example:

2-10; 81-85; 200-206

When the first number is more than 100 (in multiples of 100) but less than 110, use only the changed part for the second digit. For example:

206-8; 4003-4

When the first number (in multiples of 100) is more than 109, use the last two or three digits as needed. For example:

264-66; 206-365; 1165-281; 1790-1956

The documents in Chapters 6 through 8 show reference lists in many styles.

5.17   Some styles, such as AMathS and ASTM, number documentation in the list of references and cite the number in the text, but these styles don't determine the number in the same way. For example, in ASTM style the number is established by the order in which a writer first cites a document. Section 5.7 describes the numbering procedures.

Variations

5.18   Check reference lists for consistency on the following items:

** **Capitalization throughout;** possibilities are complete capitalization, sentence capitalization, and capitalization of important words following the rule in Section 3.31.

** **Punctuation between elements;** watch for commas, semicolons, colons, periods, parentheses, dashes, and brackets.

** **Name;** use of initials (MSN) or full first and last names and one initial (MLA, MSH); reversal of name order; and (ASA) or & (SA) between names of coauthors; use of dashes or a short line to replace author's name for second and subsequent listings by the same author (Sage).

** **Date;** order--from earliest to latest (ASA) or latest to earliest; placement either immediately after the name (ASA) or near the end of the reference (APA, ASTM); use of parentheses around date (SA).

** **Titles of articles and chapters in books;** omission (ASTM); use of quotation marks (ASA but not APA); subsequent punctuation within quotation marks (most American styles) or outside (most British styles).

** **Titles of books;** underlined (APA) or not (ASA); subsequent punctuation a period (ASA), comma (ASTM), or space and open parenthesis (MSH).

** **Ed and eds.;** placement before or after the editor's name; placed within or outside parentheses.

** **Journal titles;** underlined (APA but not ASA); abbreviated (AMathS) or not.

** **Page numbers for chapters in books;** required (ASA) or not (APA); if so, placed after title of chapter (ASA) or at end of reference; preceded by "pp." or "Pp." (ASA).

** **Page numbers for journal articles;** preceded by "pp." or by comma or colon.

** **For books, information on city, state, publisher;** all three required or some omitted; brief form or not; inside parentheses or not.

Examples are in the manuscripts in Chapters 6 through 8.

BIBLIOGRAPHIES

General Information

5.19   Bibliographies give complete data on sources used to prepare a document. The list of sources is usually alphabetically ordered by author's last name or first significant word in title (when there is no author) and is sometimes broken down into alphabetized subcategories, such as "Primary Sources" and "Secondary Sources." An author's own work is cited ahead of his or her edited works. When a bibliography contains only works cited, it is usually titled "Works Cited" (MSN) or "List of References" (many other styles; see Sections 5.14 through 5.18 above). When annotated, a bibliography is usually titled "Annotated Bibliography." When the document is a book or other long document with several parts, usually the bibliography is placed at the end, before the index. When a bibliography is more specialized, pertaining mainly to a single part or chapter, usually it is typed at the end of the part. When in doubt, type bibliographic items where they will be easiest for readers to use.

5.20   Tradition used to require that all documents contain a bibliography in addition to footnotes or endnotes. Not any more. As printing and paper costs have gone up, magazine and journal publishers and many businesses increasingly have required footnotes but not the alphabetized bibliography.

Curiously, elementary, secondary, and college instructors often still require both, as if unaware of changing practice in the real world.

Variations

5.21   The variation in elements present and placement and treatment of elements is as in Section 5.18. A second variation is annotation--summaries of the useful or especially pertinent information in a document. Annotations help readers to decide whether the information in a document would be useful to them. The bibliography for this book is annotated.

SPECIAL-PURPOSE NOTES

Substantive Notes

5.22   Substantive notes are comments about documentation or observations other than documentation that might be important to some readers but that would interrupt the flow if incorporated into the text. Sometimes substantive notes are combined with documentation. The general typing instructions are:

** Use the notes to chapters in this book as examples; for instance, see Note 1, Chapter 3.

** Follow the spacing requirements in Section 5.10.

Identifying References

5.23   Identifying references, which occur only in scholarly manuscripts, are useful when writers must disguise or remove from the text and reference lists all documentation that might identify them. Examples of such items are:

** A writer's doctoral dissertation, when the title closely resembles the manuscript title or when the writer cites it as the source of more detailed information on background, method, or specific findings.

** Unpublished articles, project reports, and letters.

5.24   General requirements are:

** Type the notes on a separate page, entitled "Identifying References." Check where in the manuscript to place it (see discussion in Sections 3.11 through 3.12).

** Number the notes in alphabetic order.

** Type "Identifying References" two inches from the top of the page. Leave three empty lines between the title and the first line of the first note.

** Double-space the notes. EXCEPTION: a few styles require triple-spacing be-tween notes.

** Order the elements, punctuate, and capitalize exactly like references in the list of references.

** In text, refer only to the note number. Use no name. For example:

The substance is toxic (identifying note 1).

Reference Notes

5.25   Reference notes, used mainly in scholarly documents being submitted to journals that follow APA style, are bibliographic data on letters, papers presented at meetings, and other materials that are not widely and easily available to readers. General instructions are:

** Type "Reference Notes" two inches from the top of the page. Quadruple-space between the title and the first line of the first note.

** Double-space the notes. EXCEPTION: same style require two empty lines be-tween notes.

** Order the elements, punctuate, and capitalize exactly like the documents in the list of references or documentation notes (described in Sections 5.14 through 5.18).

** Insert and number the page of reference notes immediately after the last page of text.

TABLES

General Requirements

5.26   The general requirements are:

** Type each table on a separate piece of paper. Never type tables onto pages with text unless the style explicitly requires it (sometimes the case for dissertations, theses, class papers, research proposals, project reports, conventions, and manuscripts to be printed directly from camera-ready copy).

** Type an indicator into the text to show where the table belongs. The best place for an indicator usually is immediately after the first mention of the table. Double-space above and below the indicator. For example:

[Table 9.9 about here]

(Table 9.9 about here)

The indicator can go either between paragraphs or between lines of a paragraph. Between paragraphs is usually preferred.

** Begin typing number and title 1 1/2 inches from the top of the page.

** Double-space between lines.

** Leave at least 3 spaces between columns.

** Line up numbers by decimals, expressed or implied, as Table 5.1 (end of chapter) shows.

** In columns of dollar amounts, place a dollar sign in front of the top entry even when the column head also indicates dollars. The sign is an additional help to readers.

** In columns of percentages, put a percent sign (%) after the top entry even when the column head also indicates percentages. The sign is an additional aid to readers. In table titles, column heads, and row stubs, use "percentage," not "%" or "percent."

** Check whether to center horizontally tables that are not wide enough to fill the whole page.

** Check how to treat continuation pages of long tables.

** Use the following conventions for empty cells and cells whose entry is zero (0):

No entry = the column head and the row stub don't apply to each other.

..... = the column head and row stub apply to each other, but no data exist. The leaders (.....) may run all the way across the column or across the same horizontal space as the widest entry in the column.

Zero (0) = the quantity entered is a numerical zero.

There is no need for dashes or "n.a." (not applicable). These conventions have their roots in the University of Chicago Press's <u>A Manual of Style</u>.

Variations

5.27   Check all tables for consistency. Table 5.1 shows the parts of a table. Not all tables have subordinate row stubs and notes.

5.28   Treatment of table number and title. Look for consistency in:

** Placement and treatment of table number. The number may be in sequence throughout or by section or chapter (5.1, 5.2, etc.). Check how to number appendix tables.

** Placement, capitalization, and underlining of title.

** Presence or absence of one or two lines separating the number and title from the body of the table.

5.29   Body. In the body of the table:

** Look for consistency in use of vertical and horizontal lines. Most styles prohibit vertical lines (although Turabian style permits them) and limit horizontal lines to positions beneath the title, boxheads, and column heads, and the body of the table.

** Never add lines that aren't explicitly permitted by the style.

** Check whether lines should be typed, drawn with a pencil, or (especially in the case of horizontal lines) drawn with permanent black ink.

** Check consistency in capitalization of row stubs and column headings.

** Check consistency in treatment of second lines in stubs and headings. When the writer has no preference and the style guide expresses none, follow the style in Table 5.1.

5.30   Notes. Treat notes consistently:

** Check division between body and notes. Most styles require a line between these two elements.

** Check the order for source, general, and specific notes. Also check capitalization and underlining. In the absence of instructions, follow the model in Table 5.1.

** Check the designation of notes that pertain to only one part of a table. Some styles require superscript numbers like the ones shown in Table 5.1. Other styles require superscript letters (a,b,c) or symbols (*, **, ***, #, etc.). Turabian, MSH, and MSN require numbers when the body of a table contains words, letters, or symbols, and symbols when the body contains a mixture of numbers and letters. Social science manuscripts often use *, **, and *** for notes that give statistical significance.

** Check indentation. In general, type notes flush with the left margin, as in Table 5.1. Note, though, that some styles require indentation of the first line. In such cases, check the number of spaces required for the indentation.

** Check superscription. In general, type "Source" and "Note" on a line with what follows. Superscript the designations of specific notes half a space.

Photoreproduction of Tables

5.31   When "camera-ready" copy (properly prepared for photoreproduction) is required, check the rules very carefully. The general requirements are:

** Use an electric or electronic typewriter or a word processing printer such as NEC, Qume, or Diablo that produces camera-ready copy.

** Clean the type face and use a carbon ribbon.

** For every table use the required type size and style. Some styles specify only type size, or pitch (pica or elite; defined in Section 2.9), leaving choice of style to the writer or typist.

** Check requirements for width of tables. For example, some journals require that tables be a specific number of pica or elite spaces wide, no more and no less.

** When "transparencies" are required, make a photocopy of the typed page. Then copy the copy onto a sheet of plastic film. Printing and copying centers usually keep the necessary supplies on hand.

ILLUSTRATIONS

5.32   Often typists do little or no typing on illustrations. Sometimes the only responsibility is to type a list of captions (titles) and legends (notes) as they should appear in print. In manuscripts for publication:

** Use paper with no rag content.

** Place each illustration on a separate piece of paper.

** With graphs to be copied, use graph paper with pale nonphoto-blue lines, which don't reproduce.

** Use a location note in the text, like those for tables (described in Section 5.26), to show where the printer should insert the illustration in the flow of printed text.

** Type gummed labels for the backs of photographs. Include the figure number, title of manuscript, senior author's name, and an arrow to show which way is up.

** Check whether to type captions and legends on the pages with illustrations or on a separate piece of paper. When a separate page is required, write lightly on the back of each illustration the number, title, and location.

** Check whether to use a page number on the illustration pages.

** Check whether to number the illustrations. When there are only few illustrations, some styles permit no numbers.

** Be consistent in placement, capitalization, and underlining of number, caption, and legends. Sentence capitalization, with capitalization of only the initial word and proper nouns, is common.

** Check whether to submit line drawings in the form of glossy photographs.

** Use dry mounting tissue to mount small illustrations on standard-sized pieces of paper.

** On manuscripts not intended for publication, check the amounts of space to leave for illustrations that will be added later.

WP Advantage: word processors allow you to experiment with the placement of illustrations by moving blocks of text and space around until you get the best possible fit. Firman Publications[2] describes how Firman's staff uses WP in these ways.

FRONT MATTER (PRELIMINARIES)

5.33   Section 3.11 lists the elements of front matter and back matter for short and long documents. Few documents contain all these parts. Some are most likely to occur in short documents; others, in long ones. The order of discussion here is the general order in which they usually occur in a manuscript.

Frontispiece

5.34   A frontispiece is an illustration at the front of a book that faces the title page. The frontispiece is counted but no page number is typed on it. Type the caption as for any other illustration.

Cover Sheet (Title Page)

5.35   As the sample manuscripts show (Chapters 6 through 8), cover sheets come in a variety of styles. In general, a separate title sheet will look like the ones in APA or ASA style. Title pages combined with first pages of text usually look like the title sheet in MLA style (end of Chapter 3). Turabian requires a blank page after the title page. When a manuscript has more than one author, give thought to the positions in which you type names. Here are some possibilities:

Two or More Authors, Same Affiliation

A. B. Lentz, C. D. Mullins, and L. C. Holt

Institutional Affiliation

Three Writers, Two Affiliations

A. B. Lentz and C. D. Mullins

Institutional Affiliation

L. C. Holt

Second Institutional Affiliation

Two Writers, Two Affiliations

A. B. Lentz

Institutional Affiliation

C. D. Mullins

Second Institutional Affiliation

5.36   The general typing rules are:

** Always include title, by-line (name and position), and date, with lines of the title and by-line centered from left to right. EXCEPTIONS: AMA style begins lines flush left. AIP style begins the title flush left; names and affiliation begin at a paragraph indent from the left margin.

** Check on possible inclusion of a running head, current address, acknowledgment, or abstract.

** Follow rules for capitalization in Section 3.31. EXCEPTION: some styles, such as Turabian, require that the title be completely capitalized.

** Don't underline.

** When the title has two lines, make the second line shorter than the first. This pattern is called "inverted pyramid style."

** Type the name in proper form. Some styles require full first and last names and a middle initial (when the writer has one). Others require initials and a last name. Some styles don't specify a preference.

** When no instructions are given, use full first and last names and a middle initial (when the writer has one).

** Begin typing the date flush with the left margin.

Articles by free-lance writers often combine the title page and the first page of text. At the top, single-spaced, flush with the left margin, are the writer's name and address. Opposite this information, on the first line near the right margin, writers may state the rights they wishes to sell (such as "First North American Rights"). On the next line, they type the word count. The article title, by-line, and text follow. Professional affiliation, if any, is often omitted. A typical first page might begin like this:

John Q. Writer
0000 Any Time Way
City, State   00000

First North American Rights
Word count: 1754

TITLE OF ARTICLE

by John Q. Writer

The text begins three or four lines below the by-line and is double-

spaced.

5.37   When a cover page has the additional items listed here, follow these
instructions:

** **Running head;** in general, center the running head (if any) from left to
right on the page.

** **Address;** type each line of the address flush with the left margin.

** **Acknowledgments;** see instructions in Section 5.48. The AMathS style manuscript shows an example.

** **Abstract;** see instructions in Section 5.43. The AMathS style manuscript
shows an example.

Half-Title and Part-Title Pages

5.38   Books and long proposals and reports often have a half-title or "bas-
tard title" page, which shows only the main title of the book, centered from
left to right on the page and typed three inches or so from the top of the
page. Although not part of the front matter, a part-title page, sometimes
also called a "half-title page," refers to a separate page that bears a part
title. Examples are the part title pages that set off related chapters in
this book.

Release

5.39   Some books, reports, and other publicly distributed documents begin with a "release" statement that describes and limits responsibility for the content. A common location is on the title page or half-title page, often at the bottom of the page. A typical statement goes something like:

> The conclusions expressed in this report are those of the authors and not necessarily those of Research Institute.

Dedication

5.40   A dedication, common in book manuscripts, usually fits on one or two lines of type and begins with "To" or "For" ("Dedicated to" is redundant). The dedication of this book is an example. General instructions are:

** Type it on a separate page.

** Center it from left to right.

** Capitalize the first letter in proper nouns. Capitalize all other words as you would in an ordinary English sentence.

Epigraph

5.41   In place of a dedication, some book writers use an epigraph--a short quotation. The general instructions are:

** Type the epigraph on a separate page.

** Type the source on the line following the quotation, flush right with the end of the longest line of the epigraph. Use no parentheses or brackets. Use only the author's name and the title of the work.

** When using epigraphs at the heads of chapters, indent and block them to the same indentation as paragraphs in the document.

Biography

5.42   Type a biography on a separate page as an ordinary paragraph. The general rules are:

** Type the heading "Biography" two inches from the top of the page.

** Check whether to capitalize "Biography" completely.

** Leave three empty spaces between the title and the first line of text.

** Include the author's present job title and location. Include past job location if that is where the work being reported was done. For an example, see the sample manuscript in ASTM style.

Abstract

5.43   Most styles require a separate abstract page. The major exception: a few styles require that the abstract be typed on the cover sheet. In such cases, check _where_ on the cover sheet to put it. In the absence of instructions, begin it four lines below the by-line. The general rules are:

** Center the word "Abstract" from left to right, about two inches from the top of the page, as the APA and ASA style abstracts (Chapter 8) show.

** Type the abstract as one double-spaced, blocked paragraph, just as APA and ASA styles show, unless the style specifically allows paragraph breaks.

Table of Contents

5.44   The table of contents briefly outlines the content of a long document. In the table of contents:

** Include chapter and part titles.

** On a draft to be submitted to a publisher for production, do not show page numbers. Simply enter "000". Page numbers will be added when the document is in page proof form.

** For an example, see the table of contents for this book, which uses part titles but no intrachapter headings. The Turabian-style manuscript shows a second example.

** Don't use the word "chapter" in the contents unless the sections are designated that way in text.

WP Advantage: some word processors enable typists to use nonprinting codes to mark chapter numbers, chapter titles, and headings to be included in a table of contents. Later, a simple request causes the processor to read the coded lines and print them in order in proper format, with the page numbers on which they appear. If later revision changes the page numbers, the same request will produce an updated version. The contents will have no error that does not also exist in the manuscript text.

Lists of Illustrations and Tables

5.45   In general, type the lists separately:

** Type "List of Tables" or "List of Illustrations" at the top of the first page, about three inches from the top of the page, centered from left to right.

** Type the numbers and titles exactly as they appear on the illustrations and tables. EXCEPTION: in manuscripts for publication, long titles may be shortened and explanatory notes omitted.

** Don't use the words "Table" or "Figure" before the number. The title of the section tells which is which.

** Capitalize the titles following the rule in Section 3.31.

When a manuscript has very few of either, as this book does, the writer may provide a combined list like the one in the front matter of this book. **WP Advantage:** as with tables of contents, some word processors enable typists to "tag" each table or figure title with a nonprinting code. Later, a simple request causes the processor to scan the text and print the coded titles in order, properly numbered and styled. The lists will contain no errors that are not also in the text.

Foreword

5.46   A foreword, which is most likely to occur in book manuscripts, is usually between two and four typed, double-spaced pages in length, and is written by someone other than the book's author. General instructions are:

** Type "Foreword" at the top of the first page, about three inches from the top of the page and centered from left to right.

** Quadruple-space from the title to the first line of text.

** At the end, type the foreword writer's name and title, both flush with the right margin. Type the institutional affiliation, if any, flush left.

Preface

5.47   Title the preface "Acknowledgments" when it contains only the writer's thanks for help with the manuscript. Other instructions are:

** Type "Preface" (or "Acknowledgments") about three inches from the top of the first page.

** At the end, type the writer's name and affiliation, both flush right. Type the month and year flush left. Some writers also want the city and state typed flush left, beneath the date, as is done in the preface to this book.

Acknowledgments

5.48   Acknowledgments of help usually are typed on the cover sheet, on a separate page immediately following either the cover sheet or the last page of text, or on the Notes page. Also check whether to type:

** Exactly like a paragraph of text.

** Like a paragraph but with the first line blocked flush left.

** As a numbered footnote--usually the first one.

** As a note preceded by an asterisk.

** As two paragraphs rather than one. Most commonly, the second paragraph includes the writer's position, place of employment, and mailing address.

The preface to this book shows one way to treat acknowledgments.

BACK MATTER

5.49   Sections 3.11 lists the elements of front matter for short and long documents. Few documents contain all of these parts. Some are most likely to occur in short documents; others, in long ones. The order of discussion here is the general order in which they usually occur in a manuscript. Notes and bibliographies, which are usually parts of back matter, are discussed earlier in this chapter.

Appendixes

5.50   The title on the first page of text is "Appendix" or "Appendix A (B, C, etc.), depending on whether there is one appendix or several. The general instructions are:

** Type the title two inches (three for a book manuscript) from the top of the page. Leave three empty lines between the title and the first line of text.

** Treat the text exactly as you would treat a page of text.

** Treat tables and illustrations exactly as you do tables and illustrations in the main text. The numbers will be either A.1, A.2, A.3 or 1', 2', 3', depending on style.

Glossary

5.51   A glossary defines foreign words and technical terms. In a glossary:

** Begin each word on a separate line.

** Use periods at the ends of definitions only when some or all consist of complete sentences. Then use a period at the end of each one.

List of Abbreviations

5.52   A list of abbreviations is needed only when a document contains arbitrarily devised abbreviations. It is not needed for commonly accepted abbreviations. Type the list according to the instructions for the glossary.

Index

5.53   Indexes are collected, organized, key words and phrases that enable readers to locate quickly topics discussed in a document. The longer the document, the more likely an index is needed.

5.54   Alphabetization. Alphabetization can be either letter by letter or word by word. Whichever you use, be consistent. Examples:

Education and sociology   [Word by word]

Educational sociology

Educational sociology   [Letter by letter]

Education and sociology

5.55   Entries and subentries. Each entry must include both a heading and either a page number or inclusive pages. **Subentries** are subcategories of entries. The following examples of subentries are typed in "run-in" style:

Indexes: alphabetization of, 000; entries in, 000; subentries in, 000

5.56   Typed in "indented" style, the same entries look like this:

Indexes

   alphabetization of, 000
   entries in, 000
   subentries in, 000

In both examples, note the lack of end punctuation and the lack of capitalization of subentries.

5.57   Cross-references. Cross-references list different places to look for information on the same topic. The following example is typed in "run-in" style. Note the use of underlining and the lack of end punctuation:

Dogs. <u>See</u> canine

Dogs. <u>See also</u> quadrupeds

5.58   Style. Style can be either run-in or indented (Sections 5.55 and 5.56 illustrate both styles):

** Check which style to follow.

** Follow the appropriate style consistently.

** Pay especially careful attention to underlining.

5.59   The final draft. On the final draft of an index:

** Type directly from the index cards that contain the entries.

** Check the style rules for all details of punctuation.

** Ask about paper and length of lines. Some publishers require a special kind of paper, or lines of specified lengths, that would be improper for the rest of the manuscript.

5.60   WP Advantage: the more sophisticated word processors and an increasing number of home computers offer automatic indexing programs. Some computer systems also use general-purpose indexing programs. One of these, BINDEX,[3] developed by Nuel Belnap at the University of Pittsburgh, is available free (to those who send Belnap a tape) and can be used by those who are typing on time-shared word procesors. Such tools vastly speed up the indexing process. Furthermore, the resulting index is of much higher quality because revisions are easy to do.

NOTES TO CHAPTER 5

1. A common though not universal custom is to use <u>forthcoming</u> in place of a date for books that have been accepted but not published; <u>in press</u> for articles that have been accepted but not published; and <u>unpublished</u> for all other unpublished manuscripts. AMathS style uses "to appear" in place of "in press." ASA style uses "forthcoming" for both journals and books.

2. Firman Publications, <u>Designing Technical Manuals</u> (Pembroke, Mass.: Firman Technical Publications, Inc, n.d.).

3. Nuel D. Belnap, "BINDEX: A Book Indexing System," <u>Scholarly Publishing</u> 9 (January 1978): 167-170.

TABLE 5.1

Title of Example Table

Stubhead	Boxhead		
	Cost in Dollars	Column Head	Percen-tages
Spanner Head[1]			
Row stub	$ 10	4	1.0%
Row stub	110	100	15.3
Subordinate stub[1]	1250	....	.1
Second subordinate stub[1]	1540	64	112.2
Row Stub	3	1	.1
Second Spanner Head			
Row stub	$ 1567	0	2.6%
Subordinate stub[1]	12	....	27.9
Subordinate stub[1]	278	1765	281.0
Row stub	1567	0	0.0

Source: James S. Smith, The Census Story (Washington, D. C.: Publishing House, 1990), p. 100.

Notes: Notes in this category apply to the entire table.

[1] Notes in this category apply only to certain entries. Subordinate stubs and spanners are not present in every table.

STYLES

chapter 6

AMaths, AMA, ASTM, MLA, GPO

6.1   Part II is mainly for typists, writers, and editors of technical and scholarly manuscripts. Typists, writers, and editors of other manuscripts will need only the instructions in Chapters 1 through 3 and sometimes 4 and 5. Chapter 6 opens Part II with requirements and examples for three styles that document by number of reference--AMathS, AMA, and ASTM--and two that document by means of endnotes or footnotes--MLA and GPO. Chapter 7 continues with four more endnote/footnote styles--Turabian, MSH, AIP, and AIEE. Chapter 8 covers five major author (date) styles--MSN, AChemS, CBE, APA, and ASA, and several similar minor styles. All these forms of documentation and their associated reference lists and bibliographies are described in Sections 5.2 through 5.25. The source of information for each style is cited at the beginning of each section. Although all the sample documents contain some useful stylistic details, most citations are fictitious. Some sample manuscripts list more citations than others. The purpose is to show the treatment of a wide variety of document types in fields such as the humanities, where variety is common. Labels beside the examples point out important characteristics. The sample documents and document fragments are grouped at the ends of Chapters 3 and 6 through 8. Where possible, the sections list journals that are known to follow a given style or a style similar to it. The associated style sheets, in the Appendix, are filled out for the sample manuscripts. Thus, the style sheet for a scholarly article won't show, say, specifications for a preface even though the sheet for a book manuscript or thesis in the same style probably would show these requirements.

6.2   Different styles emphasize different features. AMathS pays a great deal of attention to the treatment of equations and illustrations; MLA pays almost none. These differences introduce an apparent lack of systematic treatment of styles, but the lack isn't important because certain combinations of style and feature rarely occur. For example, MLA style, popular in the humanities, would rarely be used for a mathematical paper. Different styles also vary in the length of printed instructions, so the length of sections in Chapters 6 through 8 also varies. Most of the instructions have to do with documentation style, which accounts for the bulk of instructions in style books and sheets. Unless a style's instructions are unclear, I don't mention treatment of features such as headings and table titles that are obvious from the sample manuscripts and style sheets. Sponsors of styles were given a chance to check the sample manuscripts and correct ambiguities.

6.3   Most scholarly journals expect exclusive consideration of articles or right of first refusal. Some require submission of a form that grants copyright to the considering journal (see Chapter 10). Many also require submission of an evaluation fee that ranges from $10 on up. The fee is nonrefundable, and review of a manuscript won't begin until the fee has been received.

AMERICAN MATHEMATICAL SOCIETY

Ambiguities

6.4   Ambiguities in the American Mathematical Society's instructions[1] were cleared up in correspondence with the society's director of editorial services. In contrast to most scholarly publications, the society allows authors to integrate tables with text and to set their own styles for titles, column heads, row stubs, and the like. There is no rule for numbering of headings. Some authors and journals choose to number; others don't. Similarly, there is no rule for the treatment of long quotations, although the society recommends leaving extra space above and below blocked quotes. Paragraph indentation is five spaces.

Journals and General Principles

6.5   Journals published by the American Mathematical Society are:

Bulletin (New Series) of the American Mathematical Society
Mathematics of Computation
Memoirs of the American Mathematical Society
Notices of the American Mathematical Society
Proceedings of the American Mathematical Society
Transactions of the American Mathematical Society

Of these journals, Mathematics of Computation's style differs in several ways from the requirements of the American Mathematical Society. In fact, its style is much more like ASTM (see Sections 6.12-6.17). The sample manuscript ends with a few sample entries for this journal.

6.6   Because the journals vary in some details, take heading styles and treatment of equations from the journal for which an article is intended. The text of the sample manuscript describes many of these details. Strive for conceptual rather than computational proofs so as to use a minimum of symbols. For help, read the guidelines in Sections 3.25 through 3.28. Avoid long arrows, curved lines, and angles other than 45° in diagrams of groups and homomorphisms. Printers can handle short vertical and horizontal lines and 45° angle lines. Treat all such diagrams as simply as possible. Treat complex diagrams as illustrations.

6.7   Draw all illustrations and figures in permanent black ink on strong white paper.

** Make the figure and the lettering large enough that when reduced by half for printing, the entire illustration will be readable.

** Make a separate illustration of any matrix, diagram, figure, table, or displayed formula that occupies more than four lines. This will prevent the
possibility that a compositor may have to break the matrix, etc. across two
pages, thus making it hard to read.

6.8   Pay special attention to vertical alignment in matrices and tables. Enclose matrices in a pair of vertical lines and write "det" before the determinant. Thus, in this example, the left-hand expression is the matrix; the right-hand, its determinant:

$$\begin{vmatrix} a_{ih} \end{vmatrix} \qquad \det \begin{vmatrix} a_{ih} \end{vmatrix}$$

Two other acceptable methods for the matrix and determinant respectively, are to enclose (1) the matrix in brackets and the determinant in a single pair of vertical bars and (2) the matrix in two pairs of double bars and the determinant in a single pair of vertical bars.

Footnotes and Documentation

6.9   AMathS discourages footnotes, especially ones with equations in them. When a note seems necessary, insert it parenthetically in the text as a "Remark." Place acknowledgment notes on the title page, preceded by a superscript number. In text, refer to bibliographic items in forms like those in Section 5.7:

Jones [5, pp. 32-34] showed that . . .

Use boldface on the number of the document.

Bibliography

6.10   The bibliography follows the principles described in Sections 5.6 and 5.7. Except for Mathematics of Computation, which numbers entries in order of appearance (like ASTM style), alphabetize the items and number them consecutively. References to books should give in order author, title, edition (if not the first), name of series and number (if one of a series), publisher (or distributor), city, and year. When referring to journal articles, begin with author's name, article title, and journal name. Abbreviate journal names according to the list of standard abbreviations in the annual subject indexes of Mathematical Reviews. The name of the journal is followed in order by the volume number, the year, and the first and last page numbers. Don't use month of issue or issue number unless there is no other way to identify a journal precisely. When a serial number exists, give it in parentheses just before the volume number. Standard abbreviations for some of the major journals are:

Amer. J. Math.
Amer. Math. Monthly
Ann. of Math.
Bull. Amer. Math. Soc.

J. Math. Mech.
J. Symbolic Logic
Math. Reviews
Michigan Math. J.

Canad. J. Math.
Comm. Pure Appl. Math.
Duke Math. J.
Illinois J. Math.

Pacific J. Math
Proc. Amer. Math. Soc.
Proc. Nat. Acad. Sci. U.S.A.
Trans. Amer. Math. Soc.

Similar Minor Styles

6.11   The American Journal of Orthopsychiatry[2] uses a documentation method similar to AMathS but with a twist. Document numbers are typed as superscript numbers. Thus, a sentence that cited documents 5, 3, 7, and 1, in that order would look like this:

Several researchers have confirmed it.[5,3,7,1]

The list of documents closely resembles a list of references in Sage style (see Section 8.33), but without the parentheses around the date.

AMERICAN MEDICAL ASSOCIATION

Ambiguities

6.12   AMA style[3] leaves several questions for typists. These are:

** **Paper weight and quality;** what is the minimum allowed?

** **Quotations;** granting that quotations are rare, how does AMA style recommend that long quotations be typed? Or are they forbidden?

** **Tables;** how are source notes typed? Does AMA style recognize a general note ("NOTE") that applies to an entire table, not just a column or cell? If so, how is it typed and in what order relative to source and specific notes? When substubs have turnover lines, are they indented one space further than the substub?

** **Equations;** does AMA style have any rules regarding treatment of equations? If so, how are equations typed? Centered? Numbered? Left or right? Treatment in the sample manuscript represents an educated guess.

** **Key words;** is there an approved list of key words?

Journals and General Principles

6.13   AMA style is used by the following journals:[4]

American Journal of Diseases of
 Children
Archives of Dermatology
Archives of General Psychiatry
Archives of Internal Medicine
Archives of Neurology
Archives of Ophthalmology

Archives of Otolaryngology
Archives of Pathology and Laboratory
 Medicine
Archives of Surgery
Journal of the American Medical
 Association
Journal of School Health

6.14   Manuscripts containing statistical evaluations should include the name and affiliation of the statistical reviewer. Manuscripts that report the results of experimental investigation on human subjects must include a statement to the effect that informed consent was obtained after the nature of the procedures had been fully explained. All measurements must be in metric units. Keep titles short and suited to indexing. If a word processor is used, don't justify lines. For major articles, prepare an abstract of not more than 135 words and limit references to 20 items. For Brief Reports limit the abstract to 60 words and the references to 10 items. In any manuscript, avoid appendixes when possible.

6.15   Have all illustrations professionally prepared and submit high-quality glossy photographic prints of all line drawings. Acknowledge illustrations taken from other sources, including authors, title of article, title of journal or book, volume number, pages, month, and year. When using photographs of patients, get written consent that specifies the conditions of use. The maximum length of captions and legends combined is 40 words. Captions/legends should be typed separately.

Footnotes and Documentation

6.16   Content footnotes appear not to be allowed. Documentation is by citation of references numbered in order of appearance, not alphabetical order. In each reference include, at minimum, the names of all authors, complete title of article cited, name of journal abbreviated according to Index Medicus, year of publication, volume number, and first and last page numbers. References to books should include the edition (if other than the first), the city of publication, and the publisher.

Similar Minor Styles

6.17   Several journals follow a similar minor style, that of the Index Medicus,[5] which is a major index of publications in the medical field. In this style, the superscript reference number is surrounded by parentheses, like this,[5] and references to journals and books, respectively, are typed like the ones below rather than the ones in the sample manuscript:

Stein MK, Downing RW, Rickels K. Self-estimates in anxious and depressed outpatients treated with pharmacotherapy. Psychol Rep 1978 Oct;43(2):487-92.

Carlsson A, Lindqvist M. Effects of antidepressant agents on monoamine synthesis. In: Depressive disorders: symposium, Rome, May 9th-11th, 1977. Stuttgart; New York: Schattauer Verlag, c1978. (Symposia medica Hoechst; 13) W3 SY1055 v.13 1977. pp. 95-105

Differences include the boldface on the names, the lack of italics on titles of journals and books, period rather than colon between authors' names and title, greater amount of information, "c" before the copyright date, and in the case of books, addition of the National Library of Medicine (NLM) call number (begining with "W3"), which is useful on interlibrary loans. This style, in turn, follows that of the American National Standards Institute (ANSI).[6] Among the journals that use this style are:[7]

American Journal of Psychotherapy
Child Psychiatry and Human
  Development
Drugs in Health Care

Journal of Community Health
Psychiatric Journals of University of
  Ottawa
Sexuality and Disability

Biomedical journals

American Review of Respiratory
  Diseases
British Medical Journal
Canadian Journal of Public Health
  (Revue Canadienne de Sante Publique)

Canadian Medical Association Journal
Circulation
Clinical and Investigative Medicine
The Lancet
The New England Journal of Medicine

ANSI standards have also been adopted by the American Chemical Society, the American Institute of Physics, and the Council of Biology Editors, among others,[8] but uniformity still does not exist (see Chapters 7 and 8).

AMERICAN SOCIETY FOR TESTING AND MATERIALS

Ambiguities

6.18   Ambiguities in ASTM style[9] were clarified in correspondence with the managing editor of ASTM's technical journals.

Journals and General Principles

6.19   The journals of the association are:

Cement, Concrete, and Aggregates
Composites Technology Review
Geotechnical Testing Journal
Journal of Environmental Measure-
  ments and Applications

Journal of Forensic Sciences
Journal of Testing and Evaluation
Standardization News

Special technical publications are books whose style is usually the same as that for the technical journals.

6.20   The optimum size of an ASTM paper is about 5000 words. When pertinent references are unpublished, supply either enough copies for reviewers or enough of the information to enable reviewers to evaluate the manuscript. Because automated retrieval systems demand uniform terms, authors must use key words taken from an approved list.[10] Authors who lack boldface type, which is required on first-level headings, should draw a wavy line beneath those heads. In reporting results, use SI (International System of Units) metric units. Underline (1) illustration letters and numbers used as legends for identification of parts in illustrations, (2) derivatives, (3) letters in parentheses used to identify listings or subdivisions of illustrations, (4) concentrations (e.g., N = normal), (5) prefixes o, m, and p when they stand for ortho, meta, and para; sec and tert when they stand for secondary and tertiary; iso in isooctane and n in n-pentane, (6) location words in figure captions, (7) foreign words not in the dictionary, and (8) transistors. On graphs and charts, use blue ruled coordinate paper and either press-on (wax-back) lettering or black India ink with a lettering set. Submit original line drawings and sharp, high-contrast glossy prints of photographs.

6.21   For treatment of numeric expressions, read Sections 3.25 through 3.28. In addition, when typing crystal planes and directions, enclose planes in parentheses and a family of planes in curly brackets. Enclose directions in brackets and a family of directions in less-than (left side) and greater-than (right side) signs. In equations, avoid radical signs whenever possible. In ratios use "1 to 10" or "1/10." Don't use dashes or colons between the numbers. Don't use powers of 10 in table column headings or in axis legends in an illustration. Readers won't be able to tell whether the scale has been or should be multiplied by, say, 10^6. Instead, use "$X10^6$" beside the first entry in a table or the largest number in an axis scale.

Footnotes and Documentation

6.22   For notes attached to the title of a paper, use symbols (*, †, etc.). For notes in tables, use superior lowercase letters and type the notes below the table. The letter sequence begins anew for each table. For all other notes, use superior numbers. Footnote references are used for personal communications, industry codes and standards, and methods (see also Section 6.23). Type all title and text notes on a separate sheet following the references. Don't use notes in figure captions. Either cite a previous reference (e.g., "see note 4") or type out the reference as part of the caption. Documentation is in the form of bracketed numbers in text.

References and Bibliography

6.23   List and number referenced documents consecutively on a separate page in the order in which they are mentioned in the text. When a document includes a general bibliography with items that are not cited specifically but that offer useful general information, use topical divisions with the entries in alphabetical order. References may include only papers, articles, books, and reports (see also Section 6.22). Publishing societies must be given in full; names of well-known publishers, such as Harper & Row, may be abbreviated (e.g., Harper). When citing articles, do not include the title of articles in continuing periodicals that are easy to obtain. However, always include full name of journal, volume number, issue number, and month and year, even when the information seems redundant. Uncertain bibliographic data are omitted.

MLA STYLE

6.24   The information on MLA style comes from the _MLA Handbook_ (1977).[11] The main MLA examples are at the end of Chapter 3. The sample MLA research paper has many more notes listed than are used in the text. The purpose is to give a full range of examples without adding unnecessary length to the document. The sample front matter and first chapter in MLA dissertation style also serve as a guide for books in MLA style and for articles whose publishers require footnotes rather than endnotes. Again to save space, this sample has no bibliography and no footnotes past 12; except for the internal single-spacing, the notes and bibliography would be identical to those with the MLA research paper.

6.25   The partial example here shows a variant form--use of parenthesized documentation in text instead of footnotes or endnotes. Bibliographical studies and documents with very few citations sometimes benefit from use of intext documentation throughout. In such cases, include in the parentheses all information that would normally go in a note. As this sample shows, the text is hard to read when it refers to a great many documents and very few citations are to documents previously cited.

Ambiguities

6.26   The <u>MLA Handbook</u> is ambiguous on several points:[12]

** **Lists of tables and illustrations;** how to format. Unless otherwise instructed, follow the form in the preliminaries to the complete manuscript preparation style guide.

** **Headings;** how to treat turnover lines; whether to underline; how to treat headings at the second and third levels of importance (as paragraph leaders with initial caps, followed by a period?).

** **Tables and illustrations;** whether to type on pages with text even in articles for publication; whether to type lines above and below tables and figures to separate them from text; number of empty lines to leave above and below; and how to treat turnover (second and subsequent) lines on titles and captions (centered? inverted pyramid style?).

** **Tables;** how to type substubs--indented two spaces? With respect to order of notes, does MLA recognize a general note, and if so, where it is typed?

** **Illustrations;** how to type captions (centered? top or bottom?); what capitalization rule to follow; whether to end with a period; and whether to draw boxes around them.

** **Equations;** how to type (centered? indented from left?); whether to number; and if so, how.

** **Number of copies;** for publication, how many copies to submit?

In general, users of MLA style will have little need for headings at third and fourth levels, except in some theses, and little need for equations, tables, or figures.

Journals

6.27   Among the scholarly journals that use MLA style are:[13]

American Journal of Economics &
  Sociology
Journal of American Forensic
  Association
Journal of Asian Studies
Journal of Baltic Studies
Journal of Curriculum Studies
Journal of Educational Thought
Journal of Higher Education

Journal of Popular Culture
Peabody Journal of Education
Quarterly Journal of Speech
Soundings
Southern Speech Communication Journal
Women's Studies: An Interdisciplinary
  Journal
American Quarterly
Children Today

One journal, the <u>Harvard Educational Review</u>,[14] claims to use both MLA and APA style. MLA style is also used by many students and teachers in the humanities.

Documentation

6.28   Mechanics. Most MLA manuscripts document with superscript numbers in text accompanied by either endnotes (Section 5.10-5.11) or footnotes (Section 5.12; primarily used in dissertations). Unlike bibliographic listings, notes are intended to be read like sentences, without full stops inside the citation. Thus, commas separate elements, and place, publisher, and date of publication are enclosed by parentheses. In general, even when a document uses endnotes or footnotes, put very short notes into the text.

6.29   The basic mechanics for endnotes are described in Section 5.10. Use superscript numbers in the text and with the note. The sample manuscript shows details clearly. The basic mechanics for footnotes are described in Section 5.12. In addition:

** Type all notes at the bottom of the pages on which they are referenced.

** Leave three empty lines (quadruple-space) between the last line of text and the first line of the notes.

** Indent five spaces, type the note number without punctuation slightly above the line, skip a space, and begin the reference.

** Single-space the notes.

** Double space between all notes.

6.30   On occasion, as when the last note on a page occurs on the last line or two of text, you'll have to finish the note at the bottom of the next page, ahead of notes that begin on that page.   In such cases:

** Type a solid line across the new page, one full line below the last line of the text.

** Leave three empty lines (double-space twice).

** Finish the note.

** Skip a line before beginning the first note on the new page.

6.31   **Elements.**   The standard form and approximate order of elements in references to books are:

** **Author's name;** in normal order, usually first name, middle initial, last. When only initials are given, use all.   Type with a period and a space after each.

** **Title of chapter or part of book cited;** in quotes, followed by comma inside quotes.

** **Title of work;** underlined, followed by comma unless the next element is enclosed in parentheses or unless the title has its own punctuation, such as an exclamation mark.   If the title is unusually long, it may be abbreviated, but always type the first few words verbatim.   Use an ellipsis (three spaced periods) to indicate a title portion skipped within the title.   For example, see Note 3.   Follow the capitalization rule in Section 3.31 unless, as with an e. e. cummings poem, you know the author prefers lowercase.   Use of MS (manuscript) and TS (typescript) signify types of un-published document.

** **Subtitle;** should be preceded by a colon that follows the title.   Underline the colon and the subtitle.

** **Names of editor(s), translator(s), and compilers(s);** in normal order, preceded by "ed.," "trans.," or "comp." (without parentheses) and followed by a comma unless the next detail is enclosed in parentheses.

** **Edition used;** whenever it is not the first, designated by Arabic numeral, followed by comma unless the next detail is enclosed in parentheses.   Don't confuse the original date with an edition date or reprint date.

** Series; title should be followed by a comma, followed by an Arabic numeral designating the number of the work in the series, followed by a comma unless the next detail is enclosed in parentheses. Don't underline or use quotation marks.

** Number of volumes; when more than one exist and if the information is pertinent (usually not needed when reference is to a specific passage and not to the work as a whole).

** Place of publication, publisher, and date; all within parentheses. Use a colon and a single space after the place, and a comma after the publisher. Take these data from the title page or copyright page. Use an appropriate short form of the publisher's name (e.g., "Harper" for "Harper & Row"). Use "n.p." for "no place of publication" and "no publisher." Use "privately printed" for privately printed works.

** Volume numbers; if one of two or more, use capital Roman numerals, preceded and followed by a comma. If you need to give the date of publication, as for a work published over several years, place the volume number just ahead of the publication information, as in Note 4. Otherwise, put the volume number after the publication information, without "Vol." ahead of it, followed by page numbers, as in the last entry, Note 15.

** Page number(s); in Arabic numerals (unless the original has Roman numerals), preceded by a comma, followed by a period (unless another reference follows). In general, don't use "Vol." or "p." ("pp.") when both volume and page numbers are given. However, use "Vol" and "p." or "pp." when the volume number applies to the general title of a multivolume work and not to the title of a particular volume. If there is no pagination, use "n. pag." If the book has signatures in place of page numbers, use "sig." in place of "p." If it numbers columns rather than pages, use "col." rather than "p."

When connecting inclusive page numbers, give the second number in full for numbers through 99. For larger numbers, give only the last two figures of the second when it is within the same hundred or thousand: pp. 4-5, 14-15, 32-36, 103-04, 392-405, 980-1005, 2004-06, 1708-886, 1983-2010, 13345-4400.

** Uncertain data; calls for use of inclusive brackets. For instance, in Note 15, for New York City, the publication didn't contain the date, and the writer's best guess was 1973.

6.32   The general rules and approximate order of elements in references to articles in periodicals are:

** Author's name; take from first or last page of article; same mechanics as for book.

** Title; in full, enclosed with quotation marks, followed by comma inside closing quotation marks unless title has its own punctuation, such as a question mark.

** **Name of periodical**; common words may be abbreviated according to common usage; when newspaper names don't include the city name, show it in brackets after the name. For instance: <u>Herald-Telephone</u> [Ourtown, Indiana].

** **Volume and issue numbers**; not preceded by "Vol."; Arabic numeral; followed by comma or open parenthesis. When paging is continuous through volume, give volume number followed by year in parentheses, comma, and page numbers. When numbering is by issue, give month or season (in parentheses, before date) or issue number preceded by "No." For example:

> 6 (March 1988), 45
>
> 6, No. 5 (1988), 46

When a system is unfamiliar, give all the information you can find. With newspapers and weekly or monthly magazines, omit volume and issue numbers and give complete date, set off by commas, followed by page number:

> <u>Science</u>, 18 May 1984, p. 5.

Identify the edition of newspapers.

** **Year**; in parentheses, preceded if necessary by month or season.

** **Page numbers**; Arabic; preceded by "p." or "pp." only when no volume number is given. For newspapers, section numbers may be needed.

6.33   For second and subsequent references to a document, use the briefest form that is still clear. Often, author's last name and a page number will do. When a document contains more than one work by an author, use the author's last name, a word or two from the title, and the page number.

Bibliography

6.34   **Mechanics.** The bibliography comes at the end of a document and, like endnotes, begins on a new, unnumbered page with the title centered two inches below the top of the page and three empty lines between the title and the first note. The mechanics are:

** In research papers, double-space all lines. In theses, single-space the entries but double-space between them.

** Indent second and subsequent lines five spaces.

** Skip two horizontal spaces after each full stop.

6.35   Normally, entries are alphabetized following the rules in Section 5.19. Authors of historical studies occasionally list entries chronologically by publication date. When a bibliography is sizable, it may be broken into subcatetories, as noted in Section 5.19.

6.36   Elements. The treatment of elements in a bibliography is as follows:

** **Author's name;** reverse order, first author only.

** **Title and subtitle;** complete, underlined.

** **Publication data;** no parentheses, comma between publisher and date; in citations of periodicals, yearbooks, and some reference books, the year (sometimes preceded by month or season) goes in parentheses.

** **Volume numbers:** when a writer uses all volumes of a multivolume work, indicate that fact by listing volumes <u>before</u> the publication information (e.g., entry for John Q. Author). Otherwise, list volumes after publication information (e.g., entry for Great Britain. When volumes were published in different years, treat as in entry for Moses.

** **Page numbers;** give inclusive page numbers for short pieces, such as articles and book chapters. Precede with a comma to make the page numbers part of the preceding information.

** **Punctuation;** blocks of information followed by periods. Not intended to be read as a sentence.

** **Two or more works, same author;** Use author's name on first entry only. For all others, type ten hyphens followed, in turn, by a period, two spaces, and the rest of the entry. Free choice as to whether the order of entries is chronologically by date of publication or alphabetically by title.

GOVERNMENT PRINTING OFFICE (GPO) STYLE

Introduction

6.37   The U.S. Government Printing Office's <u>Style Manual</u>[15] is mainly a guide to printers and a manual on language usage. Both topics are outside the scope of this book. Thus, this section only summarizes Chapter 1, "Suggestions to Authors and Editors," and lists journals that follow GPO style. No sample manuscript and no sample style sheet are provided.

Journals

6.38   Sussman lists a few journals as following GPO style:[16]

Improving College and University
Teaching

Law and Contemporary Problems
Worklife

As readers might expect, major users of GPO style are the compilers of government documents such as the <u>Congressional Record</u>.

General Principles

6.39   Legible copies (not carbon) are required. Send copy flat, with sheets numbered consecutively, typewritten on one side of the page only. When both sides of reprint copy are to be used, submit a duplicate copy. Begin each page with a paragraph. Put tables and illustrations on separate sheets because each will be handled separately during the printing process. Write plainly all proper names, signatures, figures, foreign words, and technical terms. Especially when copy is in a foreign language, mark capitalization, punctuation, and accents carefully.

6.40   Send photographs, drawings, and other illustrations with the manuscript. See Section 5.32 for instructions on preparation and Section 9.4 for instructions on how to package. When captions and legends are typed separately from the illustrations, place the pages with captions on top of the manuscript. When illustrations are included, enclose a requisition letter certifying that the illustrations are essential and relate entirely to the transaction of public business. The letter should also indicate the total number of illustrations and the desired process for reproduction. When enlargement or reduction is needed, give instructions in the margin of each illustration.

6.41   When a publication is composed of several parts, specify in writing the desired arrangement when delivering the first installment of copy. To reduce the possibility of costly blank pages, avoid new odd pages and half-title pages whenever possible. As much as possible, provide plainly marked samples that show the desired type, size of type page, illustrations, paper, trim, lettering, and binding. Bear in mind, though, that specifications will be ignored if they conflict with GPO rules. When pages are looseleaf or perforated on folds, indicate page sequence (beginning with title page) in nonphoto-blue pencil. Specify whether to use a separate or a self cover.

6.42   Avoid oversize fold-ins by arranging the material to appear as facing pages in the text. When fold-ins are numerous and cannot be split, consider folding and inserting in an envelope pasted inside the back cover. When a job is longer than 4 pages, try to keep the complete job to some multiple of 8, 12, 16, 24, or 32 pages (these make up **signatures**--folded pages that are bound together to make up books).

NOTES TO CHAPTER 6

1. American Mathematical Society, <u>A Manual for Authors of Mathematical Papers</u>, 6th ed. (Providence, R.I.: American Mathematical Society, 1979); Ellen E. Swanson, Director, Editorial Services, American Mathematical Society, to Carolyn J. Mullins, 2 November 1981.

2. <u>American Journal of Orthopsychiatry</u>, "Information for Contributors," <u>American Journal of Orthopsychiatry</u> 51 (1, 1981).

3. American Medical Association, "Instructions for Authors," <u>Journal of the American Medical Association</u> 245 (6, 1981):560; William R. Barclay, M. Therese Southgate, and Robert W. Mayo, <u>Manual for Authors and Editors: Editorial Style and Manuscript Preparation</u> (Los Altos, California: Lange Medical Publications, 1981).

4. Barclay, Southgage, and Mayo, <u>Manual</u>, p. 138; Marvin B. Sussman, ed., <u>Author's Guide to Journals in Sociology and Related Fields</u> (New York: Haworth, 1978).

5. <u>Index Medicus</u>, "Change of <u>Index Medicus</u> Citation Format," <u>Index Medicus</u> (August 1981), p. xvii.

6. American National Standards Institute, <u>American National Standard for Bibliographic References</u> (New York: American National Standards Institute, 1977).

7. Sussman, <u>Author's Guide</u>; International Steering Committee, <u>Uniform Requirements for Manuscripts Submitted to Biomedical Journals</u> (January 1979).

8. <u>Index Medicus</u>, "Change."

9. American Society for Testing and Materials, <u>ASTM Style Manual</u> (Philadelphia: American Society for Testing and Materials, 1973); ASTM, <u>Instructions to Authors of Papers for ASTM Journals</u> (Philadelphia: American Society for Testing and Materials, n.d.); Rosemary Horstman, Managing Editor, Technical Journals, ASTM, to Carolyn J. Mullins, 16 October, 1981.

10. The list is in Engineers Joint Council, <u>Thesaurus of Engineering and Scientific Terms</u>, available from the council at 345 E. 47th Street, New York, N.Y. 10017.

11. Modern Language Association, <u>MLA Handbook for Writers of Research Papers, Theses, and Dissertations</u> (New York: Modern Language Association, 1977).

12. The MLA's Director of Book Publications expects to announce "substantial changes" in MLA style in "mid-1982"; Walter S. Achtert to Carolyn J. Mullins, 5 August 1981. Achtert declined to comment on the sample manuscripts.

13. Sussman, _Author's Guide_; Carolyn J. Mullins, _A Guide to Writing and Publishing in the Social and Behavioral Sciences_ (New York: Wiley-Interscience, 1977), Table 7.1.

14. Sussman, _Author's Guide_, p. 58.

15. Rev. ed. (Washington, D.C.: U.S. Government Printing Office, 1973).

16. Sussman, _Author's Guide_.

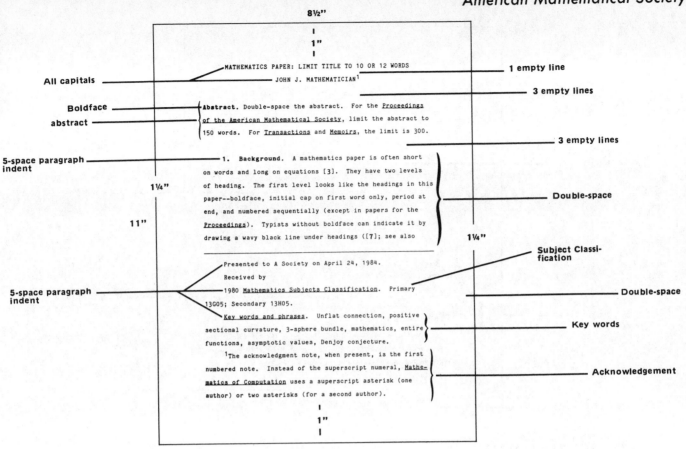

8½"

1"

All capitals

MATHEMATICS PAPER: LIMIT TITLE TO 10 OR 12 WORDS

JOHN J. MATHEMATICIAN[1]

1 empty line

3 empty lines

Boldface
abstract

Abstract. Double-space the abstract. For the *Proceedings of the American Mathematical Society*, limit the abstract to 150 words. For *Transactions* and *Memoirs*, the limit is 300.

3 empty lines

5-space paragraph indent

1¼"

1. **Background.** A mathematics paper is often short on words and long on equations [3]. They have two levels of heading. The first level looks like the headings in this paper--boldface, initial cap on first word only, period at end, and numbered sequentially (except in papers for the *Proceedings*). Typists without boldface can indicate it by drawing a wavy black line under headings ([7]; see also

11"

Double-space

1¼"

5-space paragraph indent

Presented to A Society on April 24, 1984.

Received by

1980 *Mathematics Subjects Classification.* Primary 13G05; Secondary 13H05.

Key words and phrases. Unflat connection, positive sectional curvature, 3-sphere bundle, mathematics, entire functions, asymptotic values, Denjoy conjecture.

[1]The acknowledgment note, when present, is the first numbered note. Instead of the superscript numeral, *Mathematics of Computation* uses a superscript asterisk (one author) or two asterisks (for a second author).

Subject Classification

Double-space

Key words

Acknowledgement

1"

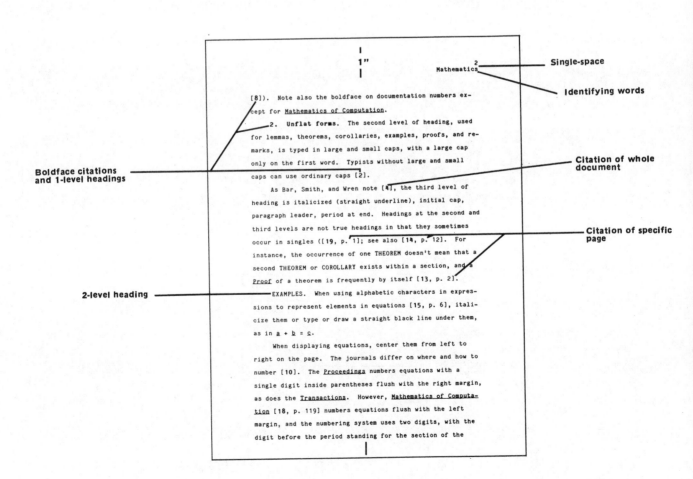

1"

Mathematics[2]

Single-space

Identifying words

Boldface citations and 1-level headings

[8]). Note also the boldface on documentation numbers except for *Mathematics of Computation.*

2. **Unflat forms.** The second level of heading, used for lemmas, theorems, corollaries, examples, proofs, and remarks, is typed in large and small caps, with a large cap only on the first word. Typists without large and small caps can use ordinary caps [2].

As Bar, Smith, and Wren note [4], the third level of heading is italicized (straight underline), initial cap, paragraph leader, period at end. Headings at the second and third levels are not true headings in that they sometimes occur in singles ([19, p. 1]; see also [14, p. 12]. For instance, the occurrence of one THEOREM doesn't mean that a second THEOREM or COROLLARY exists within a section, and a *Proof* of a theorem is frequently by itself [13, p. 2].

2-level heading

EXAMPLES. When using alphabetic characters in expressions to represent elements in equations [15, p. 6], italicize them or type or draw a straight black line under them, as in $a + b = c$.

When displaying equations, center them from left to right on the page. The journals differ on where and how to number [10]. The *Proceedings* numbers equations with a single digit inside parentheses flush with the right margin, as does the *Transactions*. However, *Mathematics of Computation* [18, p. 119] numbers equations flush with the left margin, and the numbering system uses two digits, with the digit before the period standing for the section of the

Citation of whole document

Citation of specific page

Equation mentioned in text

Equation number flush right in parenthesis

2 empty lines

Centered

3-level heading

Equation with no number

Citation of entire work

3 empty lines

Blocked 7 spaces from left margin
Quotation (Educated guess on treatment)

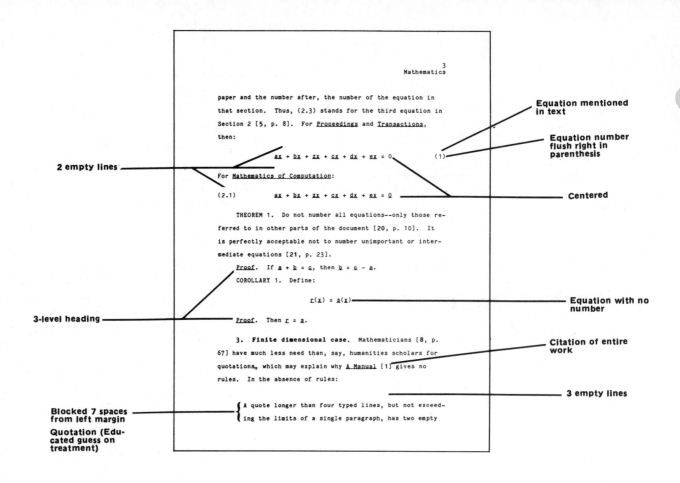

paper and the number after, the number of the equation in
that section. Thus, (2.3) stands for the third equation in
Section 2 [5, p. 8]. For Proceedings and Transactions,
then:

$$ax + bx + zx + cx + dx + ex = 0 \qquad (1)$$

For Mathematics of Computation:

$$(2.1) \qquad ax + bx + zx + cx + dx + ex = 0$$

THEOREM 1. Do not number all equations--only those referred to in other parts of the document [20, p. 10]. It
is perfectly acceptable not to number unimportant or intermediate equations [21, p. 23].
Proof. If $a + b = c$, then $b = c - a$.
COROLLARY 1. Define:

$$r(x) = a(x)$$

Proof. Then $r = a$.

3. Finite dimensional case. Mathematicians [8, p.
67] have much less need than, say, humanities scholars for
quotations, which may explain why A Manual [1] gives no
rules. In the absence of rules:

{A quote longer than four typed lines, but not exceeding the limits of a single paragraph, has two empty

3 empty lines

Underline alphabetic characters that represent elements

Sample illustration (educated guess)

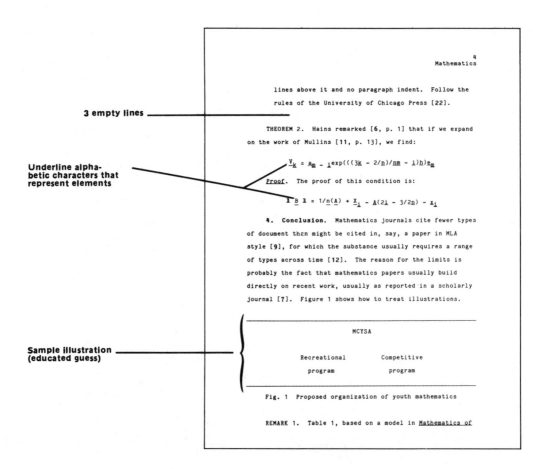

lines above it and no paragraph indent. Follow the
rules of the University of Chicago Press [22].

THEOREM 2. Hains remarked [6, p. 1] that if we expand
on the work of Mullins [11, p. 13], we find:

$$V_k = a_m - i \exp(((3k - 2/n)/nm - i)h)e_m$$

Proof. The proof of this condition is:

$$T\ B\ l = 1/n(A) + X_i - A(2i - 3/2n) - x_i$$

4. Conclusion. Mathematics journals cite fewer types
of document than might be cited in, say, a paper in MLA
style [9], for which the substance usually requires a range
of types across time [12]. The reason for the limits is
probably the fact that mathematics papers usually build
directly on recent work, usually as reported in a scholarly
journal [7]. Figure 1 shows how to treat illustrations.

```
                         MCYSA

          Recreational        Competitive

          program             program
```

Fig. 1 Proposed organization of youth mathematics

REMARK 1. Table 1, based on a model in Mathematics of

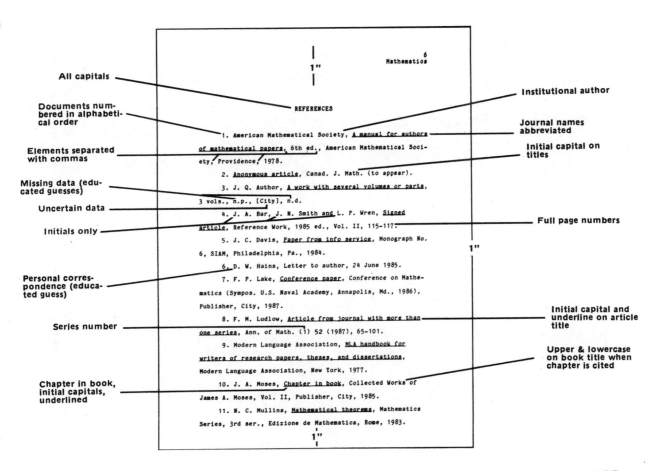

Top manuscript page:

<u>Computation</u> [8], shows large and small caps on "Table" [6].
I chose to use an initial cap in the illustration ([12];
[23]). Note the italics and sentence capitalization on the
table title even though no period follows it [16, p. 20].

Initial capital ———— Table 1

Sentence capitalization underline ———— <u>Teen-age mathematicians in Ourtown, by age group</u>

Level of Students	U-10	U-12	U-14	U-16	U-19
A-level	16	16	18	16	18
B-level	4	4	6	0	0
C-level	0[a]	0	0	0	0

Educated guess on treatment of body and notes

Note

Double-spaced

Source: Forms completed by parents and [17].
[a] Excludes players registered in Recreational League.

Table notes

Bottom references page:

1"

All capitals ———— REFERENCES

Documents numbered in alphabetical order

Elements separated with commas

Missing data (educated guesses)

Uncertain data

Initials only

Personal correspondence (educated guess)

Series number

Chapter in book, initial capitals, underlined

Institutional author

Journal names abbreviated

Initial capital on titles

Full page numbers

Initial capital and underline on article title

Upper & lowercase on book title when chapter is cited

1. American Mathematical Society, <u>A manual for authors
of mathematical papers</u>, 6th ed., American Mathematical Society, Providence, 1978.

2. <u>Anonymous article</u>, Canad. J. Math. (to appear).

3. J. Q. Author, <u>A work with several volumes or parts</u>,
3 vols., n.p., [City], n.d.

4. J. A. Bar, J. N. Smith and L. P. Wren, <u>Signed
article</u>, Reference Work, 1985 ed., Vol. II, 115-117.

5. J. C. Davis, <u>Paper from info service</u>, Monograph No.
6, SIAM, Philadelphia, Pa., 1984.

6. D. W. Hains, Letter to author, 24 June 1985.

7. F. P. Lake, <u>Conference paper</u>, Conference on Mathematics (Sympos. U.S. Naval Academy, Annapolis, Md., 1986),
Publisher, City, 1987.

8. F. M. Ludlow, <u>Article from journal with more than
one series</u>, Ann. of Math. (1) 52 (1987), 65-101.

9. Modern Language Association, <u>MLA handbook for
writers of research papers, theses, and dissertations</u>,
Modern Language Association, New York, 1977.

10. J. A. Moses, <u>Chapter in book</u>, Collected Works of
James A. Moses, Vol. II, Publisher, City, 1985.

11. N. C. Mullins, <u>Mathematical theorems</u>, Mathematics
Series, 3rd ser., Edizione de Mathematica, Rome, 1983.

1"

1"

12. Pamphlet on wave theory, rev. ed., MCYSA, Ourtown, Indiana, 1980.

13. F. X. Pert, Handbook on mathematics, Trans. S. P. Jones, Ed. Name O. Editor, 1940, Publisher, City, 1988.

14. J. R. Ramsey, Article in journal with continuous pagination through annual volume, Proc. Amer. Math. Soc. 21 (1987), 14-20.

15. _____, Article from journal that pages issues separately, Journal Name (5) 20 (1988), 2-8.

16. D. O. Ray, Computation of eigenvalues, Math. Comp. 1 (1974), 220-221.

17. S. Q. Riley, Unpublished dissertation, diss., A University, 1987.

18. D. P. Sale and E. Q. Snow, Jets of radiation, Quant. Appl. Math. 28 (1970), 116-125.

19. _____, Chapter in book edited by others, in Studies of Mathematics, ed. Susan P. Cole, Publisher, City, 1986, 4-13.

20. S. Q. Student, Published dissertation, diss. A University, 1987, Publisher, City, 1988.

21. S. W. Student, Article from dissertation abstracts, DA, 29 (1967), 3026A, University Name.

22. University of Chicago Press, A manual of style, 12th ed., University of Chicago Press, Chicago, 1969.

23. D. L. Utt, Review of Book title, by John Q. Author, in Math. Reviews 12 (1990), 223-225.

Issue number — (points to "(5)" in entry 15)

Volume boldfaced — (points to entry 14/15)

Sample Entries, Mathematics of Computation:

3. J. Q. Author, A Work with Several Volumes or Parts, 3 vols., n.p., [City], n.d.

18. D. P. Sale, "Jets of radiation," Quant. Appl. Math. 28 (1970), 116-125.

19. E. Q. Snow, "Chapter in book edited by others," in Studies of Mathematics, ed. Susan P. Cole. Publisher, City, 1986, 4-13.

Department of Mathematics, University of Anywhere, 0000 Any Time Way, Any Town, State, 00000.

Upper and lower-case book title — (points to "A Work with Several Volumes or Parts")

Initial capital and quotation marks on article title — (points to "Jets of radiation")

Author's mailing address — (points to Department of Mathematics line)

138

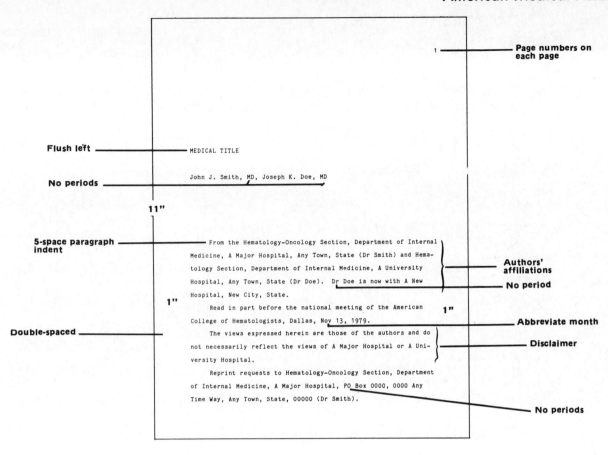

Page numbers on each page

Flush left ———— MEDICAL TITLE

No periods ———— John J. Smith, MD, Joseph K. Doe, MD

11"

5-space paragraph indent

From the Hematology-Oncology Section, Department of Internal Medicine, A Major Hospital, Any Town, State (Dr Smith) and Hematology Section, Department of Internal Medicine, A University Hospital, Any Town, State (Dr Doe). Dr Doe is now with A New Hospital, New City, State.

Authors' affiliations

No period

1"

Read in part before the national meeting of the American College of Hematologists, Dallas, Nov 13, 1979.

1"

Abbreviate month

Double-spaced

The views expressed herein are those of the authors and do not necessarily reflect the views of A Major Hospital or A University Hospital.

Disclaimer

Reprint requests to Hematology-Oncology Section, Department of Internal Medicine, A Major Hospital, PO Box 0000, 0000 Any Time Way, Any Town, State, 00000 (Dr Smith).

No periods

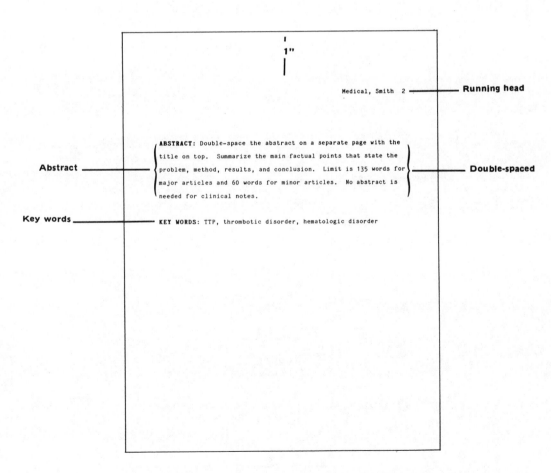

1"

Medical, Smith 2 ———— Running head

Abstract

ABSTRACT: Double-space the abstract on a separate page with the title on top. Summarize the main factual points that state the problem, method, results, and conclusion. Limit is 135 words for major articles and 60 words for minor articles. No abstract is needed for clinical notes.

Double-spaced

Key words

KEY WORDS: TTP, thrombotic disorder, hematologic disorder

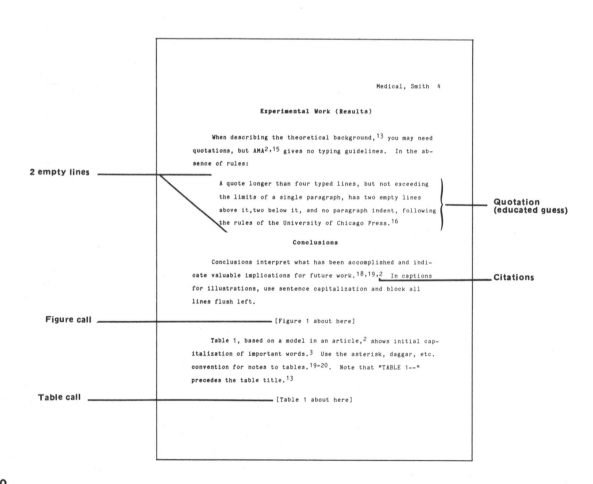

Medical, Smith 3

Statement of Problem

Cite only 20 references in entire major paper, 10 in brief note, 5 in clinical note.[1-2] First-level headings, in boldface, look like the headings in this paper. Typists without boldface can indicate it by drawing a wavy black line under headings.[3]

Method

Subjects.--The second level of heading is typed in upper- and lowercase letters and is also boldfaced.[4] As Dressendorfer et al[5] show, an unorthodox reference may be typed into the text (e.g., Sports Illustrated, Oct 8, 1979, pp 96-108).[6-8,3]

Analytic Technique.--In the reference list, note the lack of periods after initials and "pp" before page numbers.[9,1] Center displayed equations from left to right on the page (See Eq. (1)).[10] Number them inside parentheses flush with the right margin,[11-12] like this:

$$\underline{ax} + \underline{bx} + \underline{zx} + \underline{cx} + \underline{dx} + \underline{ex} = 0 \qquad (1)$$

Number only those equations that are referred to in other parts of the document.[13-14] Statements about equations represent educated guesses.[2]

5-space paragraph indent

Citation of 2 documents

2-level heading

No period

Unorthodox citation

Educated guess about treatment of equations

2 empty lines

Unjustified right margin

1-level heading

Repeat citation

Educated guess about treatment of equations

1"

Medical, Smith 4

Experimental Work (Results)

When describing the theoretical background,[13] you may need quotations, but AMA[2,15] gives no typing guidelines. In the absence of rules:

> A quote longer than four typed lines, but not exceeding the limits of a single paragraph, has two empty lines above it,two below it, and no paragraph indent, following the rules of the University of Chicago Press.[16]

Conclusions

Conclusions interpret what has been accomplished and indicate valuable implications for future work.[18,19,2] In captions for illustrations, use sentence capitalization and block all lines flush left.

[Figure 1 about here]

Table 1, based on a model in an article,[2] shows initial capitalization of important words.[3] Use the asterisk, daggar, etc. convention for notes to tables.[19-20]. Note that "TABLE 1--" precedes the table title.[13]

[Table 1 about here]

2 empty lines

Figure call

Table call

Quotation (educated guess)

Citations

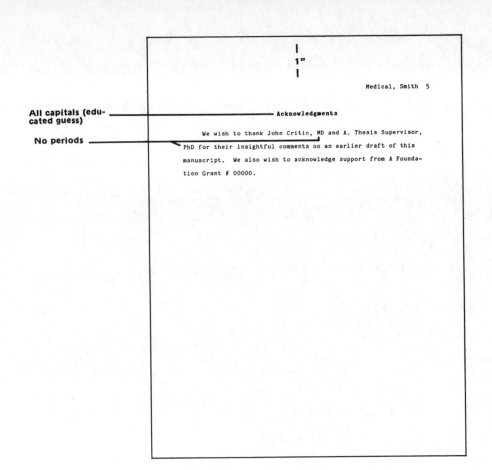

Medical, Smith 5

Acknowledgments — All capitals (educated guess)

We wish to thank John Critic, MD and A. Thesis Supervisor, PhD for their insightful comments on an earlier draft of this manuscript. We also wish to acknowledge support from A Foundation Grant # 00000. — No periods

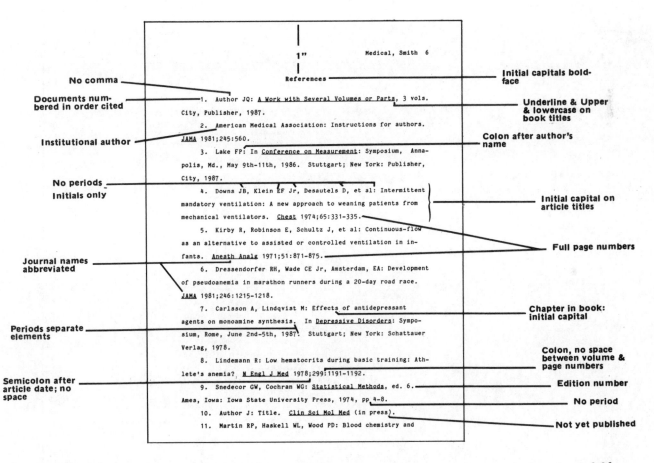

Medical, Smith 6

References — Initial capitals boldface

No comma / Documents numbered in order cited →
1. Author JQ: A Work with Several Volumes or Parts, 3 vols. City, Publisher, 1987. — Underline & Upper & lowercase on book titles

Institutional author →
2. American Medical Association: Instructions for authors. JAMA 1981;245:560. — Colon after author's name

3. Lake FP: In Conference on Measurement: Symposium, Annapolis, Md., May 9th-11th, 1986. Stuttgart; New York: Publisher, City, 1987.

No periods / Initials only →
4. Downs JB, Klein EF Jr, Desautels D, et al: Intermittent mandatory ventilation: A new approach to weaning patients from mechanical ventilators. Chest 1974;65:331-335. — Initial capital on article titles

5. Kirby R, Robinson E, Schultz J, et al: Continuous-flow as an alternative to assisted or controlled ventilation in infants. Anesth Analg 1971;51:871-875. — Full page numbers

Journal names abbreviated →
6. Dressendorfer RH, Wade CE Jr, Amsterdam, EA: Development of pseudoanemia in marathon runners during a 20-day road race. JAMA 1981;246:1215-1218.

7. Carlsson A, Lindqvist M: Effects of antidepressant agents on monoamine synthesis. In Depressive Disorders: Symposium, Rome, June 2nd-5th, 1987. Stuttgart; New York: Schattauer Verlag, 1978. — Chapter in book: initial capital

Periods separate elements →

8. Lindemann R: Low hematocrits during basic training: Athlete's anemia? N Engl J Med 1978;299:1191-1192. — Colon, no space between volume & page numbers

Semicolon after article date; no space →
9. Snedecor GW, Cochran WG: Statistical Methods, ed. 6. Ames, Iowa: Iowa State University Press, 1974, pp 4-8. — Edition number / No period

10. Author J: Title. Clin Sci Mol Med (in press). — Not yet published

11. Martin RP, Haskell WL, Wood PD: Blood chemistry and

141

Turnover line ——

Abbreviated; no period ——

|
1"
|

Caption

Fig 1.--Proposed organization. See Note 3 for source and observe treatment of turnover lines. When there is only one figure, omit numerical designation. The number is included here only for purposes of demonstration.

Center; Upper & lowercase on title ——

Upper & lowercase ——

Turnover line ——

Note symbol ——

Double-space ——

Table notes ——

Double-space throughout ——

|
1"
|

Table 1--Always Center the First Line of the Table Title;
Center the Second Line, Inverse Pyramid Style*

Level of Students	U-10	U-12	U-14	U-16	U-19
A-level	16	16	18	16	18
B-level,	4	4	6	0	0
turnover line					
C-level	0	0	0	0	...†
Substub	0	0	0	0	0
Substub	0	0	0	0	0

*Forms completed by parents.
†Use three leaders in a space that represents a blank entry. Observe the paragraph form of notes. Notes are designated, in order, by the asterisk, daggar, double daggar, section mark, parallels, paragraph mark, and number sign.

Document with more than 6 authors, list only first 3 authors ——

|
1"
|

lipid profiles of elite distance runners. NY Acad Sci 1977;301:346-360.

    12. Zar J: Biostatistical Analysis. Englewood Cliffs, NJ, Prentice-Hall Inc, 1974.

    13. Davis JC: Paper from information service. Report CR-6. Philadelphia, SIAM, August 1984, pp. 2-6, 11-12, 30-31.

    14. Student SQ: Unpublished Dissertation. Diss. A University 1986.

    15. Refsum HE, Jordfald G, Stromme SB: Hematological changes following prolonged heavy exercise. In Advances in Exercise Physiology. Basel, Switzerland, S Karger AG, 1976, vol 9, pp 91-99.

    16. University of Chicago Press: A Manual of Style, ed. 12. Chicago, University of Chicago Press, 1969.

    17. Demers RR: Rational (and irrational) approaches to weaning: A play in two acts. Respir Care 1976;21:601-602.

    18. Zwillich CW, Pierson DJ, Creagh CE, et al: Complications of assisted ventilation: A prospective study of 354 consecutive episodes. Am J Med 1974;57:161-170.

    19. Low ECY, Linn DR, Byrne JJ, et al: An article with more than six authors. Blood 1989;63:233-238.

    20. Byrnes JJ, Lian ECY: Recent therapeutic advances in thrombotic thrombocytopenic purpura. Semin Thromb Hemostas 1979;5:199-215.

|
1"
|

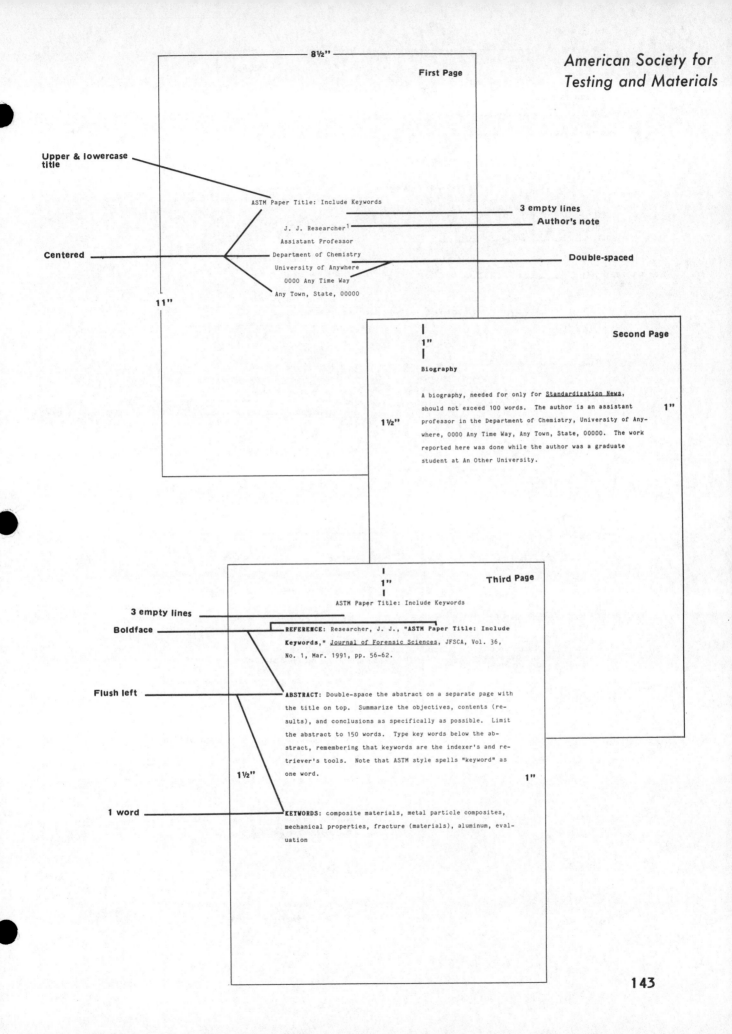

First Page

American Society for Testing and Materials

8½"

Upper & lowercase title

ASTM Paper Title: Include Keywords

3 empty lines

Author's note

J. J. Researcher[1]
Assistant Professor

Centered

Department of Chemistry
University of Anywhere

Double-spaced

0000 Any Time Way
Any Town, State, 00000

11"

Second Page

1"

Biography

1½"

A biography, needed for only for Standardization News, should not exceed 100 words. The author is an assistant professor in the Department of Chemistry, University of Anywhere, 0000 Any Time Way, Any Town, State, 00000. The work reported here was done while the author was a graduate student at An Other University.

1"

Third Page

1"

ASTM Paper Title: Include Keywords

3 empty lines

Boldface

REFERENCE: Researcher, J. J., "**ASTM Paper Title: Include Keywords**," Journal of Forensic Sciences, JFSCA, Vol. 36, No. 1, Mar. 1991, pp. 56-62.

Flush left

ABSTRACT: Double-space the abstract on a separate page with the title on top. Summarize the objectives, contents (results), and conclusions as specifically as possible. Limit the abstract to 150 words. Type key words below the abstract, remembering that keywords are the indexer's and retriever's tools. Note that ASTM style spells "keyword" as one word.

1½"

1 word

KEYWORDS: composite materials, metal particle composites, mechanical properties, fracture (materials), aluminum, evaluation

1"

143

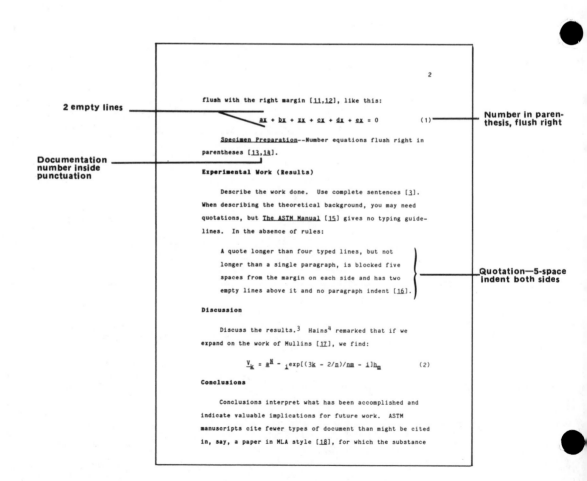

Boldface

1-level heading

5-space paragraph indent

2-level heading

3 or more authors

3-level head

Fourth Page

1"

ASTM Paper Title: Include Key Words

3 empty lines

Introduction

     Briefly present significance of current work in relation to previously published work. Do not repeat conclusion of earlier work [1]. Cite major references. First-level headings, in boldface, look like the headings in this paper. Typists without boldface can indicate it by drawing a wavy black line under headings [2,3].

Document numbers underlined, bracketed

Procedure

Data Sample   1"

     The second level of heading is typed in uppercase and lowercase letters and is underlined (italicized) [4]. As Bar et al. note [5], the third level of heading is also typed in uppercase and lowercase and underlined but is typed as a paragraph leader with two short dashes at the end (in print, one long solid dash [6-8]).

1½"

Citation of 3 documents

Analytic Technique

     Equipment--Give a general description that includes basic construction [9], principal methods of control, unique features, and so forth. Underline letters in equations that can take numerical values (see Eq 1).[2]

Note

Reference to equation. No period after "Eq"

     When displaying equations, center them from left to right on the page [10]. Number equations inside parentheses

---

2

2 empty lines

flush with the right margin [11,12], like this:

$$\underline{a}\underline{x} + \underline{b}\underline{x} + \underline{z}\underline{x} + \underline{c}\underline{x} + \underline{d}\underline{x} + \underline{e}\underline{x} = 0 \qquad (1)$$

Number in parenthesis, flush right

Specimen Preparation--Number equations flush right in parentheses [13,14].

Documentation number inside punctuation

Experimental Work (Results)

     Describe the work done. Use complete sentences [3]. When describing the theoretical background, you may need quotations, but The ASTM Manual [15] gives no typing guidelines. In the absence of rules:

     A quote longer than four typed lines, but not longer than a single paragraph, is blocked five spaces from the margin on each side and has two empty lines above it and no paragraph indent [16].

Quotation—5-space indent both sides

Discussion

     Discuss the results.[3] Hains[4] remarked that if we expand on the work of Mullins [17], we find:

$$\underline{v}_k = \underline{a}^N - {}_i\exp[(3\underline{k} - 2/\underline{n})/\underline{nm} - \underline{i}]\underline{h}_m \qquad (2)$$

Conclusions

     Conclusions interpret what has been accomplished and indicate valuable implications for future work. ASTM manuscripts cite fewer types of document than might be cited in, say, a paper in MLA style [18], for which the substance

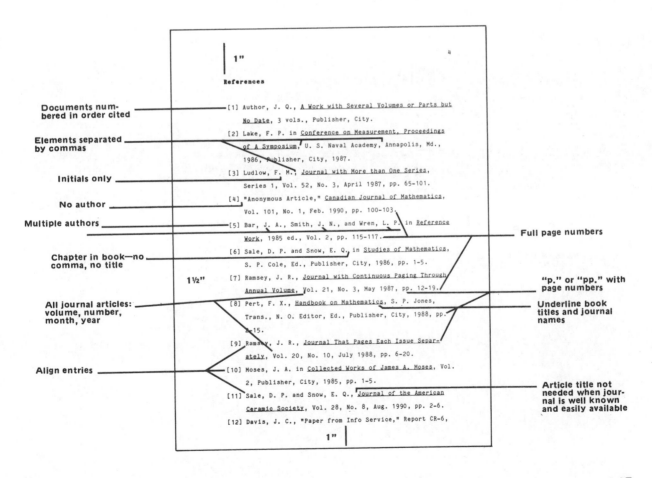

Page 3 (top manuscript)

3

usually requires a range of types across time [19]. The reason for the limits is probably the fact that ASTM papers usually build directly on recently published work [2]. Figure 1 is not shown because illustrations are usually not prepared by typists.

Figure call —————— [Figure 1 about here]

Table 1, based on a model in the ASTM Style Manual [15], shows sentence capitalization, underlining, and a terminal period. In the sample illustration, I chose to use a parallel style [19,20]. Note that "TABLE 1--" precedes the table title [21]. Appendixes, when they exist, follow the acknowledgments.

Table call —————— [Table 1 about here]

Acknowledgments

Acknowledgements —————— I wish to thank John Critic and A. Thesis Supervisor for their insightful comments on an earlier draft of this manuscript. I also wish to acknowledge support from A Foundation Grant # 00000. Do not put biographical data in acknowledgments.

Page 4 (bottom manuscript)

1"

4

References

Documents numbered in order cited — [1] Author, J. Q., A Work with Several Volumes or Parts but No Date, 3 vols., Publisher, City.

Elements separated by commas — [2] Lake, F. P. in Conference on Measurement, Proceedings of A Symposium, U. S. Naval Academy, Annapolis, Md., 1986, Publisher, City, 1987.

Initials only — [3] Ludlow, F. M., Journal with More than One Series, Series 1, Vol. 52, No. 3, April 1987, pp. 65-101.

No author — [4] "Anonymous Article," Canadian Journal of Mathematics, Vol. 101, No. 1, Feb. 1990, pp. 100-103.

Multiple authors — [5] Bar, J. A., Smith, J. N., and Wren, L. P. in Reference Work, 1985 ed., Vol. 2, pp. 115-117. **— Full page numbers**

Chapter in book—no comma, no title — [6] Sale, D. P. and Snow, E. Q., in Studies of Mathematics, S. P. Cole, Ed., Publisher, City, 1986, pp. 1-5.

1½"   [7] Ramsey, J. R., Journal with Continuous Paging Through Annual Volume, Vol. 21, No. 3, May 1987, pp. 12-19. **— "p." or "pp." with page numbers**

All journal articles: volume, number, month, year — [8] Pert, F. X., Handbook on Mathematics, S. P. Jones, Trans., N. O. Editor, Ed., Publisher, City, 1988, pp. 2-15. **— Underline book titles and journal names**

[9] Ramsey, J. R., Journal That Pages Each Issue Separately, Vol. 20, No. 10, July 1988, pp. 6-20.

Align entries — [10] Moses, J. A. in Collected Works of James A. Moses, Vol. 2, Publisher, City, 1985, pp. 1-5.

[11] Sale, D. P. and Snow, E. Q., Journal of the American Ceramic Society, Vol. 28, No. 8, Aug. 1990, pp. 2-6. **— Article title not needed when journal is well known and easily available**

[12] Davis, J. C., "Paper from Info Service," Report CR-6,

1"

145

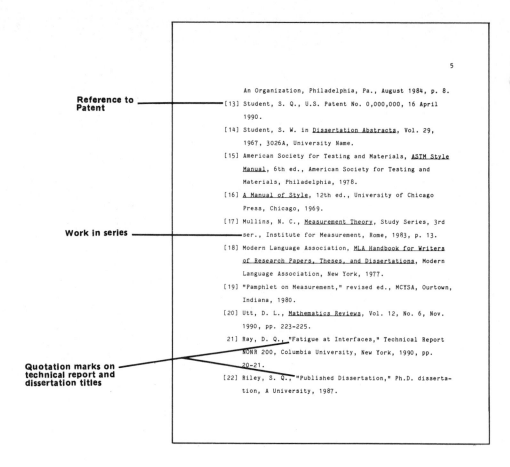

Reference to Patent

Work in series

Quotation marks on technical report and dissertation titles

5

An Organization, Philadelphia, Pa., August 1984, p. 8.

[13] Student, S. Q., U.S. Patent No. 0,000,000, 16 April 1990.

[14] Student, S. W. in _Dissertation Abstracts_, Vol. 29, 1967, 3026A, University Name.

[15] American Society for Testing and Materials, _ASTM Style Manual_, 6th ed., American Society for Testing and Materials, Philadelphia, 1978.

[16] _A Manual of Style_, 12th ed., University of Chicago Press, Chicago, 1969.

[17] Mullins, N. C., _Measurement Theory_, Study Series, 3rd ser., Institute for Measurement, Rome, 1983, p. 13.

[18] Modern Language Association, _MLA Handbook for Writers of Research Papers, Theses, and Dissertations_, Modern Language Association, New York, 1977.

[19] "Pamphlet on Measurement," revised ed., MCYSA, Ourtown, Indiana, 1980.

[20] Utt, D. L., _Mathematics Reviews_, Vol. 12, No. 6, Nov. 1990, pp. 223-225.

[21] Ray, D. Q., "Fatigue at Interfaces," Technical Report NONR 200, Columbia University, New York, 1990, pp. 20-21.

[22] Riley, S. Q., "Published Dissertation," Ph.D. dissertation, A University, 1987.

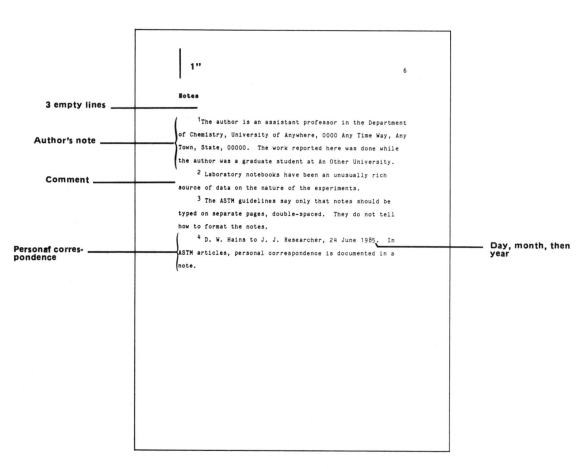

1"

6

3 empty lines

Author's note

Comment

Personal correspondence

Day, month, then year

Notes

[1]The author is an assistant professor in the Department of Chemistry, University of Anywhere, 0000 Any Time Way, Any Town, State, 00000. The work reported here was done while the author was a graduate student at An Other University.

[2] Laboratory notebooks have been an unusually rich source of data on the nature of the experiments.

[3] The ASTM guidelines say only that notes should be typed on separate pages, double-spaced. They do not tell how to format the notes.

[4] D. W. Hains to J. J. Researcher, 24 June 1985. In ASTM articles, personal correspondence is documented in a note.

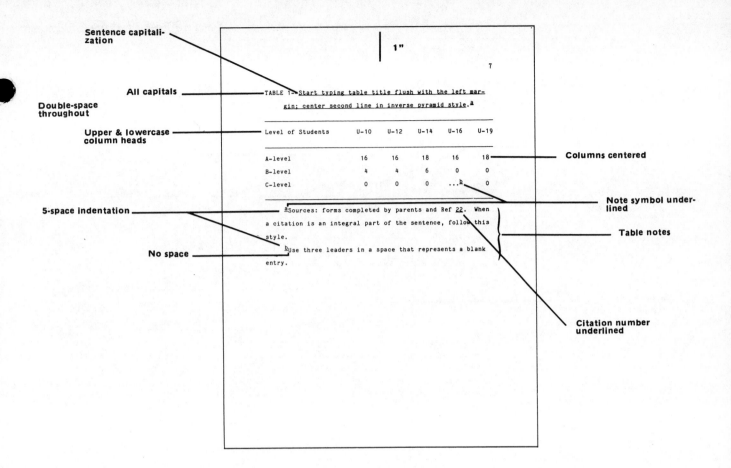

Sentence capitalization

All capitals

Double-space throughout

Upper & lowercase column heads

5-space indentation

No space

TABLE 1—Start typing table title flush with the left margin; center second line in inverse pyramid style.[a]

Level of Students	U-10	U-12	U-14	U-16	U-19
A-level	16	16	18	16	18
B-level	4	4	6	0	0
C-level	0	0	0	...[b]	0

[a]Sources: forms completed by parents and Ref 22. When a citation is an integral part of the sentence, follow this style.

[b]Use three leaders in a space that represents a blank entry.

Columns centered

Note symbol underlined

Table notes

Citation number underlined

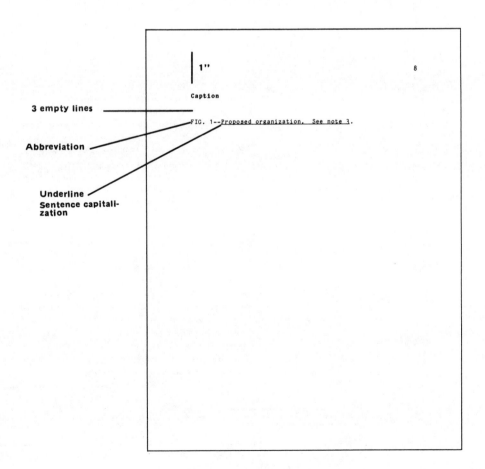

Caption

3 empty lines

Abbreviation

Underline
Sentence capitalization

FIG. 1--Proposed organization. See note 3.

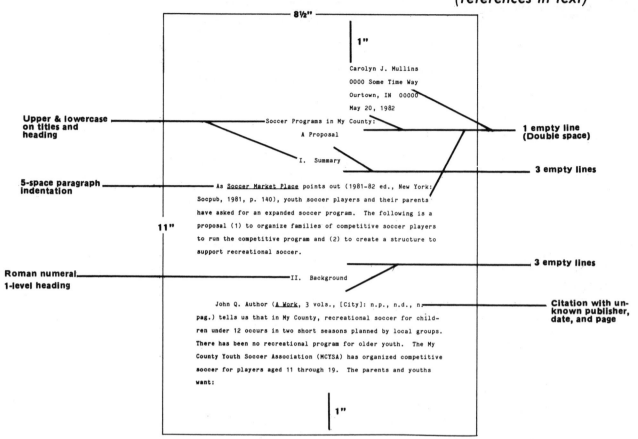

Upper & lowercase on titles and heading

5-space paragraph indentation

Roman numeral 1-level heading

8½"

1"

Carolyn J. Mullins
0000 Some Time Way
Ourtown, IN 00000
May 20, 1982

Soccer Programs in My County:
A Proposal

I. Summary

As Soccer Market Place points out (1981-82 ed., New York:
Socpub, 1981, p. 140), youth soccer players and their parents
have asked for an expanded soccer program. The following is a
proposal (1) to organize families of competitive soccer players
to run the competitive program and (2) to create a structure to
support recreational soccer.

II. Background

John Q. Author (A Work, 3 vols., [City]: n.p., n.d., n.
pag.) tells us that in My County, recreational soccer for children under 12 occurs in two short seasons planned by local groups.
There has been no recreational program for older youth. The My
County Youth Soccer Association (MCYSA) has organized competitive
soccer for players aged 11 through 19. The parents and youths
want:

11"

1"

1 empty line (Double space)

3 empty lines

3 empty lines

Citation with un-known publisher, date, and page

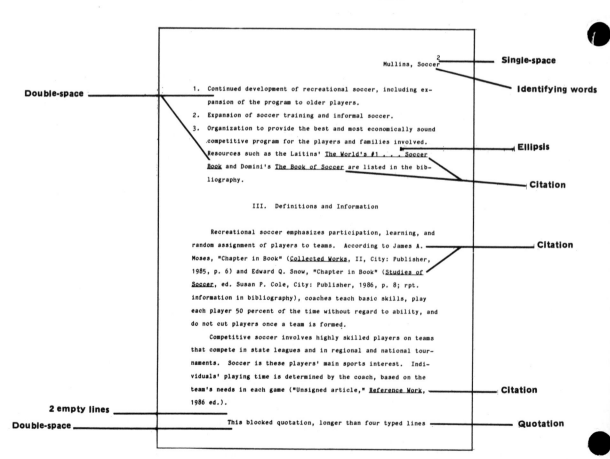

Double-space

2 empty lines

Double-space

Mullins, Soccer 2

1. Continued development of recreational soccer, including expansion of the program to older players.
2. Expansion of soccer training and informal soccer.
3. Organization to provide the best and most economically sound
   competitive program for the players and families involved.
   Resources such as the Laitins' The World's #1 . . . Soccer
   Book and Domini's The Book of Soccer are listed in the bibliography.

III. Definitions and Information

Recreational soccer emphasizes participation, learning, and
random assignment of players to teams. According to James A.
Moses, "Chapter in Book" (Collected Works, II, City: Publisher,
1985, p. 6) and Edward Q. Snow, "Chapter in Book" (Studies of
Soccer, ed. Susan P. Cole, City: Publisher, 1986, p. 8; rpt.
information in bibliography), coaches teach basic skills, play
each player 50 percent of the time without regard to ability, and
do not cut players once a team is formed.

Competitive soccer involves highly skilled players on teams
that compete in state leagues and in regional and national tournaments. Soccer is these players' main sports interest. Individuals' playing time is determined by the coach, based on the
team's needs in each game ("Unsigned article," Reference Work,
1986 ed.).

This blocked quotation, longer than four typed lines

Single-space

Identifying words

Ellipsis

Citation

Citation

Citation

Quotation

chapter 7

Turabian, MSH, AIP, AIIE

7.1 This chapter discusses Turabian, MSH, AIP, and AIIE styles. The comments that introduce Chapter 6 hold also for this chapter.

TURABIAN STYLE

Introduction

7.2 Turabian style is popular for term papers, theses, and dissertations.[1] The sample Turabian dissertation chapter has many more notes listed than are used in the text. As with MLA style, the purpose is to give a full range of examples without adding unnecessary length to the document. The sample, although for a dissertation, also serves as a guide for books in Turabian style and for articles whose publishers require footnotes rather than end-notes. Be warned, though: some journals that specify Turabian style want end-notes, not footnotes, that otherwise meet Turabian's requirements.

Ambiguities

7.3   Turabian style is ambiguous on a few points:

** **Tables and Illustrations;** whether to type tables and illustrations on pages with text even in articles for publication; whether to type lines above and below tables and figures to separate them from text; and number of empty lines to leave above and below.

** **Tables;** how to type substubs (indented two spaces?); order of notes--does Turabian style recognize a general note, and if so, where it is typed.

** **Illustrations;** how to type captions (centered? top or bottom?); how to treat turnover lines; what capitalization rule to follow; whether to end with a period; and whether to draw boxes around.

** **Equations;** how to type (centered? indented from left?); whether to number; and if so, how.

** **Number of copies;** for publication, how many copies to submit?

A caution for students: never submit your only copy of a paper. Keep a carbon, electronic, or other copy to protect you in case of loss.

Journals and General Principles

7.4   A very few journals use Turabian style:[2]

Georgia Political Science Association Journal
Journal of American Society for Public Administration
Public Administration Review

The main users of Turabian style are students in the nation's colleges, universities, and secondary schools.

7.5   Turabian points out that the form for thesis title pages varies from one institution to the next. Check it out before typing! Students who use the Turabian manuscript as a model for a term paper can use a simplified title page such as the one on the MLA dissertation sample at the end of Chapter 3. Simply substitute the course name and number and the name of the instructor for the information on the thesis advisor. Also, users of Turabian style may not need the five levels of heading that are shown in the sample manuscript. When such is the case, choose heading styles in any suitable descending order. For instance, users of three heading levels might wish to use the forms shown here for levels 1, 3, and 5.

Documentation

7.6   Mechanics. Most Turabian manuscripts document with superscript numbers in text accompanied by footnotes. The style is very much like MSH, in which this book is styled. Because notes are intended to be read like sentences, commas separate elements and place, publisher, and date of publication are enclosed by parentheses. Number notes in sequence by page, chapter, or document. Instructors in science courses may ask students to document their papers in an author (date) style that Turabian describes briefly and that is much like MSN (see Chapter 8).

7.7   The basic mechanics for footnotes are in Section 5.12. The specifics for Turabian style are:

** Leave one empty line below the last line of text.

** Type an unbroken line twenty spaces long.

** Indent eight spaces (the same as for a paragraph indentation), type the note number without punctuation slightly above the line, and begin the reference without skipping a space.

** Single-space the notes.

** Double space between the notes.

7.8   On occasion, as when the last note on a page occurs on the last line or two of text, you'll have to finish the note at the bottom of the next page, ahead of notes that begin on that page. In such cases:

** Break the note within a sentence.

** Finish the note on the next page before beginning the notes for that page.

** Don't type "Continued on next page."

** Skip a line before beginning the first note on the new page.

7.9   **Elements.** The standard form and order of elements in references is:

** **Name of cited author, compiler, or editor;** in normal order, usually first name, middle initial, last. When only initials are given, use all. Type with a period and a space after each. When an editor or compiler, follow the name with "ed." ("comp.").

** **Title of work;** if chapter or article, in quotes, followed by comma inside quotes.

** **Title of books and periodicals;** underlined, followed by comma unless the next element is enclosed in parentheses or unless the title has its own punctuation, such as an exclamation mark. Follow the capitalization rule in Section 3.31 unless, as with an e. e. cummings poem, you know the author prefers lowercase. With periodicals, common words may be abbreviated according to common usage; when newspaper names don't include the city name, show it in brackets after the name. For instance: <u>Herald-Telephone</u> [Ourtown, Indiana].

** **Names of editors, translators, and compilers of works;** in normal order, preceded by "ed.," "trans.," or "comp." (without parentheses) and followed by a comma unless the next detail is enclosed in parentheses.

** **Names of authors of prefaces, forewords, or introductions (books);** when the title page lists the name of someone who wrote the preface, foreword or introduction, list that name followed by a comma unless the next detail is enclosed in parentheses.

** **Series;** title should be followed by a comma, followed by an Arabic numeral designating the number of the work in the series, followed by a comma unless the next detail is enclosed in parentheses. Don't underline or use quotation marks.

** **Number of volumes (books);** if more than one.

** **Edition used (books);** whenever it is not the first, designated by Arabic numeral, followed by comma unless the next detail is enclosed in parentheses. Don't confuse the original date with an edition date or reprint date. There are numbered editions, named editions, reprint editions, and paperback editions.

** **Volume and issue numbers, year, and page numbers (periodicals);** not preceded by "Vol."; Arabic numeral; followed by comma or open parenthesis. When paging is continuous through volume, give volume number followed by year in parentheses, colon (a difference from MLA style), no space, and page numbers. When numbering is by issue, give month or season (in parentheses, before date) or issue number preceded by "No." For example:

    6 (1988):45

    6 (March 1988):45

    6 (No. 5, 1988):45

When a system is unfamiliar, give all the information you can find. With newspapers and weekly or monthly magazines, omit volume and issue numbers and give complete date, set off by commas, followed by page number:

    Science, 18 May 1984, p. 5.

For newspapers, edition and section numbers may be needed.

** **Place of publication, publisher, and date (books);** all within parentheses. Use a colon and a single space after the place, and a comma after the publisher. Use "n.p." for "no place of publication" and "no publisher." Use "privately printed" for privately printed works. EXCEPTIONS: classical and biblical works omit all facts of publication. Legal works and some public documents usually omit all but the date. Dictionaries, general encyclopedias, and atlases omit all but edition and date.

** **s.v.--sub verbo (books);** means "under the word"; used before article title in alphabetically arranged reference works in place of volume and page numbers.

** **Volume numbers (books);** if one of two or more, in first reference show all volumes, preceded and followed by a comma.

** **Page numbers (books);** in Arabic numerals (unless the original has Roman numerals), preceded by a comma, followed by a period (unless another reference follows). In general, don't use "Vol." or "p." ("pp.") when both volume and page numbers are given. Use "p." or "pp." when the volume number is absent. If there is no pagination, use "n. pag." If the book has signatures in place of page numbers, use "sig." in place of "p." If it numbers columns rather than pages, use "col." rather than "p."

** **Connection of inclusive page numbers;** follow the rules in Section 5.16.

** **Data that do not come from the title or copyright page;** use inclusive brackets.

7.10 For second and subsequent references to a document, use the author's last name, an abbreviated title, and a page number--the MSH format used in this book.

Bibliography

7.11 Mechanics. The bibliography comes at the end of a document and begins on a new page with the title centered two inches below the top of the page and three empty lines between the title and the first note. If the manuscript is scientific, the title is likely to be "List of References" or "References Cited." The mechanics are:

** Type the page number in the center of the fifth line from the bottom of the page.

** Begin each entry flush left.

** Single-space the entries but double-space between them. Entries may also be typed double-spaced or space and a half--the spacing used for paragraphs in this book.

** Indent second and subsequent lines six spaces (i.e., start in space 7).

** Skip two horizontal spaces after each full stop.

** Begin annotations, if any, on a new line; single-space them. Examples are in the annotated bibliography to this book.

Normally, entries are alphabetized. When any other order is used, explain it at the outset. When a bibliography is sizable, it may be broken into subcate-tories, as noted in Section 5.19.

7.12 Elements. The treatment of elements in a bibliography is as follows:

** **Author's name;** reverse order, all authors.

** **Title and subtitle;** complete, underlined.

** **Publication data;** no parentheses, comma between publisher and date; in citations of periodicals, yearbooks, and some reference books, the year (sometimes preceded by month or season) goes in parentheses.

** **Volume numbers:** in Arabic numerals.

** **Page numbers;** give inclusive page numbers for short pieces, such as articles and book chapters. Precede with a comma to make the page numbers part of the preceding information.

** **Punctuation;** blocks of information followed by periods. Not intended to be read as a sentence.

** **Two or more works, same author;** Use author's name on first entry only. For all others, type eight underlines followed, in turn, by a period, two spaces, and the rest of the entry. Free choice as to whether the order of entries is chronologically by date of publication or alphabetically by title.

MANUAL OF STYLE--HUMANITIES

Ambiguities

7.13   A Manual of Style,[3] the manual followed by many book authors and many journal editors, contains a few ambiguities:

** **Paper weight and quality;** would be helpful to have weight and rag content specified.

** **Spacing;** how many empty lines are left above the page number and between the page number and the first line of text on the first page of text and on all other pages?

** **Paragraph indentation;** would be helpful to have exact indentation specified.

** **Blocked quotations;** would be helpful to know exact number of spaces to indent for blocking.

** **Headings;** what is the spacing above and below typed headings?

Journals and General Information

7.14   At least 17 journals use MSH style:[4]

Academic Therapy
Canadian Journal of African Studies
Comparative Education Review
Educational Forum
History of Childhood Quarterly

Journal of Teacher Education
NASPA Journal
Phi Delta Kappan
Phylon
Public Administration (England)

History of Political Economy   Public Administration Review
Journal of Developing Areas   Public Welfare
Journal of Education for Social Work   Social Theory and Practice
Journal of Social History

7.15   To eliminate the need for a sample manuscript in MSH style and to provide an extended sample of book manuscript style, most of this book, including chapter notes, was typed according to the rules in <u>A Manual of Style</u>.[5] The few exceptions to these rules were noted in Chapter 1. One important exception, the bibliography in MSN style, was done for three reasons: (1) most journals that use MSH style require only the notes, not a bibliography, (2) those who need a model bibliography can use the one for the Turabian-style manuscript, and (3) the MSN bibliography provides an extended example of MSN bibliography without unnecessarily lengthening the book.

7.16   Indeed, the main differences in notes between Turabian style and MSH have to do with (1) footnotes (Turabian) vs endnotes (MSH) and (2) rules on the use of <u>ibid.</u>, <u>loc. cit.</u>, <u>idem</u>, and other Latin abbreviations in second and subsequent citations of a document or author. Turabian offers the Latin as an option (and some teachers still require students to use them). MSH recommends (and Turabian permits) the more modern practice of citing the briefest possible form of author's name, title, and page number. The Turabian manuscript shows both forms, labeled as "Repeat Citation Method A" and "Repeat Citation Method B" respectively. Minor differences in bibliographic format include the use of semicolons between authors' names when a work has three or more authors, and omission of the month and number when a journal pages by volume. Samples of these variations are given at the end of the bibliography for the Turabian manuscript.

Similar Minor Styles

7.17   One source[6] lists 181 journals that use styles similar to MSH--too many to list individually. As a whole, these journals were in the fields of African and Asian studies, business, economics, education, history, international affairs, law, peace research, philosophy, political science, and general social science. Of the many endnote styles available, MSH seems the most popular with journals in the humanities, history, and social and behavioral sciences.

AMERICAN INSTITUTE OF PHYSICS

Ambiguities

7.18   The AIP's excellent manual[7] leaves few questions for typists.   Among these are:

** **Paper weight and quality;** would be helpful to know exact standards.

** **Title page;** is the information other than the title indented the amount of a paragraph indentation? Is the title typed also on the abstract page and the first page of text?

** **Spacing;** how many empty lines are left above the page number and between the page number and the first line of text on the first page of text and on all other pages? Is extra space left between "Received" and "ABSTRACT"? Between "ABSTRACT" and the PACS numbers? Between the PACS numbers and the text?

** **Page numbers;** where are they typed? Upper, right-hand corner of page? Are the title page and other preliminaries numbered with Arabic numerals?

** **Margins;** "wide" is specified; would be helpful to have exact numbers.

** **Text;** does the text begin in a separate page or is it continued imme-diately after the abstract and PACS numbers?

** **Paragraph indentation;** does not specify exact number of spaces.

** **Quotations;** gives no instructions on how to treat quotations.

** **Tables;** does not tell how many spaces to indent turnover lines on stubs or how many spaces to indent substubs.

Journals and General Principles

7.19   The AIP publishes the following journals:[8]

AIP Conference Proceedings
American Journal of Physics
Applied Optics
Applied Physics Letters
The Astronomical Journal
Bulletin of the American Astronomi-cal Society
Bulletin of the American Physical Society

Journal of Vacuum Science and Techno-logy
Medical Physics
Optics Letters
Optics News
Physical Review A: General Physics
Physical Review B: Solid State
Physical Review C: Nuclear Physics
Physical Review D: Particles and Fields

Current Physics Index
The Journal of the Acoustical Society of America
Journal of Applied Physics
The Journal of Chemical Physics
Journal of Mathematical Physics
Journal of the Optical Society of America
Journal of Physical and Chemical Reference Data

Physical Review and Physical Review Letters Index
Physical Review Abstracts
Physical Review Letters
The Physics of Fluids
The Physics Teacher
Physics Today
Review of Scientific Instruments
Reviews of Modern Physics

7.20   Give every table and figure a title that is intelligible without reference to the text. Number tables in sequential Roman numerals. Type a separate list of figure captions with sequential Arabic numbers. On the back of each figure write lightly the authors' names and figure number. On photographs, use a very soft pencil. If the paper contains material that is supplementary but of limited interest, prepare it for deposit in the AIP's Physics Auxiliary Publication Service. Submit supplementary materials along with the manuscript so that both can be reviewed. For help with equations and symbols, see Sections 3.25 through 3.28. Authors who use AIP style frequently will probably want to acquire the AIP <u>Style Manual</u> for its extensive help with equations, its list of standard abbreviations, and its list of journal title abbreviations.

Documentation and Notes

7.21   Type all notes in a separate, double-spaced list at the end of the manuscript. Start with notes to the title and to the authors' names. Some journals use superscript letters for these notes; others use a sequence of *, †, ‡, §, etc. Put acknowledgments in the acknowledgments section of the paper. For notes in the body of the paper, use superscript Arabic numerals in sequence.

7.22   In journal references give the author's name and use the abbreviations for journal names given in Appendix G of the <u>Style Manual</u>. List volume number, the first page number (and the last, if so desired), and the year of publication. When the journal is not paginated consecutively through a volume, include the issue number. Indicate a refererence to an erratum with an "(E)" after the page number. Similarly, when referring only to a title or an abstract, use "(T)" or "(A)" after the page number. In book references, include the author's name, the title, the editor's name (when there is one), the publisher's name and location, and the year of publication. In references to reports, spell out laboratory and agency names.

AMERICAN INSTITUTE OF INDUSTRIAL ENGINEERS

Introduction

7.23   The AIIE style guide's[9] main purpose is to tell how to write a technical article. Its instructions hold for articles on computers and data processing; education; engineering and production; health, hospitals, and services; human factors (ergonomics); materials handling and transportation; management and supervision; mathematics and statistics (except for the _Journal of the American Statistical Association_); operations research and systems; quality control; safety and occupational hazards; and general science and research. The style manual lists more than 100 journals in these categories, too many to list individually here. Its few instructions on manuscript preparation style include using 8 1/2 x 11 inch letter-stock paper and 1 1/1 inch margins all around. With regard to tables and charts, the main instruction is to examine articles similar to yours and use their tables and charts as a guideline. Even the style for notes and bibliographies are labeled only as "frequently used," although they resemble ASTM style. Therefore, this book contains no sample manuscript and no sample form in AIIE style.

Documentation and Notes

7.24   Notes and references, typed together in a list of endnotes, are marked in text and in the list by sequential superscript numbers. Except for the superscript number, the documentation form is rather like ASTM style. For notes on a book and a periodical, respectively, use the following forms:

[1]John Q. Author and Susan P. Student, _Book Title_, Publisher's name, City, State, 1990, p. 165.

[2]John Q. Author and Susan P. Student, "Article Title", _Journal Title_, Institute that Publishes Periodical, City, State, Vol. 4, No. 2, July 1973, p. 36.

Note that the comma goes _outside_ the quotation marks. Craig and Yeatts[10] point out that notes to tables and charts appear at the foot of the table or chart and not at the foot of the page. Use standard symbols such as *, †, =, § unless there are more than five notes. When there are more than five, use sequential lowercase letters, beginning with "a".

Bibliography

7.25   Unlike the list of references, the bibliography may contain uncited documents that are additional readings on a topic. The form is exactly like that in the list of references except that the names are inverted, the list is alphabetized, and a colon rather than a comma separates the name of the author from the title. The form is:

Author, John Q.: _Book Title_, Publisher's Full Name, City, State, 1990.

NOTES TO CHAPTER 7

1. Summarized from <u>A Manual for Writers of Term Papers, Theses, and Dissertations</u>, 4th ed., by Kate L. Turabian by permission of The University of Chicago Press. Copyright (c) 1973. The form of this note differs from that of other notes because it was specified by The University of Chicago Press as a condition of permission to use the summaries.

2. Marvin B. Sussman, ed., <u>Author's Guide to Journals in Sociology and Related Fields</u> (New York: Haworth, 1978); Carolyn J. Mullins, <u>A Guide to Writing and Publishing in the Social and Behavioral Sciences</u> (New York: Wiley-Interscience, 1977), Table 7.1.

3. University of Chicago Press, <u>A Manual of Style</u> 12th ed. (Chicago: University of Chicago Press, 1969).

4. Mullins, <u>A Guide</u>, Table 7.1.

5. University of Chicago Press, <u>A Manual</u>.

6. Mullins, <u>A Guide</u>, Table 7.1

7. David Hathwell and A. W. Kenneth Metzner, <u>Style Manual for Guidance in the Preparation of Papers of Journals Published by the American Institute of Physics and Its Member Societies</u>, 3d ed., rev. (New York: American Institute of Physics, 1978).

8. Hathwell and Metzner, <u>Style Manual</u>, pp. 29-31.

9. Robert J. Craig and Harry W. Yeatts, <u>The Complete Guide for Writing Technical Articles</u> (Norcross, Georgia: American Institute of Industrial Engineers, Inc., 1976).

10. Craig and Yeatts, <u>The Complete Guide</u>, p. 11.

Turabian

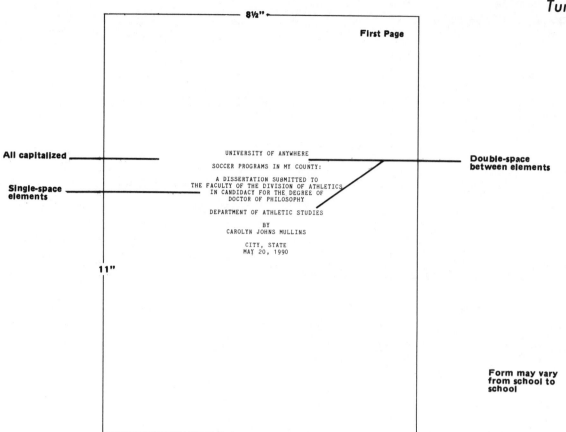

First Page

8½"

All capitalized

Single-space elements

UNIVERSITY OF ANYWHERE

SOCCER PROGRAMS IN MY COUNTY:

A DISSERTATION SUBMITTED TO
THE FACULTY OF THE DIVISION OF ATHLETICS
IN CANDIDACY FOR THE DEGREE OF
DOCTOR OF PHILOSOPHY

DEPARTMENT OF ATHLETIC STUDIES

BY
CAROLYN JOHNS MULLINS

CITY, STATE
MAY 20, 1990

Double-space between elements

11"

Form may vary from school to school

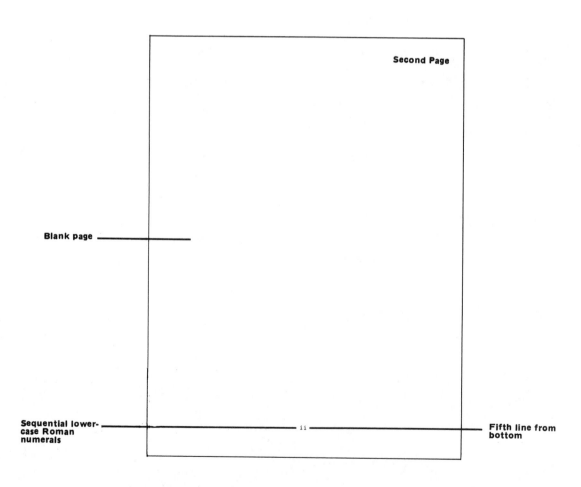

Second Page

Blank page

Sequential lower-case Roman numerals

ii

Fifth line from bottom

3

<u>Treatment of First-Level Heading</u>

Second-Level Heading

<u>Third-Level Heading</u>

Fourth-Level Heading

<u>Fifth-level heading</u>. Leave two empty lines between
text and the start of a heading. When two or more follow
each other without intervening text, leave a single empty
line between them. Always leave a single empty line between
a heading and the start of text.[7] A sample equation is:[8]

$$U-10 + U-12 + U-14 + U-16 + U-19 = \text{Total Players}$$

<u>Fifth level heading</u>. Players who commit to a competi-
tive team may have unavoidable changes in plans.[9]

Fourth-Level Heading

There is no reason to expect any season to be much
different.

This quote shows how Turabian style treats
quotations that exceed a full paragraph in length <u>and</u>
also include the beginnings of at least two full paragraphs.
In such cases, indent the first line of each paragraph four spaces beyond the required four-space indentation. When the first paragraph of a multiparagraph
quotation begins in the middle of a paragraph, do not
type the four-space indent at the beginning of the

_____

[7]<u>Encyclopedia</u>, 1985 ed., II, s.v. "Signed Article," by
Jan A. Bar.

[8]Nicholas C. Mullins, <u>Soccer Minutes Series</u>, 3rd ser.,
ed. Sam Coach (Rome: Edizione de Futbol, 1983), p. 1.

[9]Foreign X. Pert, <u>Handbook on Soccer</u>, trans. S. P.
Jones, ed. Name O. Editor (City: Publisher, 1940; reprint

4

first paragraph but <u>do</u> use it on all other paragraphs.
Single-space (no empty lines) between paragraphs (emphasis added).[10]

<u>Third-Level Heading That</u>

<u>Has a Turnover Line</u>

When a heading is flush left, the turnover line is
flush left. When a centered heading has more than 48 characters, break it into turnover lines, inverted pyramid
style.[11]

Second-Level Heading

When quoting more than one line of poetry in text, use
a virgule (/) to separate the two lines.[12] "The bird / Flew
away." Normally, when quoting two or more lines, set them
off from other text like a blocked quote.

Recreational players want to be able to play soccer
strictly for fun. Players between the ages of 12 and 19
have special needs in this regard.

<u>Divide a Centered Heading of 48 Characters or More into</u>
<u>Two or More Lines in Inverted Pyramid Style,</u>
<u>Single-Spaced, Like This</u>

Organized soccer requires players, coaches, fields,
referees, teams, and parent support. MCYSA has players,

_____

ed., 1988), p. 122.

[10]Turabian, <u>A Manual</u>, p. 64.

[11]Ibid., p. 195-96.

[12]Susan Q. Riley, "Unpublished Dissertation" (Ph.D.
dissertation, A University, 1987), p. 34; Samuel Q. Student,
"Published Dissertation," (Ph.D. Dissertation, A University,
1987; published by City: Publisher, 1988), p. 114.

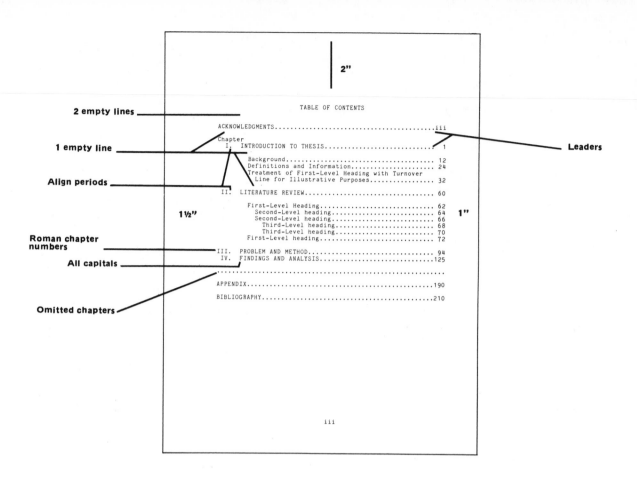

2"

2 empty lines

TABLE OF CONTENTS

ACKNOWLEDGMENTS...iii

1 empty line

Chapter
  I.   INTRODUCTION TO THESIS.......................... 1

      Background.................................. 12

Align periods

      Definitions and Information................. 24
      Treatment of First-Level Heading with Turnover
      Line for Illustrative Purposes.............. 32
 II. LITERATURE REVIEW.............................. 60

      First-Level Heading........................ 62
        Second-Level heading.................... 64
        Second-Level heading.................... 66
          Third-Level heading.................. 68
          Third-Level heading.................. 70
      First-Level heading........................ 72

1½"   **1"**

III. PROBLEM AND METHOD............................. 94
 IV. FINDINGS AND ANALYSIS.........................125
     . . . .

APPENDIX...190

BIBLIOGRAPHY..210

iii

Labels: 2 empty lines · 1 empty line · Align periods · Roman chapter numbers · All capitals · Omitted chapters · Leaders

---

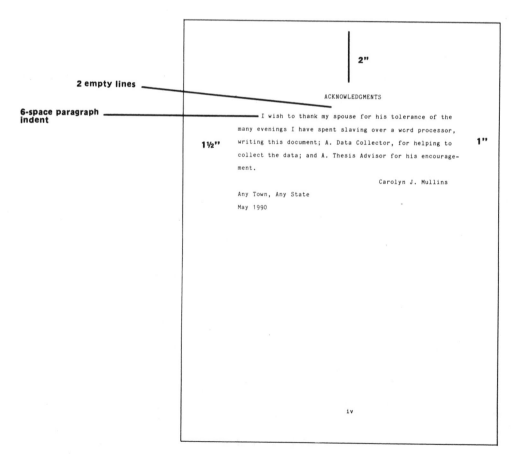

2"

2 empty lines

ACKNOWLEDGMENTS

6-space paragraph indent

      I wish to thank my spouse for his tolerance of the
many evenings I have spent slaving over a word processor,
writing this document; A. Data Collector, for helping to
collect the data; and A. Thesis Advisor for his encouragement.

                             Carolyn J. Mullins

Any Town, Any State
May 1990

1½"   **1"**

iv

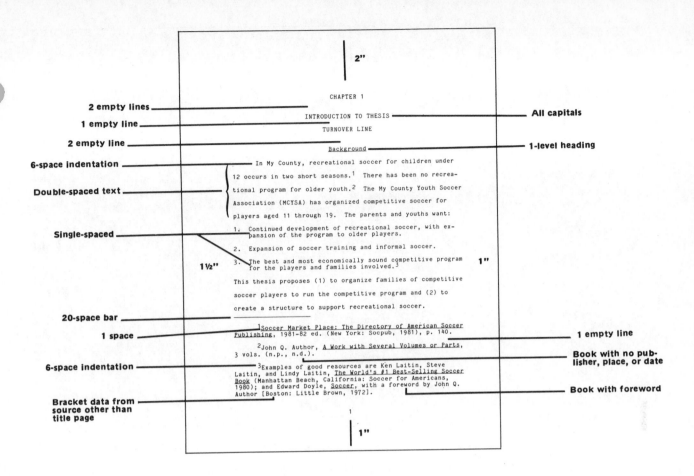

CHAPTER 1

INTRODUCTION TO THESIS

TURNOVER LINE

Background

      In My County, recreational soccer for children under 12 occurs in two short seasons.[1] There has been no recreational program for older youth.[2] The My County Youth Soccer Association (MCYSA) has organized competitive soccer for players aged 11 through 19. The parents and youths want:

1. Continued development of recreational soccer, with expansion of the program to older players.

2. Expansion of soccer training and informal soccer.

3. The best and most economically sound competitive program for the players and families involved.[3]

This thesis proposes (1) to organize families of competitive soccer players to run the competitive program and (2) to create a structure to support recreational soccer.

_____

[1]*Soccer Market Place: The Directory of American Soccer Publishing*, 1981-82 ed. (New York: Socpub, 1981), p. 140.

[2]John Q. Author, *A Work with Several Volumes or Parts*, 3 vols. (n.p., n.d.).

[3]Examples of good resources are Ken Laitin, Steve Laitin, and Lindy Laitin, *The World's #1 Best-Selling Soccer Book* (Manhattan Beach, California: Soccer for Americans, 1980); and Edward Doyle, *Soccer*, with a foreword by John Q. Author [Boston: Little Brown, 1972].

1

Labels on page: 2"; 2 empty lines; 1 empty line; 2 empty line; All capitals; 1-level heading; 6-space indentation; Double-spaced text; Single-spaced; 1½"; 1"; 20-space bar; 1 space; 1 empty line; Book with no publisher, place, or date; 6-space indentation; Book with foreword; Bracket data from source other than title page; 1"

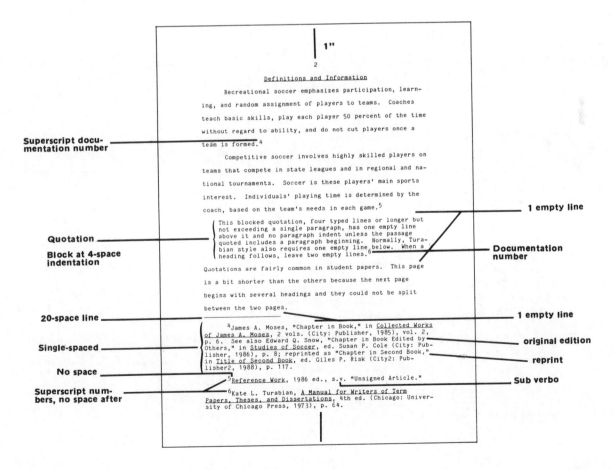

2

Definitions and Information

      Recreational soccer emphasizes participation, learning, and random assignment of players to teams. Coaches teach basic skills, play each player 50 percent of the time without regard to ability, and do not cut players once a team is formed.[4]

      Competitive soccer involves highly skilled players on teams that compete in state leagues and in regional and national tournaments. Soccer is these players' main sports interest. Individuals' playing time is determined by the coach, based on the team's needs in each game.[5]

    This blocked quotation, four typed lines or longer but not exceeding a single paragraph, has one empty line above it and no paragraph indent unless the passage quoted includes a paragraph beginning. Normally, Turabian style also requires one empty line below. When a heading follows, leave two empty lines.[6]

Quotations are fairly common in student papers. This page is a bit shorter than the others because the next page begins with several headings and they could not be split between the two pages.

_____

[4]James A. Moses, "Chapter in Book," in *Collected Works of James A. Moses*, 2 vols. (City: Publisher, 1985), vol. 2, p. 6. See also Edward Q. Snow, "Chapter in Book Edited by Others," in *Studies of Soccer*, ed. Susan P. Cole (City: Publisher, 1986), p. 8; reprinted as "Chapter in Second Book," in *Title of Second Book*, ed. Giles P. Risk (City2: Publisher2, 1988), p. 117.

[5]*Reference Work*, 1986 ed., s.v. "Unsigned Article."

[6]Kate L. Turabian, *A Manual for Writers of Term Papers, Theses, and Dissertations*, 4th ed. (Chicago: University of Chicago Press, 1973), p. 64.

Labels on page: 1"; Superscript documentation number; Quotation; Block at 4-space indentation; 20-space line; Single-spaced; No space; Superscript numbers, no space after; 1 empty line; Documentation number; 1 empty line; original edition; reprint; Sub verbo

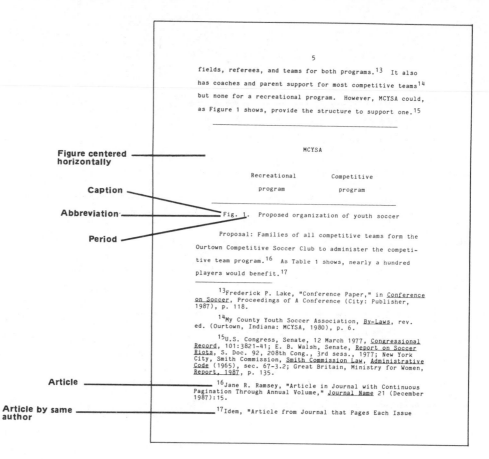

Figure centered horizontally

Caption

Abbreviation

Period

Article

Article by same author

5

fields, referees, and teams for both programs.[13] It also has coaches and parent support for most competitive teams[14] but none for a recreational program. However, MCYSA could, as Figure 1 shows, provide the structure to support one.[15]

MCYSA

Recreational program   Competitive program

Fig. 1. Proposed organization of youth soccer

Proposal: Families of all competitive teams form the Ourtown Competitive Soccer Club to administer the competitive team program.[16] As Table 1 shows, nearly a hundred players would benefit.[17]

[13]Frederick P. Lake, "Conference Paper," in Conference on Soccer, Proceedings of A Conference (City: Publisher, 1987), p. 118.

[14]My County Youth Soccer Association, By-Laws, rev. ed. (Ourtown, Indiana: MCYSA, 1980), p. 6.

[15]U.S. Congress, Senate, 12 March 1977, Congressional Record, 101:3821-41; E. B. Walsh, Senate, Report on Soccer Riots, S. Doc. 92, 208th Cong., 3rd sess., 1977; New York City, Smith Commission, Smith Commission Law, Administrative Code (1965), sec. 67-3.2; Great Britain, Ministry for Women, Report, 1987, p. 135.

[16]Jane R. Ramsey, "Article in Journal with Continuous Pagination Through Annual Volume," Journal Name 21 (December 1987):15.

[17]Idem, "Article from Journal that Pages Each Issue

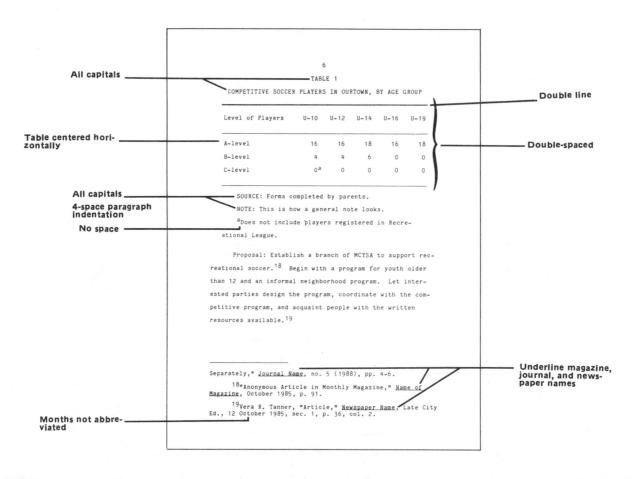

All capitals

Table centered horizontally

All capitals

4-space paragraph indentation

No space

Double line

Double-spaced

Underline magazine, journal, and newspaper names

Months not abbreviated

6

TABLE 1

COMPETITIVE SOCCER PLAYERS IN OURTOWN, BY AGE GROUP

Level of Players	U-10	U-12	U-14	U-16	U-19
A-level	16	16	18	16	18
B-level	4	4	6	0	0
C-level	0[a]	0	0	0	0

SOURCE: Forms completed by parents.

NOTE: This is how a general note looks.

[a]Does not include players registered in Recreational League.

Proposal: Establish a branch of MCYSA to support recreational soccer.[18] Begin with a program for youth older than 12 and an informal neighborhood program. Let interested parties design the program, coordinate with the competitive program, and acquaint people with the written resources available.[19]

Separately," Journal Name, no. 5 (1988), pp. 4-6.

[18]"Anonymous Article in Monthly Magazine," Name of Magazine, October 1985, p. 91.

[19]Vera R. Tanner, "Article," Newspaper Name, Late City Ed., 12 October 1985, sec. 1, p. 36, col. 2.

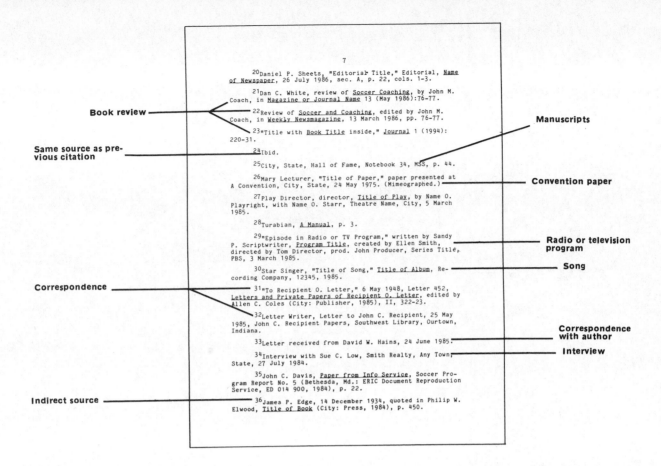

7

[20]Daniel P. Sheets, "Editorial Title," Editorial, <u>Name of Newspaper</u>, 26 July 1986, sec. A, p. 22, cols. 1-3.

[21]Dan C. White, review of <u>Soccer Coaching</u>, by John M. Coach, in <u>Magazine or Journal Name</u> 13 (May 1986):76-77.

[22]Review of <u>Soccer and Coaching</u>, edited by John M. Coach, in <u>Weekly Newsmagazine</u>, 13 March 1986, pp. 76-77.

[23]"Title with <u>Book Title</u> inside," <u>Journal</u> 1 (1994): 220-31.

[24]Ibid.

[25]City, State, Hall of Fame, Notebook 34, MSS, p. 44.

[26]Mary Lecturer, "Title of Paper," paper presented at A Convention, City, State, 24 May 1975. (Mimeographed.)

[27]Play Director, director, <u>Title of Play</u>, by Name O. Playright, with Name O. Starr, Theatre Name, City, 5 March 1985.

[28]Turabian, <u>A Manual</u>, p. 3.

[29]"Episode in Radio or TV Program," written by Sandy P. Scriptwriter, <u>Program Title</u>, created by Ellen Smith, directed by Tom Director, prod. John Producer, Series Title, PBS, 3 March 1985.

[30]Star Singer, "Title of Song," <u>Title of Album</u>, Recording Company, 12345, 1985.

[31]"To Recipient O. Letter," 6 May 1948, Letter 452, <u>Letters and Private Papers of Recipient O. Letter</u>, edited by Allen C. Coles (City: Publisher, 1985), II, 322-23.

[32]Letter Writer, Letter to John C. Recipient, 25 May 1985, John C. Recipient Papers, Southwest Library, Ourtown, Indiana.

[33]Letter received from David W. Hains, 24 June 1985.

[34]Interview with Sue C. Low, Smith Realty, Any Town, State, 27 July 1984.

[35]John C. Davis, <u>Paper from Info Service</u>, Soccer Program Report No. 5 (Bethesda, Md.: ERIC Document Reproduction Service, ED 014 900, 1984), p. 22.

[36]James P. Edge, 14 December 1934, quoted in Philip W. Elwood, <u>Title of Book</u> (City: Press, 1984), p. 450.

Labels (left to right): Book review; Manuscripts; Same source as previous citation; Convention paper; Radio or television program; Song; Correspondence; Correspondence with author; Interview; Indirect source

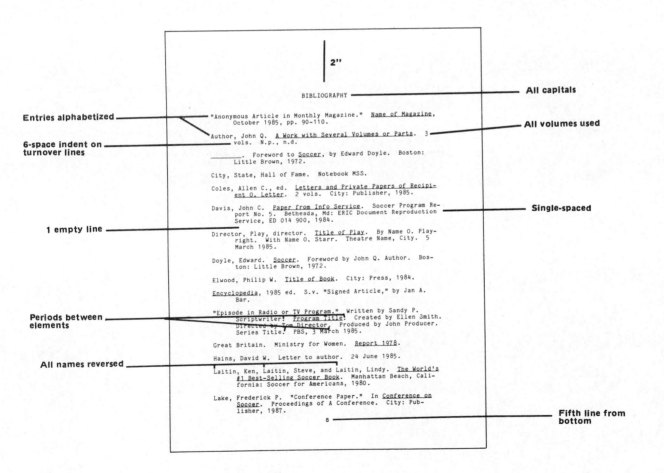

2"

BIBLIOGRAPHY

"Anonymous Article in Monthly Magazine." <u>Name of Magazine</u>, October 1985, pp. 90-110.

Author, John Q. <u>A Work with Several Volumes or Parts</u>. 3 vols. N.p., n.d.

_____. Foreword to <u>Soccer</u>, by Edward Doyle. Boston: Little Brown, 1972.

City, State, Hall of Fame. Notebook MSS.

Coles, Allen C., ed. <u>Letters and Private Papers of Recipient O. Letter</u>. 2 vols. City: Publisher, 1985.

Davis, John C. <u>Paper from Info Service</u>. Soccer Program Report No. 5. Bethesda, Md: ERIC Document Reproduction Service, ED 014 900, 1984.

Director, Play, director. <u>Title of Play</u>. By Name O. Playright. With Name O. Starr. Theatre Name, City. 5 March 1985.

Doyle, Edward. <u>Soccer</u>. Foreword by John Q. Author. Boston: Little Brown, 1972.

Elwood, Philip W. <u>Title of Book</u>. City: Press, 1984.

<u>Encyclopedia</u>, 1985 ed. S.v. "Signed Article," by Jan A. Bar.

"Episode in Radio or TV Program." Written by Sandy P. Scriptwriter. <u>Program Title</u>. Created by Ellen Smith. Directed by Tom Director. Produced by John Producer. Series Title. PBS, 3 March 1985.

Great Britain. Ministry for Women. <u>Report 1978</u>.

Hains, David W. Letter to author. 24 June 1985.

Laitin, Ken, Laitin, Steve, and Laitin, Lindy. <u>The World's #1 Best-Selling Soccer Book</u>. Manhattan Beach, California: Soccer for Americans, 1980.

Lake, Frederick P. "Conference Paper." In <u>Conference on Soccer</u>. Proceedings of A Conference. City: Publisher, 1987.

8

Labels: All capitals; All volumes used; Entries alphabetized; 6-space indent on turnover lines; Single-spaced; 1 empty line; Periods between elements; All names reversed; Fifth line from bottom

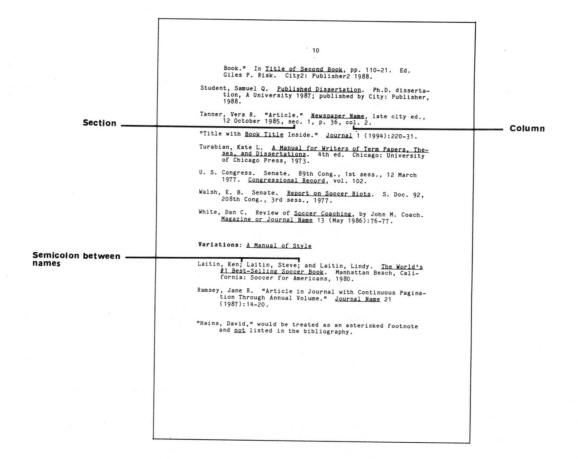

9

Lecturer, Mary. "Title of Paper." Paper presented at A
    Convention, City, State, 24 May 1975. (Mimeographed.)

Low, Sue C. Smith Realty, Any Town, Any State. Interview,
    27 July 1984.

Moses, James A. "Chapter in Book." In Collected Works of
    James A. Moses. Vol. 2, pp. 1-12. City: Publisher,
    1985.

Specific volume used; Arabic numeral

Mullins, Nicholas C. Soccer Minutes Series. 3rd ser. Ed-
    ited by Sam Coach. Rome: Edizione de Futbol, 1983.

My County Youth Soccer Association. By-Laws, Rev. ed. Our-
    town, Indiana: MCYSA, 1980.

New York, N.Y. Smith Commission. Smith Commission Law.
    Administrative Code (1965).

Ourtown, Indiana. Southwest Library. John C. Recipient
    Papers.

Pert, Foreign X. Handbook on Soccer. Translated by S. P.
    Jones. Edited by Name O. Editor. City: Publisher,
    1940; reprint ed., 1988.

Ramsey, Jane R. "Article in Journal with Continuous Pagina-
    tion Through Annual Volume." Journal Name 21 (Decem-
    ber 1987):14-20.

Inclusive page numbers

8-space underline: Same author as previous entry

_____. "Article from Journal that Pages Each Issue Sep-
    arately." Journal Name, no. 5 (1988), pp. 2-8.

Reference Work. 1986 ed. S.v. "Unsigned Article."

Review of Soccer and Coaching, edited by John M. Coach.
    Weekly Newsmagazine, 13 March 1986, pp. 76-77.

Riley, Susan Q. "Unpublished Dissertation." Ph.D. disser-
    tation, A University, 1987.

Sheets, Daniel P. "Editorial Title." Editorial. Name of
    Newspaper, 26 July 1986, sec. A, p. 22, cols. 1-3.

Soccer Market Place: The Directory of American Soccer Pub-
    lishing. 1981-82 ed. New York: Socpub, 1981.

Singer, Star. "Title of Song." Title of Album. Recording
    Company, 12345, 1985.

Snow, Edward Q. "Chapter in Book Edited by Others." In
    Studies of Soccer, pp. 4-13. Edited by Susan P. Cole.
    City: Publisher, 1986; reprint ed. "Chapter in Second

10

Book." In Title of Second Book, pp. 110-21. Ed.
    Giles P. Risk. City2: Publisher2 1988.

Student, Samuel Q. Published Dissertation. Ph.D. disserta-
    tion, A University 1987; published by City: Publisher,
    1988.

Tanner, Vera R. "Article." Newspaper Name, late city ed.,
    12 October 1985, sec. 1, p. 36, col. 2.

Section

Column

"Title with Book Title Inside." Journal 1 (1994):220-31.

Turabian, Kate L. A Manual for Writers of Term Papers, The-
    ses, and Dissertations. 4th ed. Chicago: University
    of Chicago Press, 1973.

U. S. Congress. Senate. 89th Cong., 1st sess., 12 March
    1977. Congressional Record, vol. 102.

Walsh, E. B. Senate. Report on Soccer Riots. S. Doc. 92,
    208th Cong., 3rd sess., 1977.

White, Dan C. Review of Soccer Coaching, by John M. Coach.
    Magazine or Journal Name 13 (May 1986):76-77.

Variations: A Manual of Style

Semicolon between names

Laitin, Ken; Laitin, Steve; and Laitin, Lindy. The World's
    #1 Best-Selling Soccer Book. Manhattan Beach, Cali-
    fornia: Soccer for Americans, 1980.

Ramsey, Jane R. "Article in Journal with Continuous Pagina-
    tion Through Annual Volume." Journal Name 21
    (1987):14-20.

"Hains, David," would be treated as an asterisked footnote
    and not listed in the bibliography.

168

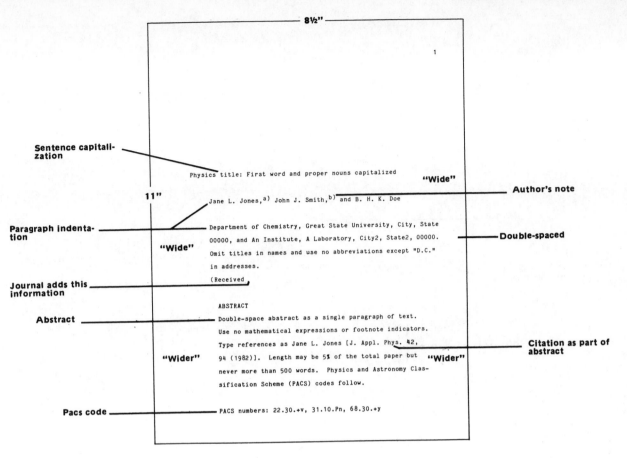

Sentence capitalization

8½"

1

Physics title: First word and proper nouns capitalized   **"Wide"**   Author's note

11"

Jane L. Jones,[a] John J. Smith,[b] and B. H. K. Doe

Paragraph indentation

"Wide"

Department of Chemistry, Great State University, City, State
00000, and An Institute, A Laboratory, City2, State2, 00000.   Double-spaced
Omit titles in names and use no abbreviations except "D.C."
in addresses.

Journal adds this information

(Received

ABSTRACT

Abstract

Double-space abstract as a single paragraph of text.
Use no mathematical expressions or footnote indicators.
Type references as Jane L. Jones [J. Appl. Phys. 42,

"Wider"

94 (1982)]. Length may be 5% of the total paper but   **"Wider"**   Citation as part of abstract
never more than 500 words. Physics and Astronomy Clas-
sification Scheme (PACS) codes follow.

Pacs code

PACS numbers: 22.30.+v, 31.10.Pn, 68.30.+y

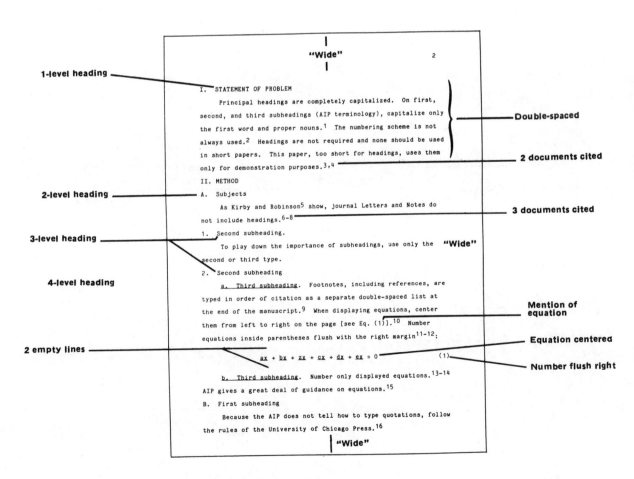

"Wide"   2

1-level heading

I. STATEMENT OF PROBLEM

    Principal headings are completely capitalized. On first,
second, and third subheadings (AIP terminology), capitalize only   Double-spaced
the first word and proper nouns.[1] The numbering scheme is not
always used.[2] Headings are not required and none should be used
in short papers. This paper, too short for headings, uses them   2 documents cited
only for demonstration purposes.[3,4]

II. METHOD

2-level heading

A. Subjects

    As Kirby and Robinson[5] show, journal Letters and Notes do   3 documents cited
not include headings.[6-8]

3-level heading

1. Second subheading.

    To play down the importance of subheadings, use only the   **"Wide"**
second or third type.

4-level heading

2. Second subheading

    a. Third subheading. Footnotes, including references, are
typed in order of citation as a separate double-spaced list at
the end of the manuscript.[9] When displaying equations, center   Mention of equation
them from left to right on the page [see Eq. (1)].[10] Number
equations inside parentheses flush with the right margin[11-12];   Equation centered

2 empty lines

$$ax + bx + zx + cx + dx + ex = 0 \qquad (1)$$

Number flush right

    b. Third subheading. Number only displayed equations.[13-14]
AIP gives a great deal of guidance on equations.[15]

B. First subheading

    Because the AIP does not tell how to type quotations, follow
the rules of the University of Chicago Press.[16]

"Wide"

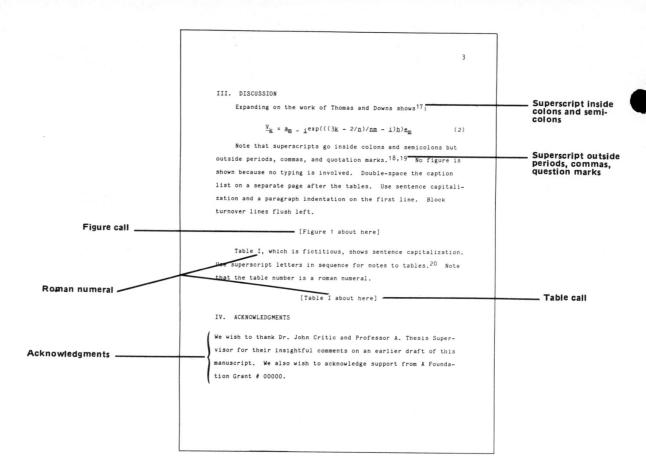

Superscript inside colons and semicolons

Superscript outside periods, commas, question marks

Figure call

Roman numeral

Table call

Acknowledgments

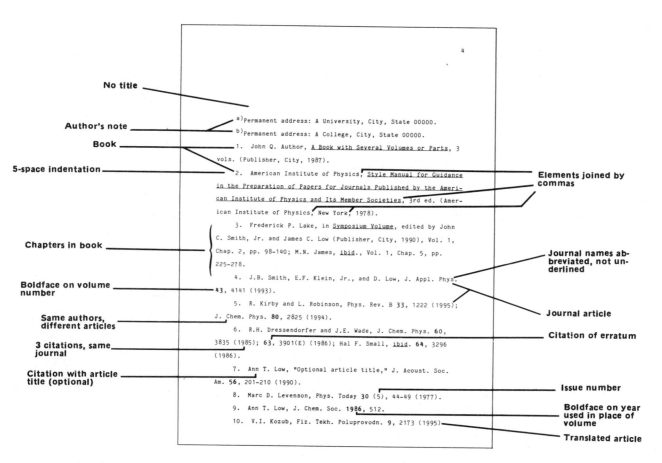

No title

Author's note

Book

5-space indentation

Elements joined by commas

Chapters in book

Journal names abbreviated, not underlined

Boldface on volume number

Journal article

Same authors, different articles

Citation of erratum

3 citations, same journal

Citation with article title (optional)

Issue number

Boldface on year used in place of volume

Translated article

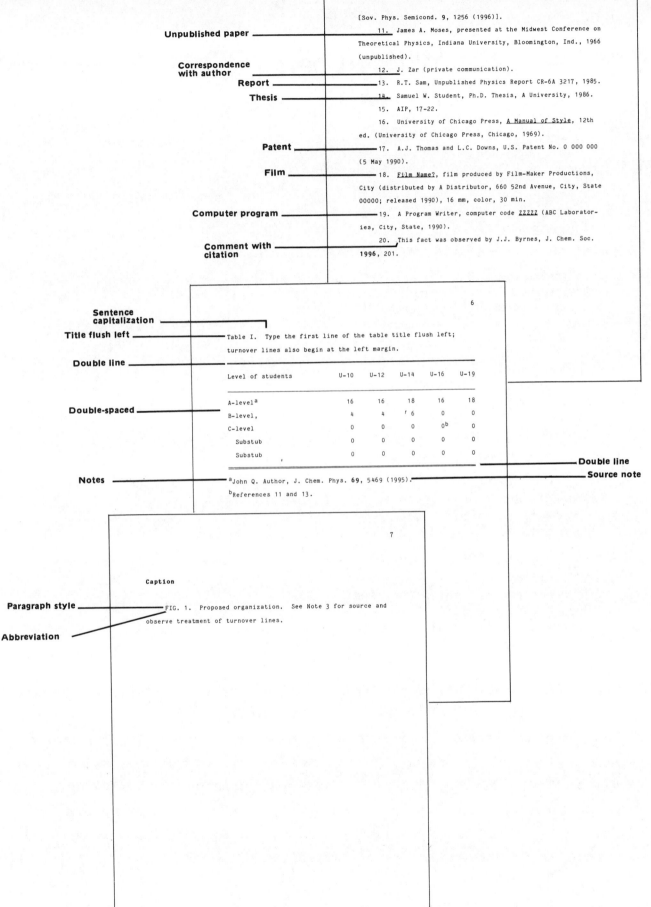

Unpublished paper

[Sov. Phys. Semicond. **9**, 1256 (1996)].

11. James A. Moses, presented at the Midwest Conference on Theoretical Physics, Indiana University, Bloomington, Ind., 1966 (unpublished).

Correspondence with author

12. J. Zar (private communication).

Report

13. R.T. Sam, Unpublished Physics Report CR-6A 3217, 1985.

Thesis

14. Samuel W. Student, Ph.D. Thesis, A University, 1986.

15. AIP, 17-22.

16. University of Chicago Press, _A Manual of Style_, 12th ed. (University of Chicago Press, Chicago, 1969).

Patent

17. A.J. Thomas and L.C. Downs, U.S. Patent No. 0 000 000 (5 May 1990).

Film

18. _Film Name?_, film produced by Film-Maker Productions, City (distributed by A Distributor, 660 52nd Avenue, City, State 00000; released 1990), 16 mm, color, 30 min.

Computer program

19. A Program Writer, computer code _ZZZZZ_ (ABC Laboratories, City, State, 1990).

Comment with citation

20. This fact was observed by J.J. Byrnes, J. Chem. Soc. 1996, 201.

5

Sentence capitalization

Title flush left

Table I. Type the first line of the table title flush left; turnover lines also begin at the left margin.

Double line

Level of students	U-10	U-12	U-14	U-16	U-19
A-level[a]	16	16	18	16	18
B-level,	4	4	6	0	0
C-level	0	0	0	0[b]	0
Substub	0	0	0	0	0
Substub	0	0	0	0	0

Double-spaced

Double line

Source note

Notes

[a]John Q. Author, J. Chem. Phys. **69**, 5469 (1995).

[b]References 11 and 13.

6

Caption

Paragraph style

FIG. 1. Proposed organization. See Note 3 for source and observe treatment of turnover lines.

Abbreviation

7

chapter 8

MSN, AChemS, CBE, APA, ASA

8.1   This chapter lists requirements for five major author (date) styles-- MSN, AChemS, CBE, APA, and ASA--and several similar minor ones. The comments that introduce Chapter 6 hold also for this chapter. In addition, to provide an example of MSN style, this chapter uses MSN style rather than endnotes for documentation. Changing styles in midstream is normally very poor practice in a book manuscript. It is done here solely to provide an example without unnecessarily lengthening the book. Rules for author (date) documentation are in Sections 5.3 through 5.5.

MANUAL OF STYLE--NATURAL SCIENCE

Introduction

8.2   MSN style (University of Chicago Press 1969, pp. 384-88) has the same ambiguities and uses the same style sheet as MSH with the exception that documentation is by author (date) citation rather than by endnotes, and documents cited are listed in a reference list rather than a bibliography.

Documentation and Notes

8.3   In author (date) style, both elements usually are enclosed within parentheses, as in the example above, although the author's name can be mentioned outside.   Also, specific reference can be made to sections and equations as well as to pages.   Examples are:

University of Chicago Press (1969) shows that . . .

This work (Smith and Jones 1990, eq. [1]) shows . . .

This work (Smith and Jones 1990, sec. 2.2) shows . . .

As Section 5.5 points out, do not use "et al." unless a work has more than three authors, and do not use "et al." at all when so doing would produce identical abbreviations of two different documents.   Put all citations either just inside a punctuation mark or at a logical break in the sentence.

8.4   Treat private communications as footnotes rather than as citations to a reference list.   Number these notes by page using the convention of *, †, ‡, §, ‖, #.   Put the symbol <u>outside</u> the punctuation mark as you would a superscript number.   The note appears as:

*John Q. Author 1990: personal communication.

References or Bibliography

8.5   A list of references is composed entirely of cited documents.   A bibliography, such as this book has, contains uncited entries that constitute additional readings on various topics. The bibliography to this book provides many examples of entries in MSN style.

Similar Minor Styles

8.6 One source (Mullins 1977, Table 7.1) lists 79 journals that use a style similar to MSN--too many to list individually. Of these, four styles merit special mention.

8.7 **LSA and AJS styles.** One style, that of the Linguistic Society of America (LSA), serves several journals and differs from MSN in two ways. (1) In reference lists, journal names are abbreviated. (2) Citations use a colon (e.g, Smith 1990:130-40) rather than ", pp." between the date and the page numbers. The second style is that of the American Journal of Sociology, one of the top journals in the field of sociology. AJS style differs in that the reference list uses (1) quotation marks on article titles and (2) upper- and lowercase on article and book titles rather than initial capitalization.

8.8 **SA style.** Suggestions to Authors (Standing Committee 1971) serves 4 British journals specifically. In addition, Mullins (1977, Table 7.1) lists 15 others that use either SA style or something quite similar. SA style requires ISO-size A4 210 x 297 mm paper, a left margin of 40 mm, and a title no longer than 80 letter spaces. References in text should be indicated by dates in parentheses after the author's name, as in "Smith (1990, 1991)," not "(Smith 1980)." Two authors are referred to as "Smith & Jones (1990)." Multiple authors are referred to in the form "Smith et al. (1990)." Two or more publications in the same year are labeled "a, b, c" as in "Smith (1990a,b,c)." The reference list differs from MSN style in capitalizing the author's name, using an ampersand instead of "and," enclosing the date in parentheses, using upper- and lowercase letters on book titles, abbreviating journal names, having a comma before page numbers, and indenting only two spaces on turnover lines. Thus:

> AUTHOR, F., AUTHOR, S., & AUTHOR, T. (1990). Article title. Br. J. soc. clin. Psychol. 9, 270-274.

BAKER, F. (1990). A Book Title. City: Publisher. (First published 1988.)

8.9 **JASA style.** JASA style (JASA 1977) is the style of the Journal of the American Statistical Association, probably the top journal in the field of statistics. JASA style requires 4 copies on 20 lb. bond paper, an abstract (on a separate page) of 100 or fewer words, at least three (no more than six) key words and phrases typed immediately after the abstract, and an Author's Footnote typed on a separate page with the author's present position, place of employment and complete address, and acknowledgments of financial and technical assistance. Headings are numbered as shown in Section 3.16. Citations are as in MSN style. The reference list differs in having parentheses around the date, quotations marks around and upper- and lowercase on article titles, a comma after book titles, commas after journal names and volume numbers, and upper- and lowercase on book titles. The reference list may include both published and unpublished works. Thus:

Author, First, and Author, Second (1990), "Title of Article," Title of Journal, 20, 44-47.

Author, First A. (1991), A Book Title. Vol. 1, City: Publisher.

----- (1973), "Convention Paper Title," paper presented at An Important Meeting in City.

AMERICAN CHEMICAL SOCIETY

Ambiguities

8.10 Ambiguities in the American Chemical Society's Handbook for Authors (1978) were cleared up in correspondence with the society. The society will accept any grade of paper except onion-skin and other lightweight papers. In many stylistic matters, such as organization of the title page and treatment of headings, the society requests the use of capitals and lowercase but has no other requirements because it uses a computer to prepare manuscripts for printing. With respect to notes, the author's address is the only kind of content note allowed in a journal article. None are allowed in books. With respect to equations, authors may number them or not, and may mix numbered and unnumbered equations in the same document. For journal-specific information, the society refers authors to the instructions for authors that are printed in the first issue of each volume; these instructions are updated annually.

Journals and General Principles

8.11   Journals of the American Chemical Society fall into three categories, depending on citation style. Groups 1, 2, and 3, respectively, are:

Biochemistry
Industrial & Engineering Chemistry
  Fundamentals
Industrial & Engineering Chemistry
  Process Design and Development

Industrial & Engineering Chemistry
  Product Research and Development
Journal of Agricultural and Food
  Chemistry

Accounts of Chemical Research
Chemical Reviews
Inorganic Chemistry
Journal of the American Chemical
  Society

Journal of Chemical Information and
  Computer Sciences
The Journal of Organic Chemistry
The Journal of Physical Chemistry
Macromolecules
Organometallics

ACS Symposia Series
Advances in Chemistry Series
Analytical Chemistry

Environmental Science & Technology
Journal of Chemical and Engineering
  Data

Group 1 documents with author (date) citation like the style of the American Sociological Association (see below). Group 2 journals use superscript numerical reference citations like the style of the American Medical Association (see Chapter 6). Group 3 journals also use numerical reference citations but they are italic (underlined) numbers typed on the line and enclosed within parentheses, like this.(1) Or this. (2-4)

8.12   The variety in citation styles and the lack of specific manuscript preparation information make a sample manuscript meaningless. However, this chapter includes a sample table and a list of sample references, and the appendix contains a sample style sheet in AChemS style. One caution about abstracts: check whether the abstract will be printed with the article or is exclusively for the Chemical Abstracts. In the former case, number the abstract immediately after the title page and before the text. In the latter, don't number the page but do type on it the paper title and the authors' names.

Documentation

8.13   For journals in Group 1, follow documentation style in the sample manuscript for the American Sociological Association. For journals in Group 2, follow the sample manuscript in AMA style. For journals in Group 3, follow the example given above of the number on the line.

Reference List

8.14   The form of reference lists is nearly the same for all three styles. The differences are (1) for author (date) style, alphabetize the references and don't number them; (2) for the other two styles, list references in the order they are mentioned and number them in that order. The sample reference list shows half the references in author (date) style ahd half in the other form. Indentation, whether paragraph style (as in AMA style) or the reverse (as in the Turabian bibliography style), varies from journal to journal. The sample reference list is done in paragraph style. Most journal names are abbreviated and article titles are omitted. Authors' full names are acceptable but not mandatory.

Similar Major Style

8.15   Like AChemS style, CBE (Council of Biology Editors) style permits a variety of documentation forms. One form is author (date) style as in MSN style. A second form is citation of document number, in parentheses. A third form is citation of document number with the documents in alphabetical order. Still a fourth form is to place the entire citation in text. The CBE <u>Style Manual</u> (1978) does not list the journals in each category.

8.16   CBE style requires margins of 1 to 1 1/2 inches all around. The order of manuscript parts is title page, abstract, first text page, other text pages, acknowledgments, list of references, notes to text, tables, caption list, and illustrations. Tables are numbered in Arabic, not Roman, numerals. Column heads are centered over column entries. Notes are designated, in order, by asterisk, dagger, double dagger, etc. with each note a separate paragraph, not run-on as in AChems style.

8.17   The reference list is much like that of AChemS. Differences include use of book chapter and article titles, no quotation marks around book titles, no italics on volume numbers or journal names, and no boldface on dates. Author's affiliation may be included in parentheses, as in item 1. Examples of CBE style are:

1. Author, J. P. (Biology Section, A great Univ., City, MI). An article about <u>Escheria coli</u>: some properties. J. Bacteriol. 130:427-434; 1985.

2. Baker, J. S. Title of article in journal paginated by issue. Sci. Amer. 254(2):96-98; 1996.

3. Low, D. P. Monograph: title. New York: Harper & Row; 1986.

4. Author, F. V.; Smith, J. P.; Jones, A. B. Title of chapter in book. Smith, J. P.; Low, D. P.; Wales, D. eds. Title of edited book. Englewood Cliffs, NJ: Prentice-Hall, Inc.; 1987: 298-325.

5. Lind, T. L.; Jones, J. P. Title of book in preparation. Proceedings of A Conference, City, Month, 1986. City: Publisher;[1987]. In preparation.

6. Tandy, B. G.; Smith, A. B., editors. Title of proceedings of a symposium; A Symposium series; 1974 June 4-7; Tampa, FL. 406 p. Available from: NTIS, Springfield, VA; ABCD-000000.

AMERICAN PSYCHOLOGICAL ASSOCIATION

Ambiguities

8.18   Correspondence from the American Psycholological Association (APA) clarified the main question not answered by the <u>Publication Manual</u> (1974): how to treat turnover lines in headings and table stubs and substubs. The preferred treatment is to type the turnover line either centered (if the first line is centered) or flush left (if the first line is either flush left or a paragraph leader). In December 1981 the APA was planning a revised version of the <u>Manual</u>, tentatively scheduled for publication in 1983. Likely changes include (1) elimination or different treatment of reference notes (possibly to be combined with references), and (2) in the reference list, typing the date immediately after the author's name and (3) using U.S. Postal Service abbreviations for state names.

Journals and General Principles

8.19   The journals of the American Psychological Association are:

American Psychologist
Contemporary Psychology
Developmental Psychology
Journal of Abnormal Psychology
Journal of Applied Psychology
Journal of Comparative and Physio-
  logical Psychology
Journal of Consulting and Clinical
  Psychology
Journal of Counseling Psychology
Journal of Educational Psychology
Journal of Experimental Psychology:
  General

Journal of Experimental Psychology:
  Learning, Memory, and Cognition
Journal of Experimental Psychology:
  Human Perception and Performance
Journal of Experimental Psychology:
  Animal Behavior Processes
Journal of Personality and Social
  Psychology
Professional Psychology
Psychological Bulletin
Psychological Review
Journal Supplement Abstract Service
  Catalog (retitled <u>Psychological
  Documents</u> in 1983)

APA (1974) lists an additional 100 nonassociation journals that also use the <u>Publication Manual</u>. This list will probably be eliminated from the 1983 revision.

8.20   Most aspects of APA style are clear in the sample manuscript and the style sheet. One point that might escape notice is that except in ratios, APA style requires <u>two</u> spaces after a colon.

8.21   Notes to tables also require special comment. Tables in APA style can have three types of note: general (about the table as a whole; preceded by <u>Note</u>), specific (to a particular column or entry; preceded by sequential lowercase letters), and probability level (the results of tests of significance; preceded by a single asterisk, double asterisk, triple asterisk, etc.). General notes are typed first, specific second, and probability third. The probability levels and number of asterisks need not be consistent among tables. When a table is from another source, indicate that fact in a general note. For instance:

> Note. Column 2 taken from "Article Title" by J. L. Smith and J. N. Jones, Journal Name, 1986, 70, 42. Copyright 1986 by Copyright Holder. Reprinted by permission.

Documentation

8.22   Documentation is much like that in this chapter except that when the citation is within parentheses (1) there is a comma between the name and the date as in "(Smith, 1981)" and (2) when there are two or more names, use an & rather than and as in "(Smith & Jones, 1981)." When a work has three or more authors, use all names for the first citation and "et al." (as in "Smith et al., 1985") unless two or more citations shorten to the same form, in which case cite all names in full all the time to avoid confusion. When there is no author, substitute the first two or three words of the entry in the reference list, as in "('Book Title,' 1985)." When a list contains publications by two or more authors with the same last name, use their initials in the citation in text to avoid confusion. When citing two or more publications by the same author, do so in chronological order as in "(Smith, 1985, 1986, in press-a, in press-b)." When citing several different authors, list the citations alphabetically by authors' last name, separated by semicolons.

8.23   APA (1974) style uses reference notes to cite documents that are not easily available. Examples are unpublished manuscripts or manuscripts that have been submitted for publication but not accepted, project working papers, meeting papers, and personal communications. The citation in text is exactly the same as a standard citation except for substitution of the note number for the date as in:

Smith (Note 2)   (Smith, Note 1)

When references and reference notes are cited together in text, list references first alphabetically by authors' last names; then list the notes in numerical order by note number.

Reference List

8.24   The reference list includes all and only documents cited in the text. The elements of a reference, in order, are author (with last names and initials, last name first), title (of article, chapter, or book), and facts of publication. For journals the facts include the full name of the journal, the date of publication, the volume number, and inclusive pages. For books the facts include city of publication, name of publisher, and publication date. Use periods, not commas, to separate the elements in the three major divisions. Use commas within divisions, as between the date and volume number in a journal entry. Use parentheses for interpretations and qualifications such as "(3rd ed.)" or "(Summary)." Journal names are not abbreviated and volume numbers are underlined. In book and article titles, capitalize only the first word, proper nouns, and the first word after a dash or colon. Underline book titles and journal names.

8.25   Organize the list of references alphabetically by authors' last names. When organizing several entries by the same author, repeat the author's name with each one. Arrange chronologically by date of publication (earliest first) several references by the same author. When the same author has two or more references published in the same year, arrange them alphabetically by title and use sequential lowercase letters in parentheses after the closing period of each entry. Use "Anonymous" in place of the author's name only when a work is actually signed "Anonymous."

AMERICAN SOCIOLOGICAL ASSOCIATION

Ambiguities

8.26   Because the ASA's style sheet for the <u>American Sociological Review</u> is only a page long, several ambiguities exist (<u>American Sociological Review</u> 1981, p. iii). These include:

** **Tables and illustrations;** should these pages be interleaved with text, according to where they appear, or collected at the end of text? If collected at the end, should they be collected in order of appearance, with tables and illustrations interleaved, or should the two be collected separately? Should illustrations be camera-ready?

** **Substubs in tables;** stubs are indented two spaces from the left margin; should turnover lines in substubs be indented an additional space from the left margin (that is, three spaces)?

** **Order of elements;** Is the correct order of elements title page, abstract, text pages, notes, appendixes, tables, and illustrations?

** **Paragraph indentation;** exact number of spaces not specified. Also, does the style require this same indentation to block quotations and indent notes to text and tables?

** **Headings;** in manuscript form, should extra space be left above and below headings, as is done in the sample manuscript?

** **Quotations;** treatment of blocked quotations is unclear.

** **Equations;** should equations be centered from left to right? Should writers number equations or not? Treatment in the sample manuscript represents an educated guess.

** **Documentation and references;** how should typists indicate bibliographic data that is uncertain as, say, when a document is not dated but someone has inferred a data of publication? How should authors cite and reference documents that have no by-line--personal or institutional?

** **Translations;** what is the preferred reference form for translations?

Journals and General Principles

8.27   The publications of the American Sociological Association are:

American Sociological Review	Social Psychology
American Soociologist	Sociological Methodology
Footnotes	Sociology of Education
Rose Monographs	Sociology of Marriage and the Family

With minor exceptions, these publications follow the requirements published in each issue of the _American Sociological Review_, which are given below.

8.28   Other journals that also follow ASA style are (Mullins 1977, Table 7.1; Sussman 1978):

Academy of Management Journal	Journal of Sociology and Social
Acta Criminologica	Welfare

Acta Sociologica
Administrative Science Quarterly
ALTERNATIVES: Marriage, Family &
 Changing Lifestyles
Berkeley Journal of Sociology
Canadian Journal of Sociology
Canadian Review of Sociology and
 Anthropology
Et al.
Ethnicity
Hueristics
Human Studies
International Journal of Comparative
 Sociology
International Journal of Sociology
 and the Family
International Review of Modern
 Sociology
Journal of American Society for
 Public Administration
Journal of the Community Development
 Society
Journal of Comparative Family Studies
Journal of Family History
Journal of Health and Social Behavior
Journal of Political and Military
 Sociology
Journal of Social Research

Kansas Journal of Sociology
Pacific Sociological Review
Political Methodology
The Prison Journal
The Public Opinion Quarterly
Quaderni di Sociologia
Qualitative Sociology
Review of Public Data Use
Review of Religious Research
Rural Sociology
Social Action
Social Problems
Social Science
Social Science Quarterly
Social Science Research
Sociological Analysis
Sociological Focus
Sociological Forum
Sociological Inquiry
Sociological Practice
Sociological Quarterly
Sociological Symposium
Sociologie et Societès
Sociology and Social Research
South African Journal of Sociology
Southeastern Review
The Southern Sociologist
Wisconsin Sociologist

8.29   Instructions on ASA style come from "Notice to Contributors," June 1981 ASR. Generally, document length ranges from 10 to 30 pages. Keep identifying material out of manuscripts (see Section 5.23 through 5.24). Clarify all symbols with encircled notes in the margin of the manuscript. Draw figures in India ink. Submit four xerox copies; retain original for the file.

Documentation

8.30   ASA style documents with author (date) citation style using author's name (or brief title where no author is given or the author is an institution), year of publication, and pagination where needed. For details, see Sections 5.3 through 5.5. Use both names for two authors; use "et al." for more than two. When authors have the same last name, use identifying initials in the text.

Reference List

8.31   List all sources by author; within author, by year of publication, earliest first. Do not use "et al."; list all authors. When there is more than one reference per author per year, distinguish them by adding the letters "a,b,c," etc. to the year as in "White (1979a)." Give the publisher's name and page numbers in as brief a form as possible. When cited material is unpublished, use "forthcoming" with the name of the future journal or publisher. When a document has not been accepted for publication, classify it as "unpublished."

Similar Minor Styles

8.32   The following journals use styles similar to that of the ASR (Mullins 1977, Table 7.1; Sussman 1978):

International Migration Review
Issues in Criminology
Journal for the Scientific Study of
 Religion
Journal of Asian and African Studies
Journal of Steward Anthropological
 Society
Linguistics
Milbank Memorial Fund Quarterly:
 Health and Society
Psychology--A Journal of Human
 Behavior*
Simulation*

Social Forces**
Western Sociological Review

Anthropological journals

  American Anthropologist
  Ethos
  Human Mosaic
  Human Organization
  Society for Applied Anthropology
  Monograph
  Urban Anthropology
Sage journals

Journals marked with a single asterisk claim to follow both ASA and APA styles (Sussman 1978, p. 143). The journal marked with two asterisks follows a modified version of ASA style that omits the date from textual citations (Sussman 1978, p. 161; Social Forces n.d.). Thus:

        Smith argues that . .   He found (Smith) that . . .

In addition, the list of references is typed in run-in fashion, rather like the entries in the bibliography to this book. Journals of the American Anthropological Association (AAA) follow the Association's style, which is much like ASA style.

8.33   Sage Publications (Sage Publications n.d.) publishes more than 50 journals in the social and behavioral sciences. Typed lines should not exceed 160 millimeters in length. Intext citations differ from ASA style in requiring a space after a colon as in "(Jones, 1986: 14)." The reference list differs in using all caps on the author's last name; parentheses around the date; single quotation marks around and upper- and lowercase on article and chapter titles; punctuation outside quotation marks; italics on book titles and journal names; and a run-in style rather like MSN. For example:

AUTHOR, John Q. (1985) 'Article Title', Inquiry, 15 (3): 4-15.

BAKER, J. L. and John Q. AUTHOR (1985) A Book Title. New York: John Wiley and Sons.

MITCHELL, J. A. (1988) 'A Dissertation Title'. PhD dissertation. City: University of Anywhere.

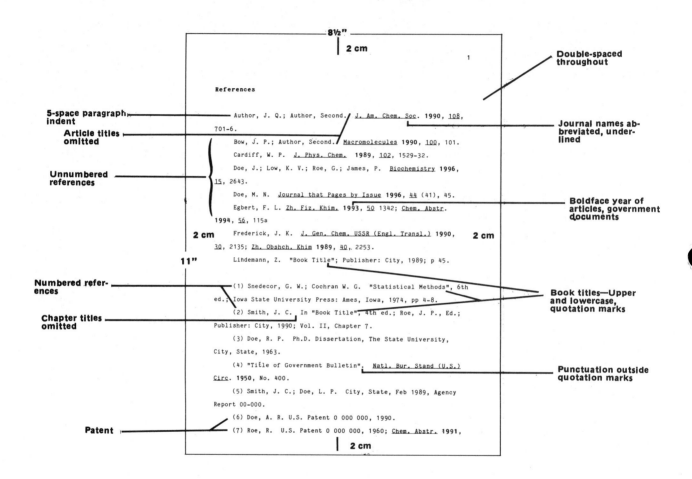

8½"

2 cm

1

Double-spaced throughout

References

5-space paragraph indent

Article titles omitted

Author, J. Q.; Author, Second. J. Am. Chem. Soc. 1990, 108, 701-6.

Bow, J. P.; Author, Second. Macromolecules 1990, 100, 101.

Cardiff, W. P. J. Phys. Chem. 1989, 102, 1529-32.

Unnumbered references

Doe, J.; Low, K. V.; Roe, G.; James, P. Biochemistry 1996, 15, 2643.

Doe, M. N. Journal that Pages by Issue 1996, 44 (41), 45.

Egbert, F. L. Zh. Fiz. Khim. 1993, 50 1342; Chem. Abstr. 1994, 56, 115a

2 cm   Frederick, J. K. J. Gen. Chem. USSR (Engl. Transl.) 1990, 2 cm
30, 2135; Zh. Obshch. Khim 1989, 40, 2253.

11"   Lindemann, Z. "Book Title"; Publisher: City, 1989; p 45.

Numbered references

(1) Snedecor, G. W.; Cochran W. G. "Statistical Methods", 6th ed.; Iowa State University Press: Ames, Iowa, 1974, pp 4-8.

Chapter titles omitted

(2) Smith, J. C. In "Book Title", 4th ed.; Roe, J. P., Ed.; Publisher: City, 1990; Vol. II, Chapter 7.

(3) Doe, R. P. Ph.D. Dissertation, The State University, City, State, 1963.

(4) "Title of Government Bulletin". Natl. Bur. Stand (U.S.) Circ. 1950, No. 400.

(5) Smith, J. C.; Doe, L. P. City, State, Feb 1989, Agency Report 00-000.

(6) Doe, A. R. U.S. Patent 0 000 000, 1990.

Patent

(7) Roe, R. U.S. Patent 0 000 000, 1960; Chem. Abstr. 1991,

2 cm

Journal names abbreviated, underlined

Boldface year of articles, government documents

Book titles—Upper and lowercase, quotation marks

Punctuation outside quotation marks

Convention paper —————

**Manuscript accepted
but not published** —————

**Manuscript not
accepted for
publication** —————

2

61, 3780.

(8) James, H. B. British Patent 0 000 000, 1996.

(9) James, A. B., presented in part at the XVIth Meeting of A
Chemical Society, City, State, Oct 1960.

(10) Smith, A. B. Spectrochim Acta, in press.

(11) Simms, N; Author, Second. "Paper Abstracts", 85th
National Meeting of A Chemical Society, City, State, Aug 1988;
American Chemical Society: Washington, D.C., 1976; INOR 83

(12) Simms, N., submitted for publication in A J. Name.

(13) Smith, P. H., Great State University, personal communication, 1989.

————— **Abstract of convention paper**

————— **Personal communi-
cation**

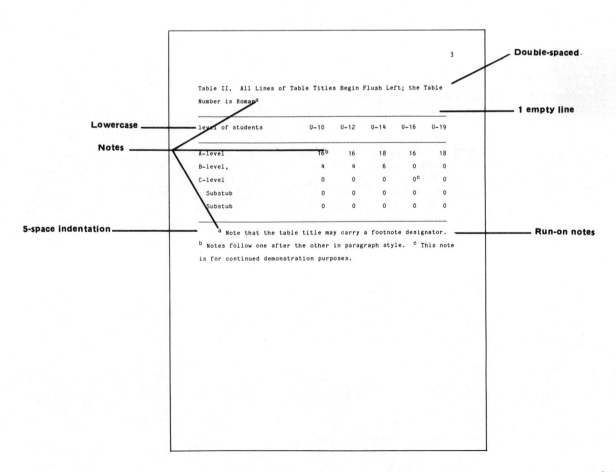

Double-spaced

1 empty line

Lowercase —————

Notes —————

5-space indentation —————

Table II. All Lines of Table Titles Begin Flush Left; the Table
Number is Roman[a]

level of students	U-10	U-12	U-14	U-16	U-19
A-level	16[b]	16	18	16	18
B-level,	4	4	6	0	0
C-level	0	0	0	0[c]	0
Substub	0	0	0	0	0
Substub	0	0	0	0	0

[a] Note that the table title may carry a footnote designator.
[b] Notes follow one after the other in paragraph style. [c] This note
is for continued demonstration purposes.

————— **Run-on notes**

3

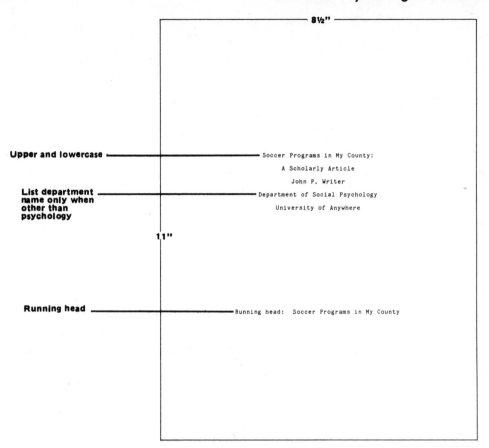

8½"

Upper and lowercase

Soccer Programs in My County:

A Scholarly Article

John P. Writer

List department name only when other than psychology

Department of Social Psychology

University of Anywhere

11"

Running head

Running head: Soccer Programs in My County

Soccer Programs

1

Abstract

3 empty lines

Blocked flush left

Youth soccer players and their parents have asked for an
expanded soccer program. The following is a proposal (a) to
organize families of competitive soccer players to run the
competitive program and (b) to create a structure to support
recreational soccer. Margins must be at least 1-1 1/2
inches (2 1/2-4 cm) wide, and typed lines should be 6 inches
(15 cm) long. Words must not be hyphenated at ends of
lines.

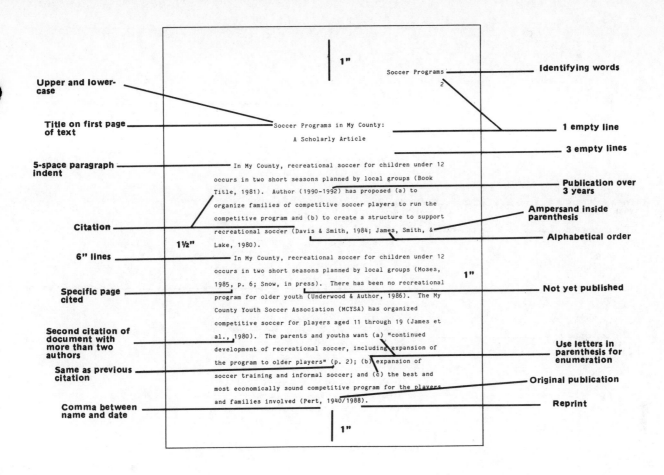

Upper and lower-case

Title on first page of text

5-space paragraph indent

Citation

6" lines

Specific page cited

Second citation of document with more than two authors

Same as previous citation

Comma between name and date

1½"

1"

1"

Soccer Programs

2

Soccer Programs in My County:

A Scholarly Article

    In My County, recreational soccer for children under 12
occurs in two short seasons planned by local groups (Book
Title, 1981). Author (1990-1992) has proposed (a) to
organize families of competitive soccer players to run the
competitive program and (b) to create a structure to support
recreational soccer (Davis & Smith, 1984; James, Smith, &
Lake, 1980).

    In My County, recreational soccer for children under 12
occurs in two short seasons planned by local groups (Moses,
1985, p. 6; Snow, in press). There has been no recreational
program for older youth (Underwood & Author, 1986). The My
County Youth Soccer Association (MCYSA) has organized
competitive soccer for players aged 11 through 19 (James et
al., 1980). The parents and youths want (a) "continued
development of recreational soccer, including expansion of
the program to older players" (p. 2); (b) expansion of
soccer training and informal soccer; and (c) the best and
most economically sound competitive program for the players
and families involved (Pert, 1940/1988).

Identifying words

1 empty line

3 empty lines

Publication over 3 years

Ampersand inside parenthesis

Alphabetical order

Not yet published

Use letters in parenthesis for enumeration

Original publication

Reprint

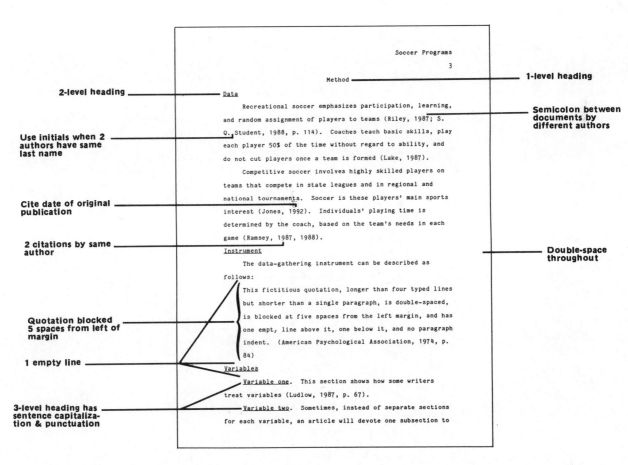

2-level heading

Use initials when 2 authors have same last name

Cite date of original publication

2 citations by same author

Quotation blocked 5 spaces from left of margin

1 empty line

3-level heading has sentence capitalization & punctuation

Soccer Programs

3

Method

Data

    Recreational soccer emphasizes participation, learning,
and random assignment of players to teams (Riley, 1987; S.
Q. Student, 1988, p. 114). Coaches teach basic skills, play
each player 50% of the time without regard to ability, and
do not cut players once a team is formed (Lake, 1987).

    Competitive soccer involves highly skilled players on
teams that compete in state leagues and in regional and
national tournaments. Soccer is these players' main sports
interest (Jones, 1992). Individuals' playing time is
determined by the coach, based on the team's needs in each
game (Ramsey, 1987, 1988).

Instrument

    The data-gathering instrument can be described as
follows:

     This fictitious quotation, longer than four typed lines
     but shorter than a single paragraph, is double-spaced,
     is blocked at five spaces from the left margin, and has
     one empty line above it, one below it, and no paragraph
     indent. (American Psychological Association, 1974, p.
     84)

Variables

    Variable one. This section shows how some writers
treat variables (Ludlow, 1987, p. 67).

    Variable two. Sometimes, instead of separate sections
for each variable, an article will devote one subsection to

1-level heading

Semicolon between documents by different authors

Double-space throughout

the dependent variable and one subsection to independent

variables (Anonymous Article, 1985, p. 91).

Analysis

Competitive Soccer

1 empty line →

Ourtown has too few top-quality, committed players and

families to field more than one genuinely competitive league

team in each age bracket. Tanner and James (1985) noted

that from at least the Under-14 (U-14) level on down,

though, each level has between 20 and 30 players who want to

play competitively. To calculate the total number of

players, Sheets (1987a, 1987b) suggested using Equation 1:

Same author, same year →

$$U-10 + U-12 + U-14 + U-16 + U-19 = \text{Total players.} \quad (1)$$

1 empty line → **Equation** →

A Great Society (1986, pp. 76-77) shows that by June

1982, state tournament time, five competitive teams had only

9-12 players left on their rosters (Reed, 1994). There is

no reason to expect any other season to be much different

(S. W. Student, 1987).[1]   ← **Footnote number**

Recreational Soccer

The values of competitive soccer do not appeal to

players and families who want recreational soccer (Reed,

1994; Lecturer & Jones, Note 1).[2]

Reference note follows standard citation →

Results and Discussion

Results

Organized soccer requires players, coaches, fields,

referees, teams, and parent support (Davis & Smith, 1984, p.

22). The MCYSA has players, fields, referees, and teams for

both programs (Coles, 1985, pp. 322-323). As Hains (Note 2)

1 empty line (annotation, top right)

Use "and" when author's names are outside parenthesis (annotation)

---

noted, the MCYSA also has coaches and parent support for

most competitive teams but none for a recreational program.

However, the MCYSA could, as Figure 1 shows, provide the

structure to support one. The figure is not shown because

figures are not typed.

_____

Figure call →   Figure 1 about here

_____

Discussion

Proposal for competitive soccer. Families of all

competitive teams form the Ourtown Competitive Soccer Club

as the arm of the MCYSA that administers the competitive

team program. As Table 1 shows, nearly 100 players would

benefit (Edge, cited in Elwood, 1984).

_____

Table call →   Table 1 about here

_____

Proposal for recreational soccer. Establish a branch

of the MCYSA to support recreational soccer (Author, Note

3). Begin with a program for youth older than 12 and an

informal neighborhood program.

Reference Notes

3 empty lines

Unpublished conference paper

Correspondence with author

1. Lecturer, N., & Jones, S. Title of paper. Paper presented at the meeting of A Psychological Association, City, May 1990.

2. Hains, D. W. Personal communication, June 22, 1990.

3. Author, J. Q. Technical report with limited availability (Tech. Rep. ABC-18). City: A State University, Psychology Laboratory, April 1990.

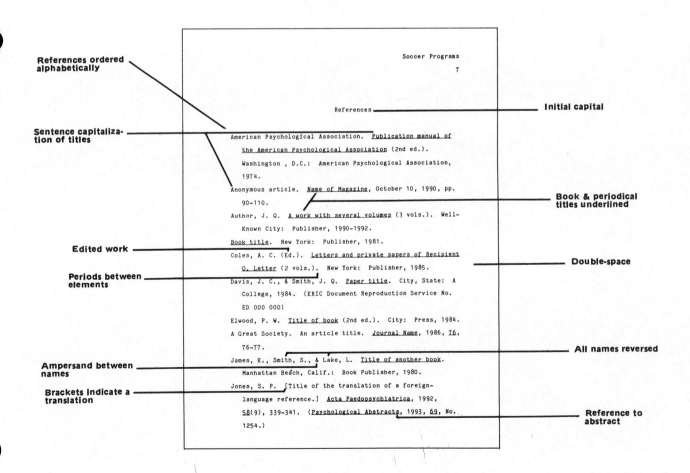

References ordered alphabetically

Sentence capitalization of titles

Edited work

Periods between elements

Ampersand between names

Brackets indicate a translation

References

Initial capital

American Psychological Association. Publication manual of the American Psychological Association (2nd ed.). Washington , D.C.: American Psychological Association, 1974.

Anonymous article. Name of Magazine, October 10, 1990, pp. 90-110.

Author, J. Q. A work with several volumes (3 vols.). Well-Known City: Publisher, 1990-1992.

Book title. New York: Publisher, 1981.

Coles, A. C. (Ed.). Letters and private papers of Recipient O. Letter (2 vols.). New York: Publisher, 1985.

Davis, J. C., & Smith, J. Q. Paper title. City, State: A College, 1984. (ERIC Document Reproduction Service No. ED 000 000)

Elwood, P. W. Title of book (2nd ed.). City: Press, 1984.

A Great Society. An article title. Journal Name, 1986, 76, 76-77.

James, K., Smith, S., & Lake, L. Title of another book. Manhattan Beach, Calif.: Book Publisher, 1980.

Jones, S. P. [Title of the translation of a foreign-language reference.] Acta Paedopsychiatrica, 1992, 58(9), 339-341. (Psychological Abstracts, 1993, 69, No. 1254.)

Book & periodical titles underlined

Double-space

All names reversed

Reference to abstract

Published summary of conference paper — Lake, F. P. Conference paper. Proceedings of A Conference, 1987, 6, 623-624. (Summary)

No quotation marks on article and chapter titles — Ludlow, F. M. Magazine article with discontinuous pages. Psychology Today, November 1987, pp. 42-43; 65-101.

Moses, J. A. Chapter in book. In, Collected works of James A. Moses (Vol. 1). City: Publisher, 1985.

Translation — Pert, F. X. Title of translated book (S. P. Jones, trans.). City: Publisher, 1988. (Originally published, 1940.)

Reprint date — **Original publication**

Ramsey, J. R. Article in journal with continuous pagination through annual volume. Journal Name, 1987, 21, 14-20.

Volume numbers underlined

Ramsey, J. R. Article from journal that paginates each issue separately. Journal Name, 1988, 20(5), 2-8.

Book review — **Issue number**

Reed, W. R. Review of Title of work by J. G. Thomas. Journal Name, 1994, 21, 220.

Dissertation — Riley, S. Q. Unpublished dissertation not available on University Microfilms. Unpublished doctoral dissertation, Name of University, 1987.

Alphabetized by title

Sheets, D. P. Technical report available from Government Printing Office (Monograph No. 2, U.S. Agency Publication No. 0000). Washington, D.C.: U.S. Government Printing Office, 1987. (a)

2 documents, same year, same author

Sheets, D. P. Technical report available from Human Resources Research Organization (HumRRO Tech. Rep. 00-00). Alexandria, Va.: Human Resources Research Organization, September 1987. (b)

Book chapter — Snow, E. Q. Chapter in book edited by others. In S. P. Cole (Ed.), Book title. City: Publisher, in press. — **Not yet published**

Book chapter — Student, S. Q. An article. In A. G. Day & D. Light (Eds.), Great State Symposium on Achievement (Vol. 17). City: Great State University Press, 1988.

Student, S. W. A doctoral dissertation available on microfilm (Doctoral dissertation, University of Anywhere, 1987). Dissertation Abstracts International, 1987, 54, 0000A-0000A. (University Microfilms No. 00-00,000)

Tanner, V. R., & James, J. M. Article in newspaper. Newspaper Name (Late City Ed.), October 12, 1985, p. 36.

Underwood, J. A., & Author, D. E. A monograph title. Monographs of A Society, 1986, 44(6, Serial No. 115).

Author Notes

This research was supported in part by Granting
Foundation Grant 00000. I wish to thank John Critic and A
Good Reader for helpful comments on an earlier version of
this article.

Footnotes

[1]In APA style, content footnotes explain or amplify the
text. Important information should be in the next, not in
the footnotes.

[2]This article lacks an appendix, which some writers use
to give detailed information on, say, methods. An appendix
should begin on a separate page and should follow the
figures in the manuscript.

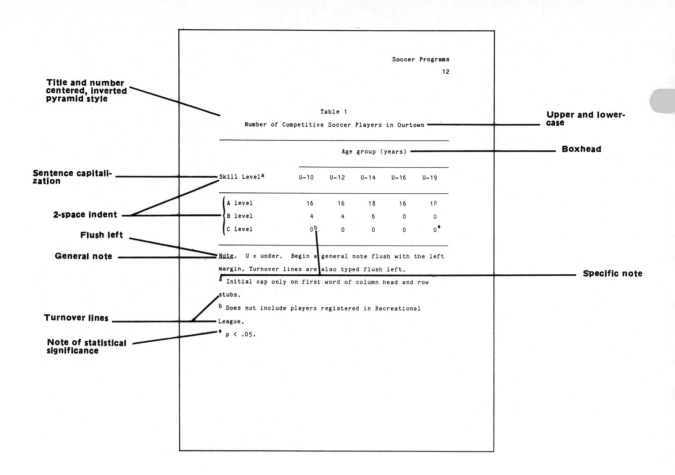

Title and number centered, inverted pyramid style

Upper and lower-case

Boxhead

Sentence capitalization

2-space indent

Flush left

General note

Specific note

Turnover lines

Note of statistical significance

Table 1

Number of Competitive Soccer Players in Ourtown

Skill Level[a]	Age group (years)				
	U-10	U-12	U-14	U-16	U-19
A level	16	16	18	16	18
B level	4	4	6	0	0
C level	0[b]	0	0	0	0*

Note. U = under. Begin a general note flush with the left margin. Turnover lines are also typed flush left.

[a] Initial cap only on first word of column head and row stubs.

[b] Does not include players registered in Recreational League.

* p < .05.

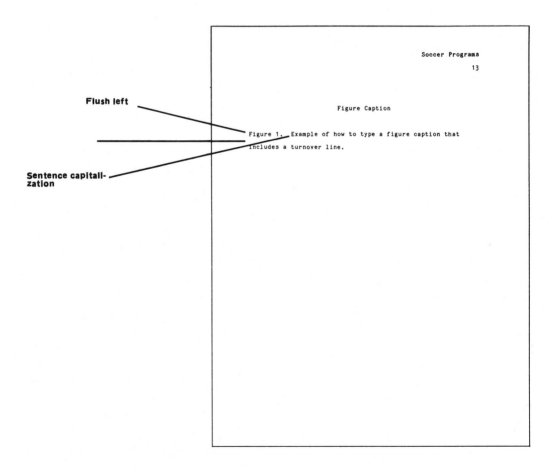

Flush left

Sentence capitalization

Figure Caption

Figure 1. Example of how to type a figure caption that includes a turnover line.

194

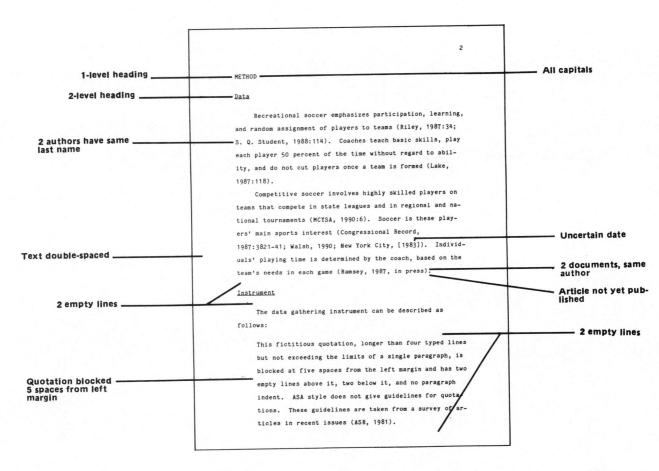

Page 1 mock-up

1"

All capitals ——— SOCCER PROGRAMS IN MY COUNTY:
A SCHOLARLY ARTICLE

——— 3 empty lines

5-space paragraph indent ———
In My County, recreational soccer for children under 12
occurs in two short seasons planned by local groups (Soccer
Market Place, 1981:140). Author (n.d.) and Bar (1985) have ——— No date
proposed (1) to organize families of competitive soccer
players to run the competitive program, and (2) to create a
structure to support recreational soccer (Laitin et al., ——— More than 2 authors
"and" between lines ——— 1980; Davis and Smith, 1984). ——— Comma separates name & date

6" lines ———
In My County, recreational soccer for children under 12
occurs in two short seasons planned by local groups (Moses,
Colon separates date & page number ——— 1985:6; Snow, 1988:117). There has been no recreational
program for older youth (Unsigned Article, 1986). The My
1½" County Youth Soccer Association (MCYSA, 1990; Bar, 1985:118)
has organized competitive soccer for players aged 11 through
19. The parents and youths want (1) continued development
of recreational soccer, including expansion of the program
to older players; (2) expansion of soccer training and informal soccer; and (3) the best and most economically sound
competitive program for the players and families involved
Specific page cited ——— (Pert, 1988:122).

1"

Page 2 mock-up

2

1-level heading ——— METHOD ——— All capitals

2-level heading ——— Data

Recreational soccer emphasizes participation, learning,
and random assignment of players to teams (Riley, 1987:34;
2 authors have same last name ——— S. Q. Student, 1988:114). Coaches teach basic skills, play
each player 50 percent of the time without regard to abil-
ity, and do not cut players once a team is formed (Lake,
1987:118).
Competitive soccer involves highly skilled players on
teams that compete in state leagues and in regional and national tournaments (MCYSA, 1990:6). Soccer is these players' main sports interest (Congressional Record, ——— Uncertain date
1987:3821-41; Walsh, 1990; New York City, [1983]). Individ-
Text double-spaced ——— uals' playing time is determined by the coach, based on the
team's needs in each game (Ramsey, 1987, in press). ——— 2 documents, same author
——— Article not yet published

Instrument
2 empty lines ———
The data gathering instrument can be described as
follows:
——— 2 empty lines

Quotation blocked 5 spaces from left margin ———
This fictitious quotation, longer than four typed lines
but not exceeding the limits of a single paragraph, is
blocked at five spaces from the left margin and has two
empty lines above it, two below it, and no paragraph
indent. ASA style does not give guidelines for quotations. These guidelines are taken from a survey of articles in recent issues (ASR, 1981).

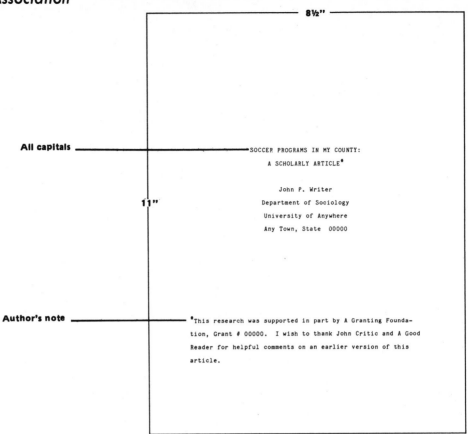

All capitals

SOCCER PROGRAMS IN MY COUNTY:
A SCHOLARLY ARTICLE*

John P. Writer
Department of Sociology
University of Anywhere
Any Town, State 00000

8½"

11"

Author's note

*This research was supported in part by A Granting Foundation, Grant # 00000. I wish to thank John Critic and A Good Reader for helpful comments on an earlier version of this article.

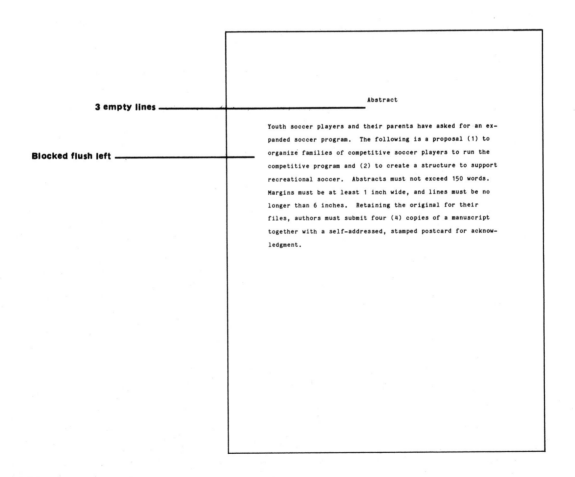

3 empty lines

Abstract

Blocked flush left

Youth soccer players and their parents have asked for an expanded soccer program. The following is a proposal (1) to organize families of competitive soccer players to run the competitive program and (2) to create a structure to support recreational soccer. Abstracts must not exceed 150 words. Margins must be at least 1 inch wide, and lines must be no longer than 6 inches. Retaining the original for their files, authors must submit four (4) copies of a manuscript together with a self-addressed, stamped postcard for acknowledgment.

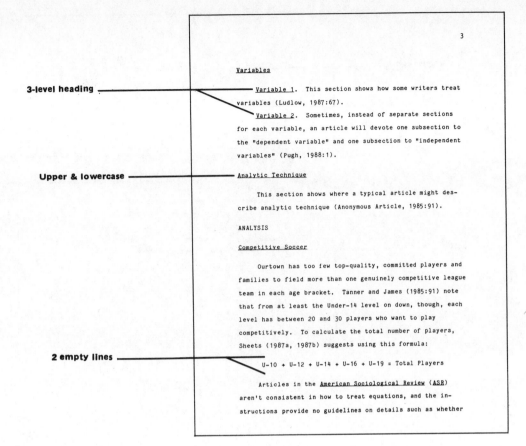

3

3-level heading ── **Variables**

Variable 1. This section shows how some writers treat variables (Ludlow, 1987:67).

Variable 2. Sometimes, instead of separate sections for each variable, an article will devote one subsection to the "dependent variable" and one subsection to "independent variables" (Pugh, 1988:1).

Upper & lowercase ── **Analytic Technique**

This section shows where a typical article might describe analytic technique (Anonymous Article, 1985:91).

ANALYSIS

Competitive Soccer

Ourtown has too few top-quality, committed players and families to field more than one genuinely competitive league team in each age bracket. Tanner and James (1985:91) note that from at least the Under-14 level on down, though, each level has between 20 and 30 players who want to play competitively. To calculate the total number of players, Sheets (1987a, 1987b) suggests using this formula:

2 empty lines ──

$$U-10 + U-12 + U-14 + U-16 + U-19 = \text{Total Players}$$

Articles in the _American Sociological Review_ (_ASR_) aren't consistent in how to treat equations, and the instructions provide no guidelines on details such as whether

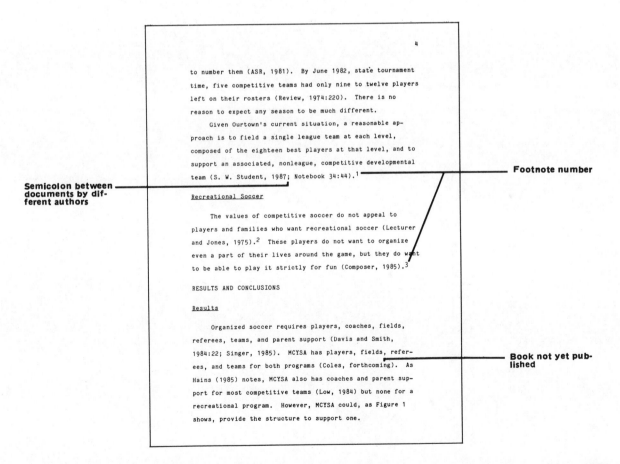

4

to number them (ASR, 1981). By June 1982, state tournament time, five competitive teams had only nine to twelve players left on their rosters (Review, 1974:220). There is no reason to expect any season to be much different.

Given Ourtown's current situation, a reasonable approach is to field a single league team at each level, composed of the eighteen best players at that level, and to support an associated, nonleague, competitive developmental team (S. W. Student, 1987; Notebook 34:44).[1]

Semicolon between documents by different authors ──

Footnote number ──

Recreational Soccer

The values of competitive soccer do not appeal to players and families who want recreational soccer (Lecturer and Jones, 1975).[2] These players do not want to organize even a part of their lives around the game, but they do want to be able to play it strictly for fun (Composer, 1985).[3]

RESULTS AND CONCLUSIONS

Results

Organized soccer requires players, coaches, fields, referees, teams, and parent support (Davis and Smith, 1984:22; Singer, 1985). MCYSA has players, fields, referees, and teams for both programs (Coles, forthcoming). As Hains (1985) notes, MCYSA also has coaches and parent support for most competitive teams (Low, 1984) but none for a recreational program. However, MCYSA could, as Figure 1 shows, provide the structure to support one.

Book not yet published ──

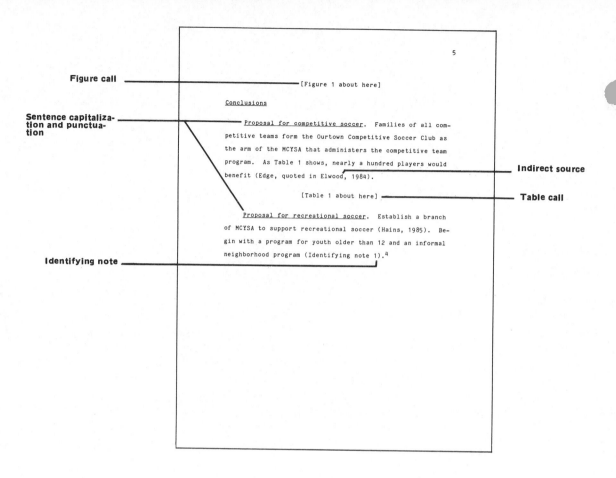

Figure call — [Figure 1 about here]

Conclusions

Sentence capitalization and punctuation — Proposal for competitive soccer. Families of all competitive teams form the Ourtown Competitive Soccer Club as the arm of the MCYSA that administers the competitive team program. As Table 1 shows, nearly a hundred players would benefit (Edge, quoted in Elwood, 1984). — **Indirect source**

[Table 1 about here] — **Table call**

Proposal for recreational soccer. Establish a branch of MCYSA to support recreational soccer (Hains, 1985). Begin with a program for youth older than 12 and an informal neighborhood program (Identifying note 1).[4]

Identifying note

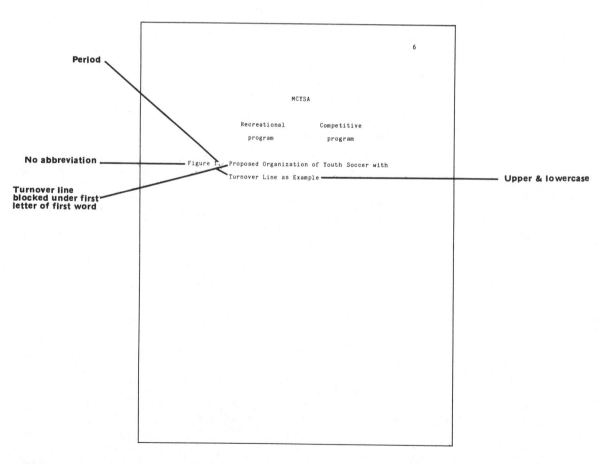

Period

MCYSA

Recreational program   Competitive program

No abbreviation — Figure 1. Proposed Organization of Youth Soccer with

Turnover line blocked under first letter of first word — Turnover Line as Example — **Upper & lowercase**

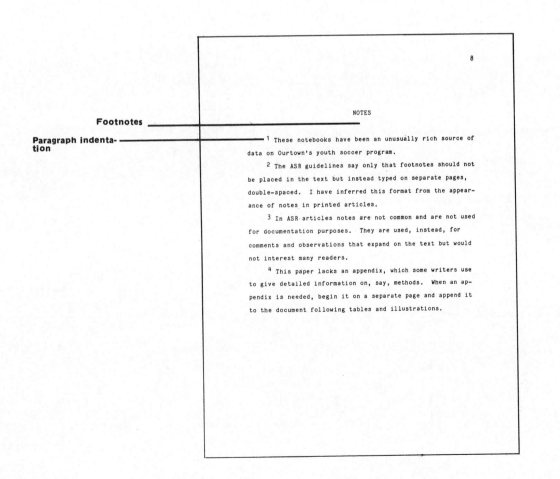

Arabic

period

Turnover line

Source

General note

Specific note

Upper & lowercase

Double line

7

Table 1. Competitive Soccer Players in Ourtown, by Age Group

Level of players	U-10	U-12	U-14	U-16	U-19
A-level, turnover line	16	16	18	16	18
B-level	4	4	6	0	0
C-level	0[a]	0	0	0	0

SOURCE: Forms completed by parents.

NOTE: Initial cap only on first word of column head and row stubs.

[a] Does not include players registered in Recreational League.

Footnotes

Paragraph indentation

8

NOTES

[1] These notebooks have been an unusually rich source of data on Ourtown's youth soccer program.

[2] The ASR guidelines say only that footnotes should not be placed in the text but instead typed on separate pages, double-spaced. I have inferred this format from the appearance of notes in printed articles.

[3] In ASR articles notes are not common and are not used for documentation purposes. They are used, instead, for comments and observations that expand on the text but would not interest many readers.

[4] This paper lacks an appendix, which some writers use to give detailed information on, say, methods. When an appendix is needed, begin it on a separate page and append it to the document following tables and illustrations.

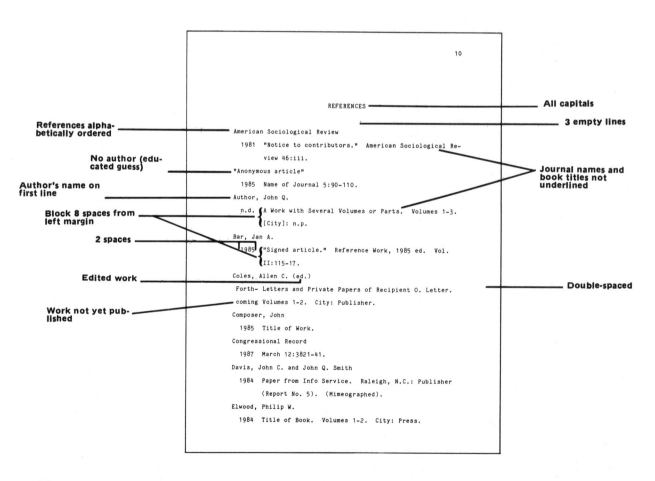

3 empty lines

5-space indent

9

IDENTIFYING NOTE

1. J. R. Smith to John P. Writer, May 1, 1984.

10

REFERENCES — **All capitals**

— **3 empty lines**

References alphabetically ordered

American Sociological Review

1981 "Notice to contributors." American Sociological Review 46:iii.

No author (educated guess)

"Anonymous article"

1985 Name of Journal 5:90-110.

Journal names and book titles not underlined

Author's name on first line

Author, John Q.

Block 8 spaces from left margin

n.d. {A Work with Several Volumes or Parts. Volumes 1-3.
       [City]: n.p.

Bar, Jan A.

2 spaces

1985 {"Signed article." Reference Work, 1985 ed. Vol.
       II:115-17.

Edited work

Coles, Allen C. (ed.)

Forth- Letters and Private Papers of Recipient O. Letter.
coming Volumes 1-2. City: Publisher.

— **Double-spaced**

Work not yet published

Composer, John

1985 Title of Work.

Congressional Record

1987 March 12:3821-41.

Davis, John C. and John Q. Smith

1984 Paper from Info Service. Raleigh, N.C.: Publisher
      (Report No. 5). (Mimeographed).

Elwood, Philip W.

1984 Title of Book. Volumes 1-2. City: Press.

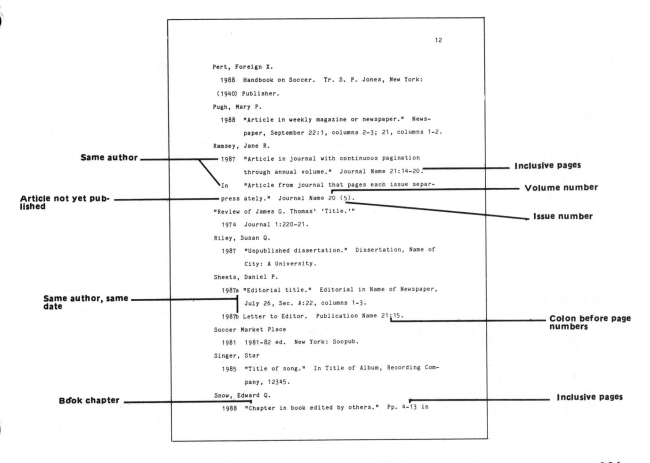

11

"And" between names

Only first name reversed

Hains, David W.
    1985. Letter to author. June 24.
Laitin, Ken, Steve Laitin, and Lindy Laitin
    1980 The World's #1 Best-Selling Soccer Book. Manhattan
        Beach, California: Soccer for Americans.
Lake, Frederick P.

Periods separate elements
    1987 "Conference paper." Conference on Soccer. Proceed-
        ings of a Conference on American Soccer, November
        1986. City: Publisher.
Lecturer, Mary and Sally Jones
    1975 "Title of paper." Paper presented at the annual
        meeting of An Association, City.
Low, Sue C.

Interview
    1984 Personal interview. July 27.
Ludlow, Francis M.

Sentence capitalization of article titles & book chapters
    1987 "Article from journal with more than one series."
        Journal Name, NS 1:65-101.
Moses, James A.
    1985 "Chapter in book." Pp. 201-51 in Collected Works of
        James A. Moses, Volume II. City: Publisher.
My County Youth Soccer Association
    1990 By-Laws. Rev. ed. Ourtown, Indiana: MCYSA.
New York City, Smith Commission
    [1983] Report with Uncertain Publication Date. New York:
        Arno.
Notebook 34
    n.d. Typescript. Soccer Hall of Fame, City, State.

12

Pert, Foreign X.
    1988 Handbook on Soccer. Tr. S. P. Jones, New York:
    (1940) Publisher.
Pugh, Mary P.
    1988 "Article in weekly magazine or newspaper." News-
        paper, September 22:1, columns 2-3; 21, columns 1-2.
Ramsey, Jane R.

Same author
    1987 "Article in journal with continuous pagination
        through annual volume." Journal Name 21:14-20.
Inclusive pages

    In   "Article from journal that pages each issue separ-
Article not yet published
    press ately." Journal Name 20 (5).
Volume number

Issue number

    "Review of James G. Thomas' 'Title.'"
    1974 Journal 1:220-21.
Riley, Susan Q.
    1987 "Unpublished dissertation." Dissertation, Name of
        City: A University.
Sheets, Daniel P.

Same author, same date
    1987a "Editorial title." Editorial in Name of Newspaper,
        July 26, Sec. A:22, columns 1-3.
    1987b Letter to Editor. Publication Name 21:15.
Colon before page numbers

Soccer Market Place
    1981 1981-82 ed. New York: Socpub.
Singer, Star
    1985 "Title of song." In Title of Album, Recording Com-
        pany, 12345.
Book chapter
Snow, Edward Q.
    1988 "Chapter in book edited by others." Pp. 4-13 in
Inclusive pages

Publication date ⎯⎯⎯⎯⎯⎯⎯⎯

Thesis date ⎯⎯⎯⎯⎯⎯⎯⎯

Studies of Soccer, Susan P. Cole (ed.). City: Publisher.

Student, Samuel Q.

1988 Published Dissertation. Dissertation, City: A
(1987) University; City2: Publisher.

Student, Susan W.

1987 "Article from dissertation abstracts." Dissertation
Abstracts 29, 3026A (University Name).

Tanner, Vera R. and John M. James

1985 "Article in daily newspaper." Newspaper Name, Late
City Ed., October 12, Sec. 1:36, column 2.

"Unsigned article"

1986 Reference Work. 1986 ed.

Walsh, E. B.

1990 Soccer Riots in South America. U.S. 208th Congress,
3rd session, House Report 106. Reprinted by New
York: Publisher.

part III
BUSINESS TIPS

chapter 9

A Primer
on Copyright
and Permissions

9.1   A copyright, "a series of exclusive, personal-property rights granted for a limited period of time to the writer of an original work,"[1] legally protects ownership of a work. The copyright owner has exclusive rights to copy, sell, adapt, translate, display, and/or perform the copyrighted work, and the right to allow others to do these things. Sometimes writers subdivide the copyright, as when one publisher brings out a hardcover book and another the paperback. Magazines that use part of a book as an article have purchased the right to use that part of the work on a one-time basis.

9.2   The information summarized in this chapter comes mainly from Chickering and Hartman's How to Register A Copyright and Protect Your Creative Work.[2] Writers who need more information will find this book a valuable resource.

A PERSPECTIVE ON COPYRIGHT

9.3   Writers need to beware of publishers that try to purchase ownership of a piece as a "work made for hire." When the publisher acquires ownership, the writer loses all rights and cannot get them back for 35 years!

9.4   Although many writers don't realize this fact, under the 1978 copyright law, work is automatically protected from the moment it is created. Because most publishers automatically copyright the documents they publish, many writers never go through the process of acquiring their own copyrights. However, there are advantages to registering a copyright before a document is published:

** Registration makes the date of creation a matter of legal record.

** Writers never know what the future holds. As Chickering and Hartman put it,[3] a work that seem insignificant at the time might catch on later to become a real money-maker or professional plum. Copyrighting protects this possibility.

** Copyrighting sometimes leads to marketing opportunities. People who are searching the copyright records on a subject may find unpublished work that they wish to publish.

The effort involved is minimal; the potential rewards, large.

WORKS THAT CAN BE COPYRIGHTED

9.5   Writers can copyright manuscripts (such as the typescript of an article), books, periodicals, phonorecords, cards, disks, tapes, poems, essays, proposals, brochures, teaching materials, bibliographies, story ideas, abstracts, and the like.

9.6   They can't copyright most fill-in-the-blank forms, information that is common property (e.g., rulers, tape measures) ideas, principles, procedures, processes, systems, modes of operation, concepts, discoveries, and the like, although they <u>can</u> copyright the tangible forms that express the ideas (manuscripts, record, etc.). Writers also can't copyright a title, even though the title may be part of a work that is copyrighted in its entirety. One further exception is publications of the U. S. government, which don't receive copyright protection.

9.7   There is one partial exception to the requirement of a tangible form--choreography, pantomime, lectures, and musical works. Until they are fixed in a tangible form, these works aren't protected by copyright, but they are protected by common-law principles of copyright law that have developed through many years of court decisions. Once fixed in tangible form, they can be copyrighted.

HOW TO REGISTER WORKS

Announcement of Copyright

9.8   To announce ownership of a work and intent to register copyright, simply write or type the copyright symbol, the year, and the writer's name on the front of the work. For example:

Copyright © 1981 Carolyn J. Mullins

© Carolyn J. Mullins

The latter form is acceptable when space for the copyright notice is limited.

9.9   The old copyright law had strict rules for the placement of the copyright notice. The new law is much more flexible. In a book, the notice can be placed on any of the following locations:

** Title page.

** Page following title page.

** Either side of the front cover or page.

** Either side of the back cover or page.

** First page of main body of the work.

** Last page of main body of the work.

** Any page between the front page and main body, if there are no more than 10 pages.

** Any page between the last page of the main body and the back page, if there are no more than 10 pages.

** Anywhere on a single-leaf work.

9.10 Similarly, in collective works, the publisher may choose any of several acceptable locations.

9.11 Copyright protection exists even when writers haven't registered their claim for copyright. Should someone publish or use unregistered works without permission, writers can still sue the illegal user <u>if</u> (1) they formally register before bringing suit and (2) registration occurs within five years of the illegal publication or use.

Registration

9.12 The U. S. Copyright Office requires that a work meet the test of "originality of expression."[4] However, this does not mean the the office acts as an artistic critic; copyright is not granted on the basis of artistic merit. It merely recognizes the writer's claim to originality and provides a legal basis for the enforcement of rights if another individual uses the work without getting permission. In general, the writer who creates a work and has not copied someone else's will pass the test of originality of expression.

9.13 Writers can register portions of a work at any time they wish before completion--however, they'll need to send a new registration fee with each new portion. For most writers, the best time to apply is after the manuscript has been completed even though it may not have been published. In general, the more widely a manuscript will be circulated, the greater the risk that the work will get out of your control. When the manuscript is published, it can be easily reregistered, with the date of actual publication recorded in the copyright office. At the very latest, register the manuscript immediately after publication.

9.14 **Procedures.** To register the copyright to a work:

** Request the appropriate forms from the Information and Publications Section, Copyright Office, Library of Congress, Washington, DC 20559. You must use the forms that became effective on January 1, 1979. The earlier forms will not be accepted.

** Don't use photocopied forms. The Copyright Office won't accept them.

** State the type of work you wish to copyright so that you are sent the proper information. Literary works use form TX; works in the performing arts are registered with form PA. If your work mixes forms, choose the form for the type of work that predominates. If the Copyright Office believes that you chose the wrong form, it will give you a chance to correct the effort.

** Complete the form.

** Add one complete copy of the manuscript (unpublished works) or two copies of the published work and the registration fee ($10). If you want more than one copy of the copyright certificate, sent an additional $4 for each additional certificate.

** Mail the fee, form, and copies to the Copyright Office. If the fee is mailed separately, make sure it goes with a letter explaining its purpose. Otherwise the Copyright Office will treat the fee as a deposit for the Library of Congress.

** If you need more detailed information, contact the Copyright Office.

Always keep a copy of documents you copyright. The Copyright Office is not required to keep any copies you deposit with it. For this reason, many writers keep a witnessed duplicate copy as legal proof of the exact document that was copyrighted.

9.15   CAUTION: If the physical size of the manuscript exceeds 96 inches in any direction, contact the Copyright Office to find out what kind of "identifying material" you should submit instead of copies. This size requirement is unlikely to affect writers.

9.16   Writers who wish may register works under a pseudonym, but they must give their nationality and their place of residence.

9.17   To avoid making many small, individual payments, writers who use copyright services frequently can open a deposit account with the Copyright

Office from which registration and service fees will be automatically deducted. To open an account:

** Write to the Copyright Office and request the required form.

** Complete the form and mail it with an initial deposit of at least $250. (All subsequent deposits must also total at least $250.)

** To keep the account alive, make a minimum of 12 transactions per year.

Writers with accounts receive regular statements showing transaction charges, deposits, and current balance. When the amount in an account is too low to cover a charge, the Copyright Office notifies the account holder. Prompt payment of such charges is very important; failure to pay a renewal fee on time will result in termination of the copyright.[5]

9.18   Precautions. When you sign a book contract, make certain that the publisher will copyright the book in your name. When you agree to publish an article in a periodical, make certain the publisher will obtain a "blanket" copyright for the issue in which the article will appear. The collective notice satisfies the requirement of notice of copyright. If you plan to register as a group all your writings within a 12-month period:

** Ask that a separate copyright notice in your name appear with the article.

9.19   Never allow publication of your work in an uncopyrighted publication. Doing so will probably invalidate your copyright. "Publication" occurs when copies of a work are distributed to the public by sale or other transfer of ownership, or by rental, lease, or lending. Similarly, _offering_ to distribute copies for the purpose of further distribution or performance also constitutes publication. When in doubt whether a distribution constitutes publication, place the copyright mark on the copies (see Section 9.8) and seek legal advice. If you inadvertently find yourself being published without proper copyright procedures, ask that a copyright notice in your name be placed on the first page of your work. Then register the work within five years of the publication date (see Section 9.21). In general, sending a manuscript to a publisher for evaluation does not constitute publication.

Reregistration

9.20   Renewal of copyright requires completion of Form RE and payment of a
$6 fee. It is possible to both register and renew a document at the same
time, as might be necessary if the document had been published with the proper
copyright mark on it but never been registered. Renewal must occur within the
28th year. For instance, a work copyrighted in 1956 would be due for renewal
in 1984. The renewal process would have to be complete by December 31, 1984.

Correction of Errors

9.21   In general, there is no way to correct errors and omissions in copyright notices for works published before January 1, 1979. (An error during
this time usually puts a work in the public domain.) The new copyright law is
more forgiving. First, omission does not invalidate copyright if any of the
following conditions is met:

** The notice was omitted from only a relatively small number of the copies
   distributed.

** Registration of the work has been made before publication or is made within
   five years after publication without copyright notice and if a reasonable
   effort is made to add the notice after the omission is discovered.

** The notice was omitted in violation of an express written request by the
   author that, as a condition of distribution, the work contain a copyright
   notice.

For most copyright holders, the most important of the three conditions is the
chance to correct the omission by registering the work and putting the notice
on copies distributed later. However, registration _must_ occur within five
years. Otherwise the work falls into the public domain. Errors in name,
date, and omission of "Copyright," "Copr.," or "©" can also be corrected.

DURATION OF COPYRIGHT PROTECTION

9.22   For works created on or after January 1, 1978, the copyright term is
the author's life plus 50 years. When a work is jointly written, the copyright doesn't expire until 50 years after the last surviving author dies.

9.23   Works made for hire, and anonymous and pseudonymous works are protected for 75 years after publication or 100 years after creation, whichever is shorter.

9.24   Works copyrighted under the old copyright law, which provided for an initial term of 28 years with a 28-year renewable term, will be protected for 75 years from the original copyright date.

9.25   Works in the "public domain" include government publications, works published before January 1, 1978, that have been published more than 75 years, and works published before July 1, 1909, that have not been copyrighted in the United States.

USE OF ANOTHER'S WORKS

9.26   In some circumstances, the "fair use" principle permits the use of a work without permission. In other circumstances, writers who wish to use the work of another person must ask for and receive permission to do so.

"Fair Use"

9.27   Fair use depends on:

** The purpose and character of use--is it for commercial or nonprofit educational purposes?

** The nature of the copyrighted work.

** The amount and substantiality of the part used in relation to the copyrighted work as a whole. A passage from a book might be fine; a few lines from a poem or song probably won't be.

** The effect on the use on the potential market or value of the copyrighted work. If the work would be devalued, the use wouldn't be fair.

Permissions

9.28   With a few exceptions (e.g., copyrighted material published within a government publication), writers need not ask for permission to use works that are in the public domain. However, don't overuse such documents. An editor friend of mine once was asked to "edit" an article that turned out to be composed almost totally of long chunks from government publications. My friend was horrified. The prospective publisher had the last word: No.

9.29   Adaptations also require the adapter to seek permission from the author of the original. The process is the same as the process for seeking permission to quote.

9.30   Types. Permission may be sought for any of several kinds of rights: First Serial Rights (also known as First Magazine Rights), Second Serial Rights (sometimes termed Syndicate Rights), Book Rights, Paperback Book Rights, Foreign Rights, Translation Rights, Motion Picture Rights, Dramatic Rights, Television Rights, and All Rights. Most writers won't find a purchaser for each and every right--I, for instance, can't imagine finding anyone who wanted Motion Picture Rights, Dramatic Rights, or Television Rights to this book. However, when a work does appear promising in several areas, the owner of the work faces the pleasant possibility of earning lots of money.

9.31   For example, a novel (Book Rights) might be picked up by a paperback publisher (Paperback Book Rights), a movie maker, a play or television producer (Motion Picture, Dramatic, and Television Rights, respectively), and a magazine that wanted to publish one or more episodes as articles (First Magazine Rights). The novel might also be translated into foreign languages (Translation Rights). One day my mail contained a totally unexpected surprise: a small, neatly done Japanese-language book. With thanks for my editorial help, no less! When I finally began searching from back to front, I discovered that the book was a business publication on which I had worked several years before. Its success in English had prompted translation into Japanese.

9.32   An article published in the United States could also be published in foreign countries (Foreign Rights) and reprinted in other U. S. Publications (Second Serial Rights). In fact, "Once is Not Enough" should be the motto of every free-lance writer who wants to survive at his or her craft.

9.33   Procedures. General principles notwithstanding, the best conservative advice is to seek permission <u>whenever</u> you quote copyrighted material. Writers who have signed book contracts often receive forms for writers to use when they request permission. Other writers will have to use a simple form letter. Always specify the exact text you wish to quote, the work it will be quoted in, the nature of that work, and the kind of rights desired. You will need to seek permission from both the writer and the publisher (if any) of the work. A letter like the following will work just fine:

Dear _____:

I want to quote 300 lines from: Susan Writer, "Chapter Six," <u>Title</u>, City, Publisher, 1989. Copyright held by Susan Writer.

I want to quote from two sections. On page 101, I want to begin quoting with the words "Starting with", line 6, and ending with the word "end" in line 25. On page 150 I want to quote beginning with "Start", line 8, and ending with "stop" on line 30. For your convenience I have attached copies of the pages and circled the parts I want to quote.

My book, _____, to be published by XYZ Publishers in June 1988, is a trade book in the Music Lovers' Series. I would like nonexclusive world publication rights.

I look forward to hearing from you.

Often writers have to pay for the rights. Especially when the work is likely to be a smashing success on the trade market, the copyright holder may expect to be handsomely reimbursed for having granted permission.

9.34   Be warned that more than one letter may be needed. I am still waiting for a permission I requested in 1975. I never received an answer despite several follow-up notes and eventually withdrew an illustration from my manuscript. Other writers have recounted similar tales.

9.35   When you receive a letter granting permission, keep it in a safe place such as a safe deposit box. Copy it and send a copy to your publisher. <u>Never</u> send your only copy of a permission through the mails.

9.36   In your published work, explicitly note the granting of permissions you have received. In a book, the usual place is the Preface. When the borrowed text is a table or illustration, the acknowledgment often goes at the bottom. In an article the usual place is a brief note on the first or last page.

NOTES TO CHAPTER 9

1. Robert B. Chickering and Susan Hartman, <u>How to Register a Copyright and Protect Your Creative Work</u> (New York: Scribner's, 1980), p. 1.

2. Robert B. Chickering and Susan Hartman, <u>How to Register a Copyright and Protect Your Creative Work</u>. Copyright (c) 1980 Robert B. Chickering and Susan Hartman (New York: Scribner's, 1980). Adapted with the permission of Charles Scribner's Sons. The form of this note differs from that of other notes because it was specified by Charles Scribner's Sons as a condition of permission to use the adaptation.

3. <u>How to Register</u>, p. 7.

4. <u>How to Register</u>, p. 6.

5. Chickering and Hartman, <u>How to Register</u>, p. 19.

chapter 10

Wrapping It Up

10.1   This chapter is for writers and typists who put the finishing touches on manuscripts. When a manuscript is ready for final typing, attach to the draft a checklist like the following to help you keep track of progress (scratch out the steps that don't apply). After each step has been completed, check it off. The steps are:

** Typed in proper style.

** Pages properly ordered and numbered.

** pages proofread.

** Errors corrected.

** Illustrations prepared in camera-ready form.

** Duplication in acceptable manner and in enough copies for recipient and for filing.

** If the document was typed on a word processor, file name and identifying index code for tape, disk, or cassette (if used) written on checklist.

** Cover added.

** Document bound, stapled, banded, or clipped.

** Material for deposit in national archives prepared (a possibility with AIP and APA styles).

** Letter of transmittal prepared.

** With scholarly documents, processing fee and copyright release form, if required, attached to letter.

** Letter attached to appropriate number of copies of document.

** Envelope or box prepared for mailing.

** When manuscript is an article, self-addressed and stamped return envelope and acknowledgment card enclosed.

** For any manuscript intended for publication, a permanent record established in the form of a 3 x 5 card, a file folder, or both.

** Mailed:

```
First class          _____
Third class          _____
Special fourth class _____
Certified            _____
Registered           _____
Date                 _____
```

** Form filed with file copies of the manuscript.

If last-minute checking reveals errors, refer to Sections 2.27 through 2.29 for help in correcting them. Caution: with manuscripts for publication, do not submit to more than one possible publisher unless all publishers explicitly permit multiple submission.

REPRODUCTION OF MANUSCRIPT

10.2   When you specify requirements for reproduction:

** Ask for the highest quality paper that will give a clear, dark copy.

** Check requirements for number and kind of copies. When the manuscript is for publication, remember that publishers and editors prefer photo- or xerographic copies to carbon copies. Most need at least two copies, and some need five or six. With other kinds of document, you might need hundreds or even thousands of copies.

** When possible, check the clarity of reproduction on each page of each copy.

** For journals and other publishers, <u>reproduce on only one side of each page</u>. In other circumstances, reproduction on both sides may be not only desirable but required to save postage.

** Check the number of copies needed. Most writers want a copy for each person who has read drafts and one or two file copies in addition to copies for the intended recipient.

** Don't staple copies for a publisher without first asking whether you should do so. Particularly when a manuscript is about to be put into production, publishers prefer that you fasten copies with a paper clip, paper press, or rubber bands.

** On documents that are not to be published, add a cover (if required) and bind the document together.

PACKAGING AND MAILING

10.3 When the manuscript is to be mailed, take precautions to ensure that the document arrives in pristine condition:

** Type a brief letter of transmittal. When more than one author is involved, indicate who is to receive correspondence. Something like the following will do nicely:

Enclosed is a copy of "Title," which we are submitting for consideration for possible publication in your journal. We am submitting it to your journal because [give reason].

We look forward to hearing from you. Please send correspondence to John Jones at the address above.

* * * * *

As I promised, I am enclosing herewith the final report of the Task Force on _____. Let me know if you have questions.

* * * * *

Enclosed is the manuscript on [topic] that you requested for your June issue. I trust that you will find it acceptable.

We agreed on a fee of $___. When may I expect your check?

I look forward to publication and to future assignments from you.

** Place the letter of transmittal on top of the copies of the manuscript.

** When the document is to be considered for publication, include a self-addressed, stamped, 9 x 12 envelope (the SASE; used for articles only) for return of the manuscript. Also include a postcard, addressed and stamped, whose return will acknowledge that the manuscript has arrived.

** Wrap the manuscript securely.

** Check mailing instructions to be sure you are sending the document to the proper person.

10.4   For small documents, such as articles and short proposals, a heavy brown envelope, about 9 x 12, usually is adequate. For a book manuscript or thick report with several copies:

** Wrap the manuscript in stout cord and make sure no edges stick out.

** When the document is intended for publication, you will probably need to tie the illustrations in a separate bundle. Send photographs separately. Mark the package "Photographs; Do Not Bend." Insure these for the cost of replacement. Send original slides, which can't be replaced, by registered mail.

** Stack copies of the manuscript in a sturdy cardboard box. For bulky manuscripts, use one box for each copy.

** Wrap the box in heavy paper, seal it tightly, fasten with strong cord or tape, and address the package.

** When time is short, you might want to use one of the same-day or next-day delivery services.

** When you want to guarantee an acknowledgment, register or certify the parcel.

Your post office can supply you with leaflets that list current postage rates in every category.

PREPARING A RECORD CARD OR FOLDER

Record Card

10.5   When a manuscript is being submitted for publication, prepare a 3 x 5 record card with the manuscript title, date of submission, and publisher's name. If the document was typed on a word processor, add the document's file name and the index name of the disk, tape, or cassette that contains the electronic copy of the manuscript. Use the card to record the manuscript's subsequent history and, eventually, complete bibliographic data.

10.6   In the meantime, find a mechanism that will remind you when the manuscript has been out for six weeks or so. If you have heard nothing from the publisher at this point, you'll want to send a gentle reminder. Writers who send out large numbers of manuscripts often use a "tickler" filing system, which lets them file the cards on a date six weeks ahead. When that day comes, pulling the file for that date automatically reminds them of the manuscript. Writers who send out fewer manuscripts may find it easier to file the cards alphabetically and write the title on their calendars on the date when they would want to write a reminder letter. For them, simply checking the calendar provides all the reminder they need.

Record Folder

10.7   Professional writers who send out several manuscripts and query letters per month may want to start a file of magazine or book publishers in addition to a card file. This idea, suggested by Arturo Gonzalez, who teaches Writer's Digest workshops for nonfiction writers, records your success or failure with each potential publisher to help you (1) identify what causes success and (2) remember that the relationship with the publisher is more important than the manuscript per se. Tape a sheet of lined paper inside the folders. On each line write the title of the manuscript or proposed manuscript, the date you sent it, the date you received a response, and the nature of the response. Keep your correspondence for the manuscript in the file.

chapter 11

Survival Tips: Managing a Typing Business

11.1   Where Chapter 9 is mainly for writers, this chapter is mainly for part- and full-time typists who are trying to run their own businesses. It provides tips that range from the personal to the technical. All have one goal: to help you do the best possible job at the highest possible earning level and with the greatest possible personal satisfaction.

PROFESSIONAL GOALS

11.2   To sharpen your business thinking, read articles and books on planning and managing a small business. Articles of this type abound in magazines
such as <u>Savvy</u> and <u>Working Woman</u>.[1] Some typists may wish to take a business
school course or two (an accounting course is particularly valuable). These
activities help you to focus on the larger issues that will determine whether
you succeed or fail in your business.

Setting Goals

11.3   Short-range goals define choices for the immediate year or two of a
business. Set goals about the amount of income you want to earn (gross and
net, or total and after expenses), the number of hours you want to work, the
schedule you wish to keep, the kind and amount of promotion to do, the number
of clients you want, and so forth.

11.4   Long-range goals help you to think about choices up through the next
five years or so into the future. While these goals also should address earn-
ings, number of clients, and the like, they should focus most strongly on the
directions you want you and your business to grow. For instance, do you want
to continue to be a typist? Would you like to become a word processing operator? Have you always liked to edit what you type, perhaps dreaming of some-
day being an editor? The specifics don't matter. What is important is:

** Identify those long-term wishes so that the day-to-day choices you make
   move you in the direction of those long-range goals.

Reaching for Goals

11.5   Next, look for concrete ways to reach those goals. For instance, if
you want to become an editor, buy the University of Chicago Press's <u>Manual of
Style</u> and read it carefully.[2] Look for typing clients who want the editorial
help you can give them. Advertise your willingness to edit, correct spelling,
and so forth as you type. Give preference to clients who want editorial help.
Look for courses that would help you develop editorial skill.[3]

Matching Personal Needs and Professional Goals

11.6   Plan a regular time each month to check your professional goals with your personal needs. Small nagging feelings of discontent have a way of mushrooming into serious trouble when we ignore them. Your feelings and instincts can be your best guide to problems as well as to successful career goals.

11.7   For instance, suppose you want to become an editor. You have been choosing your clients accordingly, and you like the work, but something inside you is uneasy. Analyzing that feeling might show that you aren't earning enough income for the hours you are working. You are spending editorial hours for which you aren't charging because they don't contribute to your number of pages typed per hour. As a result, your financial ends are barely meeting, and you don't have any time left over for your family or yourself.

11.8   What can you do about the situation? Plenty. You could raise your typing rate a bit to pay for the extra service you render. (Most clients who need editorial help are more than willing to pay for it, yet many typists make the mistake of providing this service free.) You could add an editorial charge. You might even decide that for a fixed period of time, you need money most and you'll choose typing/editing jobs only if you get adequately reimbursed for them. If you can't attract any on this basis, you'll live without them. In short, balance your need to eat and pay the rent with your need to offer a kind and level of service that pleases you. Whatever the situation:

** Make a decision that resolves the situation and helps you get rid of the uneasy feelings.

** Make sure your clients understand any changes you make in your operating practices.

FREE-LANCE TIME AND INCOME

Disadvantages

11.9   Free-lance time and income differ from those that go with a regular job. Disadvantages include uncertainty and lack of benefits. Specifically:

** Because free-lancers are usually paid as independent contractors, their employers usually don't pay an employer's share of their social security taxes, and taxes of any kind aren't withheld. Thus, free-lancers have to keep their own social security records and pay a higher social security tax rate.

** Because income tax usually isn't withheld, free-lancers have to keep their own income records and arrange for either quarterly estimated tax payments or some form of compensating savings.

** For the same given hourly rate, a full-time salaried typist earns about 25% more that a free-lancer because salaried jobs provide paid vacation, paid holidays, insurance, and other benefits.

** Free-lancers usually have to provide their own equipment.

** Free-lancers have to run their own errands, buy their own supplies, keep their own accounting records, promote their own services, and so forth.

** Work time isn't necessarily set by fixed starting and stopping times.

Advantages

11.10   For many free-lance typists, the difference between success and failure in business is determined by their success at exploiting the advantages of free-lance status. The potential advantages include:

** A home office devoted wholly to the typing business; a percentage of the cost of the home and maintenance is tax deductible as a business expense.

** Tax deductible business expenses for mileage (or transportation cost) used to run errands away from the office, pick up and deliver work, and so forth.

** Tax deduction of nonreimbursed cash costs, costs of service and supplies, and costs of capital investment.

** Tax credits on capital investments such as typewriters and word processors.

** Savings on clothes and transportation from working at home.

SETTING AND CHANGING RATES

11.11   The biggest mistake of many free-lancers, typists included, is to charge too little for their services. This section tells how to set and change rates and how to earn more for the work you do. Typists can charge in one of two ways: by the hour and by either the job (a whole manuscript) or some reasonable job unit, such as a page. Each has its advantages, depending on the situation.

By the Hour vs By the Job

11.12   When adhered to faithfully, hourly charges have the advantage of paying typists for all the hours they work. However, local custom may limit the hourly rate and, thus, the total amount you can earn. Typists lose money when they charge the same hourly rate as salaried employees because their hourly rate includes no benefits. Yet in some areas, charging a higher rate costs typists jobs. Sections 11.17-11.24 suggest ways to get around these problems. Charging by the hour or day may be the best arrangement for typists who are likely to encounter unavoidable delays such as a sick computer or late manuscript.

11.13   Charging by the job is beneficial if you work fast and accurately and like competing with yourself or if you know how much time a specific kind of job will take and you expect no uncontrollable delays. If you have a word processor, charging by the job gives you an advantage because some of the work is automated and you don't have to commit paper and ribbons until you are sure the manuscript is correct. If both you (with word processing) and a competitor with a typewriter charge the same rate per page, you will earn more because you can process more jobs in a given amount of time. Even if you charge a bit more per page, you probably won't lose business because you can promise perfectly clean copy, corrected pages with no new errors from retyping, and faster completion of the job.

How to Set and Change Rates

11.14   When you set rates, take into account both the going local rates and your needs. Find out what others are charging for the services you want to offer. Figure out the total income (after taxes and expenses) you need to live and pay your bills. Remember to include the effect of a tax deduction for a home office. Divide the total to find out what you need to earn per month or week, and divide that figure by either the number of hours you want to work or the number of jobs or job units. This calculation tells what you need to charge per hour or per job. Now compare your figure with the going rate. If your rate is high, look for ways to lower costs, charge differently, or justify the charge.

11.15   Once you have set a rate, plan to change it regularly to cope with inflation, rising expenses, your increasing skill and knowledge, and failure to have priced the service high enough to start with. In promotional material, include a statement that guarantees rates only until a specific date. Alternatively, include a statement that rates may change without notice. Make the same statement in promotional letters.

11.16   When you plan a price change, tell all current clients in advance. You might even offer the benefit of service at the old rate for jobs that are in your hands before the specified date. This might bring in quite a rush of work.

How to Earn More for Your Work

11.17   Suppose the local rate is lower than your rate, but you can't find any way to cut your rate any lower. Here are some suggestions to help you earn higher rates for your work.

11.18   Sell your ideas. One possibility is to sell your ideas, not just your time. Yes, you charge more, but the client receives something extra. Possible benefits might include editorial services, design and layout services (as for brochures), and faster or more accurate typing.

11.19   Sell your technology. As the **WP Advantage** statements show, typists with word processors can offer a whole host of technological advantages--readability analyses (see Section 2.33 through 2.37), word counts (Section 2.30 through 2.32), proportional print and spacing (Section 2.11), boldface (Section 2.13), automatic indexes (Section 5.60), automatic tables of contents (Section 5.44) and lists of tables and illustrations (Section 5.45), ability to adapt documents easily from the requirements of one style to the requirements of another, ability to use parts of old documents in new documents, spelling checks (Section 3.29), and the like. The simple ability to correct without introducing new errors will persuade many clients to pay more. Others will be attracted by your ability to store electronically documents they may need again.

11.20   Sell contracts. Some typists are able to make contracts with clients that guarantee a fixed rate of pay and a fixed minimum number of hours per week. The contract gives stability—a certain amount of work will exist no matter how much or how little promoting the typist does. The contractor gets guaranteed availability and a high quality of service because the typist doesn't have to relearn requirements with each new job.

11.21   Get paid on a part-time salary. Try to get paid as a part-time employee to get social security and tax withholding—an arrangement that is often possible in work for a company but rarely possible in work for individuals.

11.22   Other possible off-setting advantages to seek are:

** Time plus expense arrangements to reimburse the costs of typewriter ribbons, correction fluid, paper, diskettes, xeroxing, and so forth.

** "Door-to-door" charges—that is, charge not only for time spent at the typewriter but for time spent picking up supplies, picking up and delivering work, and the like.

** Free use of a firm's equipment. For instance, a typist who was saving money for a typewriter might seek jobs in which the employer would allow use of the company's typewriters during evening hours.

One enterprising typist with design skills got a part-time job with a print shop. Because she was the only one who used the typewriter, she asked for permission to use it and certain of the design tools for her free-lance work. The typist's benefits are obvious. The printer also benefited when typing clients began choosing the shop as a convenient place to do their printing.

11.23   Set minimum charges. A one- or two-page job can be more of a nuisance than a moneymaker. For 30 minutes' typing, you spend 15 minutes preparing a bill and making entries in your accounting books. Set a minimum charge--say, twice your hourly rate--to keep the small jobs from eating up your profit. You'll lose a few jobs but save money in the long run. Don't let horrified clients shame you into dropping the charge, either!

11.24   Try promotional gimmicks. If your geographic area is over-loaded with free-lance typists (many college towns are), you might want to try a promotional trick or two to keep customers coming back. For instance, you might offer bonuses such as one free hour's service for every 24 paid hours or every new customer a client brought in. Supply clients with a record sheet that you fill in and initial it each time you do a job. The kind or amount of bonus matters less than the "hook" it provides to keep customers coming back. Another promotional idea is the "I'm about to raise my rates" special mentioned in Section 11.16.

11.25   CAUTION: don't fall into the trap of charging different rates for different kinds of work. I knew one typist who charged $8/hour for editing, $4/hour for typing, and $3/hour for proofreading! For your sake and the sake of your accounting and bookkeeping, set a single rate that you charge for any work, regardless of what it is. Charge that rate for all hours spent, whether editing, typing, or proofing. Otherwise, you'll find yourself shirking the cheap work and looking for the more highly paid.

TIME MANAGEMENT

Daily Diary

11.26   Every self-employed person needs an efficient system for recording and analyzing time spent at various tasks. To control your time, use some sort of daily diary that has spaces for you to list appointments, hours spent at different tasks, and the like. Get a diary that you can carry with you. Other useful features to look for in a diary are monthly planning pages, a telephone list, annual planning pages, note pages, monthly summary sheets, and the like. If you have children younger than 15, keep a systematic record of child care expenses. Start keeping records _when_ you start the business and keep it up daily. Don't let record-keeping get out of hand.

Categories of Work

11.27   Develop categories that describe the tasks you have to do. For instance:

** **Management;** includes work on filing systems, mailing lists, correspondence, keeping records, getting supplies, choosing new equipment, hiring
and firing, and analyzing how you spend time and money.

** **Accounting;** includes maintaining an accurate record of income and expense,
paying bills, doing income taxes, keeping salary records on employees, taking inventory, and analyzing cost per unit of production.

** **Promotion;** includes letters and visits to potential clients, purchase or
development and use of mailing lists, free samples (of either work or
time), lectures and talks that allow you do display your talents,
developing and keeping brochures up to date, and entertaining.

** **Development;** unpaid work or learning time that you expect to increase
your earning power at a later time. For instance, taking an editing course
wouldn't earn current income and probably would cost tuition money.

** **Running errands;** includes buying supplies, picking up and delivering
work, and so forth.

** **Task categories;** includes the kinds of paid work you do--editing, typing,
proofreading.

** **Miscellaneous;** anything that doesn't fit anywhere else.

The categories matter less than your ability to find out where your time is
going and what return it is bringing. If you discover, for instance, that you
spend only 20 hours per week typing and 20 hours doing accounting, management,
and other tasks, chances are you aren't earning a living wage. You may need
to find ways to both charge more and work more efficiently.

Summaries

11.28   The next step is an accounting system that enables you to summarize
categories, analyze figures, and use the information. Once a week, record the
information from your diary either on an accountant's multicolumn "spread"
sheet or in a computer program. (Many personal computers come with prepack-
aged programs for recording this kind of data.)

11.29   The summaries tell how much of your time is earning money, now and (projected) in the future; how much time you are spending on specific kinds of work (so you can make more accurate estimates for future jobs); whether you are charging enough for your work; and what, if any, time you are wasting. For instance, if you are making five trips a week to the same shopping location, chances are you need to organize you trips more efficiently to save both time and money.

11.30   You might also find that you are earning less on certain kinds of work or certain clients. For instance, Client A keeps coming back with small corrections that he needs "right away." You charge for them by the hour, but the additional billing takes time, and he disrupts other work. Solutions might include billing him for additional time outright (so you don't have to bill him again), setting a minimum rate for corrections, charging him a higher rate, telling him to leave the manuscript with you (you'll have it ready tomorrow), and some combination of these techniques. The important factors are:

** Identify the money makers.

** Identify the time wasters.

** Identify the minimum-pay jobs and money-losing tasks.

Keep your job choices moving in the direction of getting more of the money-making jobs and cutting down on wasted time. The longer you keep records, the more useful they'll be and the more pieces of information you'll want, so keep your system flexible. Leave room for a few more categories. On these tasks, typists with a microcomputer word processor have a great advantage over others. Once the time management system exists, keeping records takes little more than the time to type in the data from a personal diary.

CONTROL OF INCOME AND EXPENSES

11.31   Financial accounting, also available in microcomputer programs, provides the basis for tax returns and indicates the degree of success your business is having. As with time management, there is no way to avoid keeping records. The question, then, is: what is the easiest, most efficient way to keep them. For many typists, the best basic record-keeper is the same daily diary used for time management. For instance, mine has spaces for cash expenses, mileage, child care, and so forth. Carry the diary with you. Don't trust yourself to remember mileage and cash expenses until you get home.

11.32   When you first start out, get help with your taxes from a qualified accountant. Learn from him or her as much as possible about ways to save on tax money. Often, an accountant's services cost less than the tax savings you recover, and the bill is tax deductible in the next tax year. Furthermore, having an accountant do your taxes may reduce the liklihood of an audit.

Expenses and Mileage

11.33   Record in either a small notebook or a daily diary all trips and every business-related cash expense. For mileage record:

** Destination.

** Purpose of trip.

** Speedometer start.

** Speedometer stop.

** Total miles, door to door.

** Job or work category to be charged.

11.34   For expenses less than $25, the Internal Revenue Service considers a properly kept diary a legitimate record. Save all receipts (ask for them if the cashier doesn't volunteer one). Write on them what you bought. Save them in a shoe box or envelope. The reason for recording in the diary is to save you from a massive sorting job at tax time. It also allows you to keep track of expenses for various jobs so that you can get all expenses reimbursed on jobs that pay time and expenses. Once a month, summarize the expenses on a summary accounting sheet.

11.35   To keep track of expenses, consider some form of "one-write" system that writes on an accounting sheet when you write a check. Look for a system that will let you write the address on the check and use window envelopes for mailing. I use a system whose accounting sheet gives me 23 columns for categorizing expenses. An alternative to a one-write system is 3-on-a-page checks with carbon paper and blank paper slipped under each page so you automatically keep a duplicate of every check you write.

Billing

11.36 For billing, use carbonless, color-coded multiple-copy invoice forms with your letterhead and logo, numbered beginning with 100 (so that your first few customers don't realize that theirs is a first job). Print on the bill a statement that payment is due 10 days from date of issue and that overdue accounts are charged an additional fee at the rate of, say, 1.5% per month. As with the checks, plan the form so that the client's address shows through the window in a window envelope. The multiple copy (1) provides a tax record and (2) enables you to send reminders without typing a new bill (you simply pull off the next copy, fold it so the address shows through the window, and mail). The letterhead and logo on the bills advertise your services.

11.37 Most people find a formal printed bill an easy way to tell clients when they expect payment and what the penalties of nonpayment are. To save postage, deliver the top copy of the bill with the work.

PROMOTION

11.38 In college towns, often the only advertising necessary is a 3 x 5 card tacked on bulletin boards with your rates, name, and telephone number. It's also wise to have a small supply of stationary with a letterhead and logo (these can be copied onto good quality paper), matching invoices, and window envelopes (it wastes time to type an address twice).

11.39 If competition is stiff in your geographic area, consider a well-designed brochure that advertises your services. Emphasize:

** The employer's benefits from hiring you (you don't take up space or overhead; he pays you only when he needs you).

** Your special services (see Sections 11.18-11.24).

11.40 For help in reaching the five major typing markets (academic, business, medical, legal, and professional writing) and for more detailed help with establishing and managing a typing business, read Peggy Glenn's <u>How to Start and Run a Successful Home Typing Business</u>.[4] You may also want to join the typist's network that Glenn sponsors and subscribe to her newsletter, <u>ProToType</u>.

11.41 There's no need to restrict yourself to local business. Many national magazines have classified advertising space in which typists frequently advertise. Examples are <u>The Atantic</u> and <u>Writer's Digest</u>.

NOTES TO CHAPTER 11

1. Savvy can be ordered from 111 Eighth Avenue, New York, NY, 10021. Working Woman can be ordered from Hal Publications, Inc., 1180 Avenue of the Americas, New York, NY, 10036.

2. University of Chicago Press, A Manual of Style, 12th ed. (Chicago: University of Chicago Press, 1969).

3. You might also want to read Carol L. O'Neill and Avima Ruder's The Complete Guide to Editorial Free-Lancing, 2d ed. (New York: Dodd-Mead, 1979); also of interest is Dorothy Bestor's "Starting Out as a Freelance Editor," Scholarly Publishing 13 (October 1981): 55-69.

4. (Huntington Beach, California: PIGI Publishing, n.d.). Glenn can be reached at 924 Main Street, Huntington Beach, CA, 92648.

Appendix:
Specifications
for Major Styles

Style sheets are presented in the order in which they appear in Chapters 6, 7, and 8. No sheet is completely filled out. The information given in the sheets is included in either a style manual or corresponce from the organization that sponsors a style. For reasons explained in Chapters 6-8, there are no style sheets for GPO style, AIIE style, MSN style (which is identical to MSH except for documentation style), or CBE style.

Style Sheet

1

STYLE SHEET

Name _____ Address _____

Phones _____ Color of handwriting is: _____

Consultation desired? Y/N   Edit check: Spelling, Y/N   Punctuation, Y/N

Comma rules: Serial? Y/N   After short intro clauses? Y/N

Type of ms. *scholarly paper*   Style *Maths*   Draft/Final copy/Camera-Ready/OCR

Corrections: Eraser/Fluid/Tape/Cut-Ins/Strikeovers   Hyphenation: Y/N

Paper wt., qual./Master (type) *good quality white*   Size: (Ltr)/Legl/ISO

Ribbon: (Carbon)/Cloth/None   Self-corr OK? (Y)/N   Color: (Black)/Other: _____   Boldface: (Y)/N

Margins: Left 1 1/4"   Right 1 1/4"   Top 1"   Bottom 1"

Pitch: Pica/Elite/Propor.   Style _____ Tabs _____   Boldface: (Y)/N

Underline: Words/Solid; For'n wrds? Y/N   Spelling: Webster/Oxford/Other

Spacing of text: Triple/(Double)/Single/One and a half/Other

Chp/(Art)/title (All caps)/Up-Low/Init cap   (Centered left to right)/flush left

Chapter # Arabic/Roman/None   With/Above ttl/NA _____ empty lines

Word "Chapter" before number?   Caps/Up-Low/NA/Other

Spaces: Top to # _____ # to title _____   Title to text _____

Running Hds: Lt/Rt/Alt/NA   Top/Bottom   Title pgs? Y/N   Spaces to RH _____

Text page #s Lt/(Rt)/Alt/Ctr   (Top)/Bottom   Title pgs? Y/(N)   Ident wrds? Y/N

Prelim. #s   Lt/Rt/Alt/Ctr   Top/Bottom   Title pgs? Y/N   Ident wrds? Y/N

Part	Exist?	Seq. #2	Separate? Y/N	Counted? Y/N	Pg. # Typed On? Y/N
Frontispiece	Y/N	Y/N	Y/N	Y/N	Y/N; Rom/Ara.
Title page	(Y)/N	1	Y/(N)	(Y)/N	Y/N; Rom/Ara.
Half-title	Y/N	Y/N	Y/N	Y/N	Y/N; Rom/Ara.
Dedication	Y/N	Y/N	Y/N	Y/N	Y/N; Rom/Ara.
Epigraph	Y/N	Y/N	Y/N	Y/N	Y/N; Rom/Ara.

2

Style Sheet

Part	Exist?	Seq.	Separate? Y/N	Counted? Y/N	Pg. # Typed On?
Tbl of Cnts	(Y)/N	Y/N	Y/N	Y/N	Y/N; Rom/Ara.
List of ill	Y/N	Y/N	Y/N	Y/N	Y/N; Rom/Ara.
List of Tbls	Y/N	Y/N	Y/N	Y/N	Y/N; Rom/Ara.
Foreword	Y/N	Y/N	Y/N	Y/N	Y/N; Rom/Ara.
Preface	Y/N	Y/N	Y/N	Y/N	Y/N; Rom/Ara.
Acknowl	(Y)/N	(Y)/N 5	Y/(N)	Y/N	Y/N; Rom/(Ara).
Biography	Y/N	Y/N	Y/N	Y/N	Y/N; Rom/Ara.
Abstract	(Y)/N	(Y)/N 2	(Y)/N	Y/N	Y/N; Rom/Ara.
Classif schem	(Y)/N	(Y)/N 4	(Y)/N	Y/N	Y/N; Rom/Ara.
Part ttl pg	Y/N	Y/N	Y/N	Y/N	Y/N; Rom/Ara.
Text	(Y)/N	(Y)/N 3	(Y)/N	Y/N	Y/N; Rom/Ara.
Chp ttl pgs	Y/N	Y/N	Y/N	Y/N	Y/N; Rom/Ara.
Each table	(Y)/N	(Y)/N 6	(Y)/N	Y/N	Y/N; Rom/Ara.
Each illus	(Y)/N	(Y)/N 6	(Y)/N	Y/N	Y/N; Rom/(Ara).
Caption list	Y/N	Y/N	Y/N	Y/N	Y/N; Rom/Ara.
Notes	Y/N	Y/N	Y/N	Y/N	Y/N; Rom/Ara.
Chp notes	Y/N	Y/N	Y/N	Y/N	Y/N; Rom/Ara.
Ref notes	Y/N	Y/N	Y/N	Y/N	Y/N; Rom/Ara.
Ident refs	Y/N	Y/N	Y/N	Y/N	Y/N; Rom/Ara.
List of refs	Y/N	Y/N	Y/N	Y/N	Y/N; Rom/Ara.
Bibliography	(Y)/N	(Y)/N 7	(Y)/N	(Y)/N	Y/N; Rom/(Ara).
Appendix	Y/N	Y/N	Y/N	Y/N	Y/N; Rom/Ara.
Budget	Y/N	Y/N	Y/N	Y/N	Y/N; Rom/Ara.
Glossary	Y/N	Y/N	Y/N	Y/N	Y/N; Rom/Ara.
List of abbr	Y/N	Y/N	Y/N	Y/N	Y/N; Rom/Ara.
Index	Y/N	Y/N	Y/N	Y/N	Y/N; Rom/Ara.
Supplem Text	Y/N	Y/N	Y/N	Y/N	Y/N; Rom/Ara.

Text: empty lines, running head/pg. # to text _____   Par. Ind. 5   Just. Y/N

Documentation: Author (date)/[#] (#) #/superscript: *,**,#/#s/a,b,c

Notes typed: Footnotes/End of subunit/Collected, end of doc./(Not allowed)

Designate by: *,#/1,2/a,b   Superscript? Y/N   Spaces after? _____

First line: Flush left/Para. Ind.   Period after #?   Y/N

Turnovers: Flush left/Block, hang under first letter

Style Sheet

Comments, examples: *Title underlined*

Figures: Models? Y/N #ed? Y/N, Rom/Ara. #, capt: L/Ctr/Ind ___ /U-Line

Number: With "Figure" or "Fig."? Y/N Caps/Init Top/Btm Per. after? Y/N

Caption: Caps/U-L/Init Top/Btm On line w/#? Y/N Per. after? Y/N

First line: Flush left/Indent ___ spaces

Turnovers: Flush left/Centered/Hanging Ind. ___ spaces.

Comments, examples:

Displayed equations: (Centered) Indented ___ spaces from left margin

Equation Numbers: (L)/R/None/NA; In Brackets/(Parens)/Open

Comments: *Number only significant equations*

Readability analyses? Y/N Word count? Y/N

Key words: (Y)/N Total # of copies, including original: 1/2/3/4/5/6

Treatment of uncertain bibliographic data:

Other comments:

Check which classification scheme to use.

Copyright transfer required.

Style Sheet

Symbols: (Handwritten)/Type only/Rub-on Accents: Handwritten/Type/Rub-on

Rules for numbers in text: Hum./(Tech.)/Other: ___ Percent/(%)

Headings: Empty lines above ___ below ___ Turnovers: Block/Indent 1 space

Boldface

1-level Caps/U-L/(Init. cap)/ed Underline Y/N C/L/(Para. leader)

2-level (Caps)/U-L/Init. cap/#ed Underline Y/N C/L/(Para. leader)

3-level Caps/U-L/(Init. cap)/#ed Underline (Y)/N C/L/(Para. leader)

4-level Caps/U-L/Init. cap/#ed Underline Y/N C/L/Para. leader

Quotations: Brit/Amer Block 5/7/10 L/R/Both Indnt 1st line 0/3/5 sp.

Empty lines: Above ___ Below ___ Spacing: Dbl/Sngl/Other ___

Emphasis: [_]ed Inside quotes/( ) at end/in note

Comments:

Tables: Models? (Y)/N #ed? Y/N, (Rom)/Ara. #, ttl: Fl. Left/(Ctr)/U-Line

Number: W/"Table"? (Y)/N Per. after? Y/N Spcs to ttl ___

Title: Caps/U-L/(Init) On line with number? Y/(N) Per. at end? Y/(N)

Turnovers: Flush left/Centered/Hanging Ind. ___ spaces.

Bars: Above #? Y/(N) Below: (ttl) (1) or 2 lines/(Col. hds)/(Body)/notes

Cl. hds: Caps/U-L/Init Ctr/Lft Turnovers: Ctr/Lft

Stubs: Caps/U-L/Init Turnovers: Flush/Indent ___ spaces

Substb: Caps/U-L/Init Indent ___ spaces Turnovers: Ind. ___ more sp.

Notes: Which comes first: Source ___ General ___ Specific ___

"SOURCE" and "NOTE" as labels? Y/N Caps/Initial cap only

Specific: *,#/1,2/a,b Superscript? Y/N Spaces after?

First line: Flush left/Indent ___ spaces

Turnovers: Flush left/Ind. ___ sp./Ind. to first letter of note

Tables in text: ___ spaces above and below

Panel 1

STYLE SHEET

Name _____ Address _____

Phones _____ Color of handwriting is: _____

Consultation desired? Y/N   Edit check: Spelling, Y/N   Punctuation, Y/N

Comma rules: Serial? Y/N   After short intro clauses? Y/N

Type of ms. _Scholarly paper_   Style _AMA_   Draft/Final copy/Camera-Ready/OCR

Corrections: Eraser/Fluid/Tape/Cut-ins/Strikeovers   Hyphenation: Y/N

Paper wt., qual./Master (type) _White bond_   Size: (Ltr)/Legl/ISO

Ribbon: (Carbon)/Cloth/None   Self-corr OK? (Y)N   Color: (Black)/Other: ____

Margins: Left 1"   Right 1"   Top 1"   Bottom 1"   Boldface: (Y)N

Pitch: Pica/Elite/Proport.   Style ____   Tabs ____

Underline: Words/Solid; For'n wrds? Y/N   Spelling: Webster/Oxford/Other

Spacing of text: Triple/(Double)/Single/One and a half/Other

Chp/(Artcl) title (All caps)/Up-Low/Init cap   Centered left to right/(flush left)

Chapter # Arabic/Roman/Other   With/Above ttl/NA ____ empty lines

Word "Chapter" before number?   Caps/Up-Low/NA/Other

Spaces: Top to ____ # to title   Title to text

Running Hds: Lt/(Rt)/Alt/NA   (Top)/Bottom   Title pgs? Y(N)   Spaces to RH

Text page #s Lt/(Rt)/Alt/Ctr   (Top)/Bottom   Title pgs? (Y)N   Ident wrds? Y/N

Prelim. #s Lt/Rt/Alt/Ctr   Top/Bottom   Title pgs? Y/N   Ident wrds? Y/N

Part	Exist?	Seq. #?	Separate? Y/N	Counted? Y/N	Pg. # Typed On? Y/N
Frontispiece	Y/N	Y/N	Y/N	Y/N	Y/N; Rom/Ara.
Title page	(Y)N	(Y)N	(Y)N	(Y)N	(Y)N; Rom/(Ara.)
Half-title	Y/N	Y/N	Y/N	Y/N	Y/N; Rom/Ara.
Dedication	Y/N	Y/N	Y/N	Y/N	Y/N; Rom/Ara.
Epigraph	Y/N	Y/N	Y/N	Y/N	Y/N; Rom/Ara.

Panel 2

Tbl of Cnts	Y/N	Y/N	Y/N	Y/N	Rom/Ara.
List of Ill	Y/N	Y/N	Y/N	Y/N	Rom/Ara.
List of Tbls	Y/N	Y/N	Y/N	Y/N	Rom/Ara.
Foreword	Y/N	Y/N	Y/N	Y/N	Rom/Ara.
Preface	Y/N	Y/N	Y/N	Y/N	Rom/Ara.
Acknowl	(Y)N	(Y)N	(Y)N	(Y)N	Rom/(Ara.)
Biography	Y/N	Y/N	Y/N	Y/N	Rom/Ara.
Abstract	(Y)N 2	(Y)N	(Y)N	(Y)N	Rom/(Ara.)
Classif schem	Y/N	Y/N	Y/N	Y/N	Rom/Ara.
Part ttl pg	(Y)N 3	(Y)N	(Y)N	(Y)N	Rom/(Ara.)
Text	(Y)N	(Y)N	(Y)N	(Y)N	Rom/Ara.
Chp ttl pgs	Y/N	Y/N	Y/N	Y/N	Rom/Ara.
Each table	(Y)N 6	(Y)N	(Y)N	(Y)N	Rom/(Ara.)
Each Illus	(Y)N	(Y)N	(Y)N	Y(N)	Rom/(Ara.)
Caption list	(Y)N 7	(Y)N	(Y)N	(Y)N	Rom/(Ara.)
Notes	Y/N	Y/N	Y/N	Y/N	Rom/Ara.
Chp notes	Y/N	Y/N	Y/N	Y/N	Rom/Ara.
Ref notes	Y/N	Y/N	Y/N	Y/N	Rom/Ara.
Ident refs	Y/N	Y/N	Y/N	Y/N	Rom/Ara.
List of refs	(Y)N 5	(Y)N	(Y)N	(Y)N	Rom/(Ara.)
Bibliography	Y/N	Y/N	Y/N	Y/N	Rom/Ara.
Appendix	Y/N	Y/N	Y/N	Y/N	Rom/Ara.
Budget	Y/N	Y/N	Y/N	Y/N	Rom/Ara.
Glossary	Y/N	Y/N	Y/N	Y/N	Rom/Ara.
List of abbr	Y/N	Y/N	Y/N	Y/N	Rom/Ara.
Index	Y/N	Y/N	Y/N	Y/N	Rom/Ara.
Supplem Text	Y/N	Y/N	Y/N	Y/N	Rom/Ara.

Text: empty lines, running head/pg. # to text __ Par. Ind. __ Just. Y/N

Documentation: Author (date)/[L#] (#) (#) superscript: *,**,#/#s/a,b,c

Notes typed: Footnotes/End of subunit/Collected, end of doc. (Not allowed)

Designate by: *,#/1,2/a,b   Superscript? Y/N   Spaces after?

First line: Flush left/Para. Ind.   Period after #? Y/N

Turnovers: Flush left/Block, hang under first letter

Style Sheet

Comments, examples:

*Sequence of notes: * † ‡ §*

Figures: Models? (Y)/N, Rom/(Ara) #, capt: (1)/Ctr/Ind ___ /U-Line
Number: With "Figure" or "Fig."? (Y)/N Caps/(Init) Top/(Btm) Per. after? (Y)/N
Caption: Caps/U-L/(Init) Top/(Btm) On line w/#? (Y)/N Per. after? (Y)/N
First line: Flush left/Indent ___ spaces
Turnovers: (Flush left)/Centered/Hanging Ind. ___ spaces.

Comments, examples:

Captions limited to 40 words
Typed in separate list

Displayed equations: Centered/Indented ___ spaces from left margin
Equation Numbers: L/R/None/NA; In Brackets/Parens/Open
Comments:

Readability analyses? (Y)/N Word count? Y/N; Typed where? ___
Key words? (Y)/N Total # of copies, including original: 1/2/(3)/4/5/6
Treatment of uncertain bibliographic data:

Other comments: *Either letter- or ISO-size paper is OK.*
No right justification allowed.
Copyright transfer required.

Style Sheet

Symbols: Handwritten/Type only/Rub-on   Accents: Handwritten/Type/Rub-on
Rules for numbers in text: Hum./Tech./Other: ___   Percent/%
Headings: Empty lines above ___ below ___   Turnovers: Block/Indent 1 space

(1-level) Caps/(U-L)/Init. cap/#ed Boldface Under-line Y/(N) (C)/L/Para. leader
(2-level) Caps/(U-L)/Init. cap/#ed Boldface Under-line Y/(N) C/L/(Para. leader)
3-level Caps/U-L/Init. cap/#ed Under-line Y/N C/L/Para. leader
4-level Caps/U-L/Init. cap/#ed Under-line Y/N C/L/Para. leader

Quotations: Brit/Amer Block 5/7/10 L/R/Both Indnt 1st line 0/3/5 sp.
Empty lines: Above ___ Below ___ Spacing: Dbl/Sngl/Other
Emphasis: [ ]ed inside quotes/( ) at end/in note
Comments:

Tables: Models? (Y)/N #ed? (Y)/N, Rom/(Ara) #, ttl: Fl. Left/(Cntr)/U-Line *Dashes*
Number: W/"table"? (Y)/N Caps/(U-L)/Init On line with number? (Y)/N Per. after? (Y)/N Spcs to ttl ___
Title: Caps/(U-L)/Init Turnovers: Flush left/(Centered)/Hanging Ind. ___ spaces.
Bars: Above #? (Y)/N Below: (ttl)/(1) or 2 lines)/(Col. hds)/(Body) notes
Cl. hds: Caps/(U-L)/Init (Ctr)/Lft Turnovers: (Ctr)/Lft
Stubs: Caps/(U-L)/Init Turnovers: Flush/Indent (2) spaces
Substb: Caps/(U-L)/Init Indent ___ spaces Turnovers: Ind. ___ more sp.
Notes: Which comes first: Source ___ General ___ Specific ___
"SOURCE" and "NOTE" as labels? Y/N Caps/Initial cap only
Specific: (*,#)1,2/a,b Superscript? Y/N Spaces after? ___
First line: (Flush left)/Ind. (5) spaces
Turnovers: (Flush left)/Ind. ___ sp./Ind. to first letter of note (Not allowed)
Tables in text: ___ spaces above and below (Not allowed)

Style Sheet (1)

STYLE SHEET

Name _____ Address _____
Phones _____ Color of handwriting is: _____

Consultation desired? Y/N   Edit check: Spelling, Y/N   Punctuation, Y/N
Comma rules: Serial? Y/N   After short intro clauses? Y/N
Type of ms. *Scholarly Paper*   Style *ASTM*   Draft/Final copy/Camera-Ready/OCR
Corrections: Eraser/Fluid/Tape/Cut-Ins/Strikeovers   Hyphenation: Y/N
Paper wt., qual./Master (type) *75 g/m*   Size: (Ltr)/Legl/ISO
Ribbon: (Carbon)/Cloth/None   Self-corr OK? (Y)/N   Color: (Black)/Other: ___   Boldface: (Y)/N
Margins: Left *1½"*   Right *1"*   Top *1"*   Bottom *1"*
Pitch: Pica/Elite/Proport.   Style ___   Tabs ___
Underline: Words/Solid; For'n wrds? Y/N   Spelling: Webster/Oxford/Other
Spacing of text: Triple/(Double)/Single/One and a half/Other
Chp/(Artcl) title   All caps/(Up-Low)/Init cap   (Centered left to right)/flush left
Chapter # Arabic/Roman/None   With/Above ttl/NA ___ empty lines
Word "Chapter" before number?   Caps/Up-Low/NA/Other
Spaces: Top to # ___   # to title ___   Title to text

Running Hds: Lt/Rt/Alt/NA   Top/Bottom   Title pgs? Y/N   Spaces to RH
Text page #s *Any clear system is ok* ~~Lt/Rt/Alt/Ctr Top/Bottom~~   Title pgs? Y/N   Ident wrds? Y/N
Prelim. #s   Lt/Rt/Alt/Ctr Top/Bottom   Title pgs? Y/N   Ident wrds? Y/N

Part	Exist? Seq. #?	Separate? Y/N	Counted? Y/N	Pg. # Typed On? Y/N
Frontispiece	Y/N Y/N	Y/N	Y/N	Y/N; Rom/Ara.
Title page	(Y)/N Y(N) *1*	Y/N	Y/N	Y/N; Rom/Ara.
Half-title	Y/N Y/N	Y/N	Y/N	Y/N; Rom/Ara.
Dedication	Y/N Y/N	Y/N	Y/N	Y/N; Rom/Ara.
Epigraph	Y/N Y/N	Y/N	Y/N	Y/N; Rom/Ara.

Style Sheet (2)

Part					
Tbl of Cnts	Y/N	Y/N	Y/N	Y/N; Rom/Ara.	
List of Ill	Y/N	Y/N	Y/N	Y/N; Rom/Ara.	
List of Tbls	Y/N	Y/N	Y/N	Y/N; Rom/Ara.	
Foreword	Y/N	Y/N	Y/N	Y/N; Rom/Ara.	
Preface	Y/N	Y(N)	Y/N	Y/N; Rom/Ara.	
Acknowl	(Y)N *5*	(Y)N	(Y)N	(Y)N; Rom/(Ara.)	
Biography	(Y)N *2*	Y(N)	(Y)N	(Y)N; Rom/(Ara.)	
Abstract	(Y)N *3*	Y(N)	(Y)N	(Y)N; Rom/(Ara.)	
Classif schem	Y/N	Y/N	Y/N	Y/N; Rom/Ara.	
Part ttl pg	*4*	(Y)N	(Y)N	Y/N; Rom/Ara.	
Text	(Y)N	(Y)N	(Y)N	Y/N; Rom/(Ara.)	
Chp ttl pgs	Y/N	(Y)N	(Y)N	Y/N; Rom/(Ara.)	
Each table	(Y)N *9*	(Y)N	(Y)N	(Y)N; Rom/(Ara.)	
Each illus	(Y)N *11*	(Y)N	(Y)N	(Y)N; Rom/(Ara.)	
Caption list	(Y)N *10*	(Y)N	(Y)N	(Y)N; Rom/(Ara.)	
Notes	(Y)N *8*	(Y)N	(Y)N	(Y)N; Rom/Ara.	
Chp notes	Y/N	Y/N	Y/N	Y/N; Rom/Ara.	
Ref notes	Y/N	Y/N	Y/N	Y/N; Rom/Ara.	
Ident refs	Y/N	Y/N	Y/N	Y/N; Rom/Ara.	
List of refs	(Y)N *7*	(Y)N	(Y)N	(Y)N; Rom/(Ara.)	
Bibliography	Y/N	Y/N	Y/N	Y/N; Rom/Ara.	
Appendix	Y(N) *6*	(Y)N	(Y)N	(Y)N; Rom/(Ara.)	
Budget	Y/N	Y/N	Y/N	Y/N; Rom/Ara.	
Glossary	Y/N	Y/N	Y/N	Y/N; Rom/Ara.	
List of abbr	Y/N	Y/N	Y/N	Y/N; Rom/Ara.	
Index	Y/N	Y/N	Y/N	Y/N; Rom/Ara.	
Supplem Text	Y/N	Y/N	Y/N	Y/N; Rom/Ara.	

Text: empty lines, running head/pg. # to text ___ Par. Ind. ___ Just. Y/N
Documentation: Author (date)([#]) (#) #/superscript: *,**,#/#s/a,b,c
Notes typed: Footnotes/End of subunit/(Collected, end of doc)/Not allowed
Designate by: *,#/1,2/a,b   Superscript? (Y)N   Spaces after? *None*
First line: Flush left/(Para. Ind.)   Period after #? Y/N
Turnovers: (Flush left)/Block, hang under first letter

Style Sheet

Comments, examples:
Use "a,b,c" for all notes. Underline title

Figures: Models? (Y)/N, Rom/(Ara) #, capt:(L)Ctr/Ind — (U-Line)
Number: With "Figure" or "Fig." (Y)/N (Caps)/Init Top/Btm Per. after? Y/N
Caption: Caps/U-L/Init Top/Btm On line w/#? (Y)/N Per. after?(Y)/N
First line: Flush left/Indent — spaces
Turnovers: (Flush left)/Centered/Hanging Ind. — spaces.

Comments, examples: *Figures must be camera-ready*
Captions go on caption list.

Displayed equations: (Centered)Indented — spaces from left margin
Equation Numbers: (L)R/None/NA; In Brackets?(Parens)Open
Comments: *Number only those referred to*

Readability analyses? (Y)/N Word count? Y/N; Typed where?
Key words? (Y)/N Total # of copies, including original: 1/2/3/4/(5)6
Treatment of uncertain bibliographic data: *Omit it.*

Other comments:
Keywords go on abstract page
Numbers: use words from one to twelve.
Use numerals for other numbers.
Copyright transfer required.

Style Sheet

Symbols: Handwritten/Type only/Rub-on   Accents: Handwritten/Type/Rub-on
Rules for numbers in text: Hum./(Tech)/Other: *See Comm.* (Percent)/%
Headings: Empty lines above 2 below 2   Turnovers: Block/Indent 1 space

1-level	Caps/(U-L)/Init. cap/#ed	Boldface Underline (Y)/N C/(L)/Para. leader
2-level	Caps/(U-L)/Init. cap/#ed	Underline (Y)/N C/(L)/Para. leader
3-level	Caps/(U-L)/Init. cap/#ed	Underline (Y)/N C/(L)/Para. leader *Dashes after*
4-level	Caps/U-L/Init. cap/#ed	Underline Y/N C/L/Para. leader

Quotations: Brit/Amer   Block (5)/7/10 L/R/(Both) Indnt 1st line 0/3/5 sp.
Empty lines: Above ___ Below ___   Spacing: (Dbl)/Sngl/Other
Emphasis: []ed Inside quotes/() at end/in note
Comments: *Leave extra space above and below*

Tables: Models? (Y)/N #ed?(Y)/N, Rom/(Ara) #, ttl: Fl. Left/(Cntr)/U-Line
Number: W/"table"?(Y)/N *Dashes* Per. after?(Y)/N Spcs to ttl ___
Title: Caps/U-L/(Init) On line with number?(Y)/N Per. at end?(Y)/N
Turnovers: Flush left/(Centered)/Hanging Ind. ___ spaces.
Bars: Above #? Y/(N) Below: (ttl)/(1)/or 2 lines)/Col. hds/(body)/notes
Cl. hds: Caps/(U-L)/Init Turnovers: (Flush)/Indent ___ spaces
Stubs: Caps/(U-L)/Init Turnovers: (Flush)/Indent ___ spaces
Substb: Caps/U-L/Init Indent ___ spaces Turnovers: Ind. ___ more sp.
Notes: Which comes first: Source 1 General ___ Specific 2
"SOURCE" and "NOTE" as labels? (Y)/N Caps (Initial cap only)
Specific: *,#/1,2/(a,b) Superscript? Y/N Spaces after? 2
First line: (Flush left)/Indent 5 spaces
Turnovers: (Flush left)/Ind. ___ sp./Ind. to first letter of note (Not allowed)
Tables in text: ___ spaces above and below

Style Sheet

Tbl of Cnts	Y/N	Y/N	Y/N	Y/N	Y/N; Rom/Ara.
List of Ill	Y/N	Y/N	Y/N	Y/N	Y/N; Rom/Ara.
List of Tbls	Y/N	Y/N	Y/N	Y/N	Y/N; Rom/Ara.
Foreword	Y/N	Y/N	Y/N	Y/N	Y/N; Rom/Ara.
Preface	Y/N	Y/N	Y/N	Y/N	Y/N; Rom/Ara.
Acknowl	Y/N	Y/N	Y/N	Y/N	Y/N; Rom/Ara.
Biography	Y/N	Y/N	Y/N	Y/N	Y/N; Rom/Ara.
Abstract	Y/N	Y/N	Y/N	Y/N	Y/N; Rom/Ara.
Classif schem	Y/N	Y/N	Y/N	Y/N	Y/N; Rom/Ara.
Part ttl pg	Y/N	Y/N	Y/N	Y/N	(Y)/N; Rom/(Ara).
Text	(Y)/N 2	(Y)/N	Y/N	(Y)/N	Y/N; Rom/Ara.
Chp ttl pgs	Y/N	Y/N	Y/N	Y/N	Y/N; Rom/Ara.
Each table	(Y)/N 2	(Y)/N	(Y)/N	Y/N	Y/N; Rom/Ara.
Each illus	(Y)/N 2	(Y)/N	(Y)/N	Y/N	Y/N; Rom/Ara.
Caption list	(Y)/N 3	(Y)/N	(Y)/N	Y/N	(Y)/N; Rom/(Ara).
Notes	(Y)/N	Y/N	Y/N	Y/N	Y/N; Rom/Ara.
Chp notes	Y/N	Y/N	Y/N	Y/N	Y/N; Rom/Ara.
Ref notes	Y/N	Y/N	Y/N	Y/N	Y/N; Rom/Ara.
Ident refs	Y/N	Y/N	Y/N	Y/N	Y/N; Rom/Ara.
List of refs	Y/N	Y/N	Y/N	Y/N	Y/N; Rom/Ara.
Bibliography	(Y)/N 4	(Y)/N	(Y)/N	Y/N	(Y)/N; Rom/(Ara).
Appendix	Y/N	Y/N	Y/N	Y/N	Y/N; Rom/Ara.
Budget	Y/N	Y/N	Y/N	Y/N	Y/N; Rom/Ara.
Glossary	Y/N	Y/N	Y/N	Y/N	Y/N; Rom/Ara.
List of abbr	Y/N	Y/N	Y/N	Y/N	Y/N; Rom/Ara.
Index	Y/N	Y/N	Y/N	Y/N	Y/N; Rom/Ara.
Supplem Text	Y/N	Y/N	Y/N	Y/N	Y/N; Rom/Ara.

Text: empty lines, running head/pg. # to text __3__ Par. Ind. __5__ Just. Y/N

Documentation: Author (date)/[#] (#) #(Superscript) *, **, #(s) a,b,c

Notes typed: Footnotes/End of subunit/(Collected, end of doc.)/Not allowed

Designate by: *, #(1,2) a,b Superscript? (Y)/N Spaces after? __1__

First line: (Flush left)/Para. Ind. ___ Period after #? Y/(N)

Turnovers: (Flush left)/Block, hang under first letter

Style Sheet

S T Y L E   S H E E T

Name _____ Address _____

Phones _____ Color of handwriting is: _____

Consultation desired? (Y)/N Edit check: Spelling, Y/N Punctuation, Y/N

Comma rules: Serial? (Y)/N After short intro clauses? Y/N

Type of ms. _Research Paper_ Style _MLA res. paper_ Draft/Final copy/Camera-Ready/OCR

Corrections: Eraser/Fluid/Tape/Cut-Ins/Strikeovers Hyphenation: Y/N

Paper wt., qual./Master (type) _20 pound white_ Size: (Ltr)/Legl/ISO

Ribbon: Carbon/Cloth/None Self-corr OK? Y/N Color: (Black)/Other: ___

Margins: Left _/"_ Right _/"_ Top _/"_ Bottom _/"_ Boldface: Y/N

Pitch: Pica/Elite/Proport. Style ___ Tabs ___

Underline: Words/Solid; For'n wrds? Y/N Spelling: Webster/Oxford/Other

Spacing of text: Triple/(Double)/Single/One and a half

Chp (Artcl)/title All caps/(Up-Low)/Init cap (Centered left to right)/flush left ___ empty lines

Chapter # Arabic/Roman/None With/Above ttl/NA Caps/Up-Low/NA/Other

Word "Chapter" before number? ___ Title to text _3 empty lines_

Spaces: Top to # ___ # to title ___

Running Hds: Lt/Rt/Alt/NA Top/Bottom

Text page #s Lt/(Rt)/Alt/Ctr (Top)/Bottom Spaces to RH ___ Ident wrds? (Y)/N

Prelim. #s Lt/Rt/Alt/Ctr Top/Bottom Ident wrds? Y/N

Part	Exist?	Seq. #2	Separate? Y/N	Counted? Y/N	Pg. # Typed On? Y/N
Frontispiece	Y/N	Y/N	Y/N	Y/N	Y/N; Rom/Ara.
Title page	(Y)/N 1	Y/(N)	Y/N	Y/N	Y/N; Rom/Ara.
Half-title	Y/N	Y/N	Y/N	Y/N	Y/N; Rom/Ara.
Dedication	Y/N	Y/N	Y/N	Y/N	Y/N; Rom/Ara.
Epigraph	Y/N	Y/N	Y/N	Y/N	Y/N; Rom/Ara.

Style Sheet

Comments, examples: *Use double lines under column heads. Indent only specific notes. "Source" and "note" are flush left.*

Figures: Models? Y/N #ed? Y/N, Rom/Ara. #, capt: L/Ctr/Ind ___ /U-Line

Number: With "Figure" or "Fig."? Y/N Caps/Init Top/Btm Per. after? Y/N

Caption: Caps/U-L/Init Top/Btm On line w/#? Y/N Per. after? Y/N

First line: Flush left/Indent ___ spaces

Turnovers: Flush left/Centered/Hanging Ind. ___ spaces.

Comments, examples:

Displayed equations: Centered/Indented ___ spaces from left margin

Equation Numbers: L/R/None/NA; In Brackets/Parens/Open

Comments:

Readability analyses? Y/N Word count? Y/N; Typed where?

Key words: Y/N Total # of copies, including original: 1/2/3/4/5/6

Treatment of uncertain bibliographic data:

Other comments: *Don't type page number on first page of text, notes, bibliography.*

Style Sheet

Symbols: (Handwritten)/Type only/Rub-on Accents: (Handwritten)/Type/Rub-on

Rules for numbers in text: (Hum)/Tech./Other: _____ (Percent)%

Headings: Empty lines above **3** below **3** Turnovers: Block/Indent 1 space

Rom.

1-level Caps(U-L)/Init. cap/(ed) Underline Y(N) C(L)/Para. leader
2-level Caps(U-L)/Init. cap/#ed Underline Y(N) C(L)/Para. leader
3-level Caps/U-L/Init. cap/#ed Underline Y/N C/L/Para. leader
4-level Caps/U-L/Init. cap/#ed Underline Y/N C/L/Para. leader

Quotations: Brit/(Amer) Block 5/7/(10) (L)/R/Both Indnt 1st line 0/(3)/5 sp.

Empty lines: Above **2** Below **2** Spacing: (Dbl)/Sngl/Other

Emphasis: [ ]ed inside quotes(.) at end in note

Comments:

Tables: Models? (Y)/N #ed? (Y)N, Rom/(Ara.) #, ttl: Fl. Left/(Cntr)/U-Line **1**

Number: W/"table"? (Y)N Per. after? Y(N) Spcs to ttl (N)

Title: (Caps)/U-L/Init On line with number? Y(N) Per. at end? Y(N)

Turnovers: Flush left/(Centered)/Hanging Ind. ___ spaces. (Col. hds)/Body/Notes

Bars: Above #? Y(N) Below: (ttl)/(1 or 2 lines) Ctr(Lft)

Cl. hds: Caps/U-L(Init) Turnovers: Flush/(Indent **3** spaces)

Stubs: Caps/U-L(Init) Turnovers: Flush/(Indent **3** spaces)

Substb: Caps/U-L/Init Indent ___ spaces Turnovers: Ind. ___ more sp.

Notes: Which comes first: Source **1** General ___ Specific **2**

"SOURCE" and "NOTE" as labels? Y/N Caps/(Initial cap only)

Specific: *,#/1,2/(a,b) Superscript? (Y)N Spaces after? **1**

First line: (Flush left)/Ind. ___ sp./Ind. to first letter of note

Turnovers: (Flush left)/Ind. ___ spaces/(Indent **5** spaces)

Tables in text: **3** spaces above and below

Style Sheet

Page 1

STYLE SHEET

Name _____ Address _____

Phones _____ Color of handwriting is: _____

Consultation desired? Y/N   Edit check: Spelling, Y/N   Punctuation, Y/N

Comma rules: Serial? Y/N   After short intro clauses? Y/N

Type of ms. _Dissertation_ Style _MLA Diss._   Draft/Final copy/Camera-Ready/OCR

Corrections: Eraser/Fluid/Tape/Cut-ins/Strikeovers   Hyphenation: Y/N

Paper wt., qual./Master (type) _20 pound white_   Size: (Ltr)/Legl/ISO

Ribbon: Carbon/Cloth/None   Self-corr OK? Y/N   Color: Black/Other: _____

Margins: Left _2"_   Right _1"_   Top _1"_   Bottom _4_

Pitch: Pica/Elite/Proport.   Style _____   Tabs _____   Boldface: Y/N

Underline: Words/Solid; For'n wrds? Y/N   Spelling: Webster/Oxford/Other _____

Spacing of text: Triple/(Double)/Single/One and a half/Other _____

(Chp)/Artcl title   All caps/(Up-Low)/Init cap   (Centered left to right)/flush left

Chapter # (Arabic)/Roman/None   With (Above tt)/NA _3_ empty lines

Word "Chapter" before number? _Yes_   Caps/(Up-Low)/NA/Other _____

Spaces: Top to # _2"_   # to title _3 empty lines_   Title to text _3 empty lines_

Part	Exist? Seq. #2	Separate? Y/N	Counted? Y/N	Pg. # Typed On? Y/N
Frontispiece	Y/N	Y/N	Y/N	Y/N; Rom/Ara.
Title page	(Y)/N 1	(Y)/N	(Y)/N	Y/(N); (Rom)/Ara.
Half-title	Y/N	Y/N	Y/N	Y/N; Rom/Ara.
Dedication	Y/N	Y/N	Y/N	Y/N; Rom/Ara.
Epigraph	Y/N	Y/N	Y/N	Y/N; Rom/Ara.

Running Hds: Lt/Rt/Alt/(NA)   Top/Bottom   Title pgs? Y/N   Spaces to RH _____

Text page #s Lt/(Rt)/Alt/Ctr   (Top)/Bottom   Title pgs? Y/(N)   Ident wrds? Y/(N)

Prelim. #s   Lt/(Rt)/Alt/Ctr   (Top)/Bottom   Title pgs? Y/(N)   Ident wrds? Y/(N)

Page 2

Part	Exist?	Seq. #	Separate?	Counted?	Rom/Ara
Tbl of Cnts	(Y)/N	(Y)/N 3	(Y)/N	Y/(N)	(Rom)/Ara.
List of Ill	Y/N	Y/N	Y/N	Y/N	Rom/Ara.
List of Tbls	Y/N	Y/N	Y/N	Y/N	Rom/Ara.
Foreword	Y/N	Y/N	Y/N	Y/N	Rom/Ara.
Preface	(Y)/N	(Y)/N 4	(Y)/N	Y/(N)	(Rom)/Ara.
Acknowl	(Y)/N	(2)/N 4	Y/(N)	Y/N	Rom/Ara.
Biography	Y/N	Y/N	(Y)/N	Y/N	Rom/Ara.
Abstract	(Y)/N	(Y)/N 2	(Y)/N	Y/(N)	(Rom)/Ara.
Classif schem	Y/N	Y/N	Y/N	Y/N	Rom/Ara.
Part ttl pg	Y/N	Y/N	Y/N	Y/N	Rom/Ara.
Text	(Y)/N	(Y)/N 6	(Y)/N	(Y)/N	Rom/(Ara).
Chp ttl pgs	(Y)/N	(Y)/N 5	(Y)/N	(Y)/N	Rom/Ara.
Each table	(Y)/N	(Y)/N 6	Y/(N)	Y/(N)	Rom/Ara.
Each illus	(Y)/N	(Y)/N 6	Y/(N)	Y/(N)	Rom/Ara.
Caption list	Y/N	Y/N	Y/N	Y/N	Rom/Ara.
Notes	(Y)/N	(Y)/N 6	Y/(N)	Y/(N)	Rom/Ara.
Chp notes	Y/N	Y/N	Y/N	Y/N	Rom/Ara.
Ref notes	Y/N	Y/N	Y/N	Y/N	Rom/Ara.
Ident refs	Y/N	Y/N	Y/N	Y/N	Rom/Ara.
List of refs	Y/N	Y/N	Y/N	Y/N	Rom/Ara.
Bibliography	(Y)/N	(Y)/N 7	(Y)/N	Y/N	Rom/(Ara).
Appendix	Y/N	Y/N	Y/N	Y/N	Rom/Ara.
Budget	Y/N	Y/N	Y/N	Y/N	Rom/Ara.
Glossary	Y/N	Y/N	Y/N	Y/N	Rom/Ara.
List of abbr	Y/N	Y/N	Y/N	Y/N	Rom/Ara.
Index	Y/N	Y/N	Y/N	Y/N	Rom/Ara.
Supplem Text	Y/N	Y/N	Y/N	Y/N	Rom/Ara.

Text: empty lines, running head/pg. # to text _3_ Par. Ind. _5_ Just. Y/N

Documentation: Author (date)/[#]   (#)   [#]   (#)   (superscript)   *,**,#(#s)a,b,c

Notes typed: (Footnotes)/End of subunit/Collected, end of doc./Not allowed

Designate by: *,#,(1,2)a,b   Superscript? (Y)/N   Spaces after? _1_

First line: Flush left/(Para. Ind.)   Period after #? Y/N

Turnovers: (Flush left)/Block, hang under first letter   _single-space_

Comments, examples: *Use double line under column heads. Indent only specific notes. "Source" and "note" are flush left.*

Figures: Models? Y/N #ed? Y/N, Rom/Ara. #, capt: L/Ctr/Ind ___ /U-Line

Number: With "Figure" or "Fig."? Y/N Caps/Init Top/Btm Per. after? Y/N
Caption: Caps/U-L/Init On line w/#? Y/N Per. after? Y/N
First line: Flush left/Indent ___ spaces
Turnovers: Flush left/Centered/Hanging Ind. ___ spaces.

Comments, examples:

Displayed equations: Centered/Indented ___ spaces from left margin
Equation Numbers: L/R/None/NA; In Brackets/Parens/Open

Comments:

Readability analyses? Y/N Word count? Y/N; Typed where?
Key words: Y/N Total # of copies, including original: 1/2/3/4/5/6
Treatment of uncertain bibliographic data:

Other comments: *Single-space notes, double-space between them. Don't type page numbers on first page of abstract, table of contents, preface, chapters, bibliography.*

Style Sheet

Style Sheet

Symbols: (Handwritten)/Type only/Rub-on Accents: (Handwritten)/Type/Rub-on
Rules for numbers in text: (Hum)/Tech./Other: ___ (Percent)/%
Headings: Empty lines above ___ below ___ Turnovers: Block/Indent 1 space

1-level Caps (U-L)/Init. cap/(#ed) Underline Y/(N) (C)/L/Para. leader
2-level Caps (U-L)/Init. cap/(#ed) Underline Y/(N) C/(L)/Para. leader
3-level Caps/U-L/Init. cap/#ed Underline Y/N C/L/Para. leader
4-level Caps/U-L/Init. cap/#ed Underline Y/N C/L/Para. leader

Quotations: Brit/(Amer) Block 5/7/(10) (L)/R/Both Indnt 1st line 0/(3)/5 sp.
Empty lines: Above 2 Below 2 Spacing: Dbl/(Sng)/Other ___
Emphasis: []ed inside quotes/(( ) at end)/(in note)
Comments:

Tables: Models? (Y)/N
Number: W/"table"? (Y)/N (Caps)/U-L/Init On line with number? (Y)/N Per. after? Y/(N) Spcs to ttl 1
Title: (Caps)/U-L/Init Turnovers: Flush left/(Centered)/Hanging Ind. ___ spaces.
Bars: Above #? Y/(N) Below: (ttl) (1)/or 2 lines) (Col. hds.)/body notes Turnovers: Ctr/(Lft)
Cl. hds: Caps/U-L/(Init) Turnovers: Ctr/(Lft)
Stubs: Caps/U-L/(Init) Turnovers: Flush/(Indent 3) spaces
Substb: Caps/U-L/Init Indent ___ spaces Turnovers: Ind. ___ more sp.
Notes: Which comes first: Source 1 General ___ Specific 2
"SOURCE" and "NOTE" as labels? Y/N Caps/(Initial cap only) Superscript? (Y)/N Spaces after? 1
Specific: *,#/1,2(a,b) Superscript? (Y)/N Spaces after? 1
First line: (Flush left)/Ind. ___ sp./Ind. to first letter of note
Turnovers: Flush left/Ind. ___ sp./Ind. to first letter of note
Tables in text: 3 spaces above and below

Style Sheet

Part	Exist?	Seq. #?	Separate?	Counted?	Pg. # Typed On?
Tbl of Cnts	(Y)/N	(Y)/N 3	(Y)/N	(Y)/N	(Y)/N; (Rom)/Ara.
List of ill	Y/N	Y/N	Y/N	Y/N	Y/N; Rom/Ara.
List of Tbls	Y/N	Y/N	Y/N	Y/N	Y/N; Rom/Ara.
Foreword	Y/N	Y/N	Y/N	Y/N	Y/N; Rom/Ara.
Preface	Y/N	Y/N	Y/N	Y/N	Y/N; Rom/Ara.
Acknowl	(Y)/N	(Y)/N 4	(Y)/N	(Y)/N	(Y)/N; (Rom)/Ara.
Biography	Y/N	Y/N	Y/N	Y/N	Y/N; Rom/Ara.
Abstract	Y/N	Y/N	Y/N	Y/N	Y/N; Rom/Ara.
Classif schem	Y/N	Y/N	Y/N	Y/N	Y/N; Rom/Ara.
Part ttl pg	Y/N	Y/N	Y/N	Y/N	Y/N; Rom/Ara.
Text	(Y)/N	(Y)/N 6	Y/(N)	(Y)/N	(Y)/N; Rom/(Ara).
Chp ttl pgs	(Y)/N	(Y)/N 5	(Y)/N	(Y)/N	(Y)/N; Rom/(Ara).
Each table	(Y)/N	(Y)/N 6	(Y)/(N)	Y/N	Y/N; Rom/Ara.
Each illus	(Y)/N	(Y)/N 6	(Y)/(N)	Y/N	Y/N; Rom/Ara.
Caption list	Y/N	Y/N	Y/(N)	Y/N	Y/N; Rom/Ara.
Notes	(Y)/N	(Y)/N 6	Y/N	(Y)/N	Y/N; Rom/Ara.
Chp notes	Y/N	Y/N	Y/N	Y/N	Y/N; Rom/Ara.
Ref notes	Y/N	Y/N	Y/N	Y/N	Y/N; Rom/Ara.
Ident refs	Y/N	Y/N	Y/N	Y/N	Y/N; Rom/Ara.
List of refs	Y/N	Y/N	Y/N	Y/N	Y/N; Rom/Ara.
Bibliography	(Y)/N	(Y)/N 7	Y/N	(Y)/N	(Y)/N; Rom/(Ara).
Appendix	Y/N	Y/N	Y/N	Y/N	Y/N; Rom/Ara.
Budget	Y/N	Y/N	Y/N	Y/N	Y/N; Rom/Ara.
Glossary	Y/N	Y/N	Y/N	Y/N	Y/N; Rom/Ara.
List of abbr	Y/N	Y/N	Y/N	Y/N	Y/N; Rom/Ara.
Index	Y/N	Y/N	Y/N	Y/N	Y/N; Rom/Ara.
Supplem Text	Y/N	Y/N	Y/N	Y/N	Y/N; Rom/Ara.

Text: empty lines, running head/pg. # to text __1__ Par. Ind. _6-8 spaces_ Just. Y/N

Documentation: Author (date)/[#] (#) #(Superscript): *,**,#/$/a,b,c

Notes typed: (Footnotes)/End of subunit/Collected, end of doc./Not allowed

Designate by: *,#/(1,2)a,b Superscript? (Y)/N Spaces after? _Nona_

First line: Flush left/(Para. Ind.) Period after #? Y/(N)

Turnovers: (Flush left)/Block, hang under first letter

STYLE SHEET

Name _____

Address _____

Phones _____ Color of handwriting is: _____

Consultation desired? Y/N Edit check: Spelling, Y/N Punctuation, Y/N

Comma rules: Serial? (Y)/N After short intro clauses? Y/N

Type of ms. _Dissertation_ Style _Turabian_ Draft/Final copy/Camera-Ready/OCR

Corrections: Eraser/Fluid/Tape/Cut-Ins/Strikeovers Hyphenation: Y/N

Paper wt., qual./Master (type) _20 pound, 50% Rag_ Size: (Ltr)/Legl/ISO

Ribbon: Carbon/Cloth/None Self-corr OK? Y/N Color: (Black)/Other: _____ Boldface: Y/N

Margins: Left _1½"_ Right _1"_ Top _1"_ Bottom _1"_

Pitch: Pica/Elite/Proport. Style _(unfamiliar ones)_ Tabs _____ Boldface: Y/N

Underline: Words/Solid; For'n wrds? (Y)/N Spelling: (Webster)/Oxford/Other _____

Spacing of text: Triple/(Double)/Single/One and a half/Other

(Chp)/Artcl title (All caps)/Up-Low/Init cap (Centered left to right)/flush left

Chapter # (Arabic)/Roman/None With/(Above ttl)/NA _2 empty lines_

Word "Chapter" before number? _Yes_ # to title _2 empty lines_

Spaces: Top to # _2"_ # to text _2 empty lines_

Running Hds: Lt/Rt/Alt/(NA) Top/Bottom

Text page #s Lt/Rt/Alt/(Ctr) (Top)/Bottom

Prelim. #s Lt/Rt/Alt/(Ctr) (Top)/Bottom

Part	Exist?	Seq. #?	Separate? Y/N	Counted? Y/N	Pg. # Typed On? Y/N
Frontispiece	Y/N	Y/N	Y/N	Y/N	Y/N; Rom/Ara.
Title page	(Y)/N	(Y)/N 1	Y/(N)	(Y)/N	Y/(N); (Rom)/Ara.
Half-title	Y/N	Y/N	Y/N	Y/N	Y/N; Rom/Ara.
Dedication	Y/N	Y/N	Y/N	Y/N	Y/N; Rom/Ara.
Epigraph	Y/N	Y/N	Y/N	Y/N	Y/N; (Rom).
Blank page	(Y)	(Y) 2	(Y)	(Y)	(Y)

Style Sheet

4

Comments, examples: *Try to get each table on a single page. Single-space body, double-space rest unless 1½ space will squeeze long table onto one page*

Figures: Models? (Y)N, Rom/(Ara.) #, capt: L/Ctr/(Ind 6-8sp) U-line

Number: With "Figure" or "Fig." (Y)N Caps/(Init) Top/(Btm) Per. after? (Y)N

Caption: Caps/U-L/(Init) Top/(Btm) On line w/#? 6-8 spaces Per. after? (Y)N

First line: Flush left/(Indent) ___ spaces.

Turnovers: (Flush left)/Centered/Hanging Ind. ___ spaces.

Comments, examples: *Center short Captions flush to right with no period. For long ones use paragraph indent on first line.*

Displayed equations: Centered/Indented ___ spaces from left margin

Equation Numbers: L/R/None/NA; In Brackets/Parens/Open

Comments:

Readability analyses? Y/N Word count? Y/N; Typed where?

Key words: Y/N Total # of copies, including original: 1/(2)/3/4/5/6

Treatment of uncertain bibliographic data:

Other comments: *On first page of abstract, table of contents, acknowledgments, chapters, and bibliography, type page number in center of bottom margin.*

Style Sheet

3

Symbols: Handwritten/Type only/Rub-on Accents: Handwritten/Type/Rub-on

Rules for numbers in text: (Hum.)/Tech./Other: ___ Percent/%

Headings: Empty lines above 1 below 1 Turnovers: (Block)/Indent 1 space
Center if first line is centered

1-level Caps/(U-L)/Init. cap/#ed Underline (Y)N C/(L)/Para. leader

2-level Caps/(U-L)/Init. cap/#ed Underline Y/(N) C/(L)/Para. leader

3-level Caps/(U-L)/Init. cap/#ed Underline (Y)N C/(L)/Para. leader

4-level Caps/(U-L)/Init. cap/#ed Underline Y/(N) C/(L)/Para. leader
5-level *U-L* (4) *Underline (Y)* (4) *Para. leader*

Quotations: Brit/(Amer) Block B/7/10 (L)R/Both Indnt 1st line 0/3/4/5sp.

Empty lines: Above 1 Below 1 Spacing: Dbl/(Sng)/Other

Emphasis: []ed Inside quotes/(() at end)/In note

Comments:

Tables: Models? (Y)N #ed? (Y)N, Rom/(Ara) #, ttl: Fl. Left/(Cntr)/U-Line Spcs to ttl 1

Number: W/"table"? (Y)N (Caps)U-L/Init Per. after? Y/(N) Per. at end? Y/(N)

Title: (Caps)U-L/Init On line with number? (Y)N Turnovers: Flush left/(Centered)/Hanging Ind. ___ spaces... *one line*

Bars: Above #? Y/(N) Below: (ttl)/(1 or 2 lines)/(Col. hds)/(body)/notes Turnovers: Ctr/(Lft)

Cl. hds: Caps/U-L/(Init) Turnovers: Flush/(Indent 2 spaces)

Stubs: Caps/U-L/(Init) Indent no spaces Turnovers: Ind. 2 more sp.

Substb: Caps/U-L/(Init) Which comes first: Source 1 General 2 Specific 3

Notes: "SOURCE" and "NOTE" as labels? Y/N (Caps)/Initial cap only

Specific: *,#/1,2/(a,b) Superscript? (Y)N Spaces after? 0

First line: (Flush left) Ind. ___ sp./Ind. to first letter of note

Turnovers: (Flush left) Ind. ___ sp./Ind. to first letter of note

Tables in text: ___ spaces above and below

STYLE SHEET

1

Name _____ Address _____

Phones _____ Color of handwriting is: _____

Consultation desired? Y/N   Edit check: Spelling, Y/N   Punctuation, Y/N

Comma rules: Serial? Y/N   After short intro clauses? Y/N

Type of ms. _Trade book_ Style _MSH_ Draft/Final copy/Camera-Ready/OCR

Corrections: Eraser/Fluid/Tape/Cut-Ins/Strikeovers   Hyphenation: Y/N

Paper wt., qual./Master (type) _Good quality_ Self-corr OK? Y/N   Color: (Black)/Other: ___ Size: (Ltr)/Legl/ISO

Ribbon: (Carbon)/Cloth/None

Margins: Left 1"   Right 1"   Top 1"   Bottom 1"

Pitch: (Pica)/Elite/Proport.   Tabs ___   Style ___   Boldface: Y/N

Underline: Words/Solid; For'n wrds? Y/N   Spelling: (Webster)/Oxford/Other ___

Spacing of text: Triple/(Double)/Single/One and a half/Other

(Chp)/Artcl title   All caps   (Up-Low)   Init cap   (Centered left to right)/flush left

Chapter # (Arabic)/Roman/None   With/(Above) ttl/NA   _3_ empty lines

Word "Chapter" before number? _Yes_   Caps-(Up-Low) NA/Other

Spaces: Top to # _17_   # to title _3_   Title to text _3_

Running Hds: Lt/Rt/Alt/NA   Top/Bottom   Title pgs? Y/N   Spaces to RH ___

Text page #s   Lt/(Rt)/Alt/Ctr   (Top)/Bottom   Ident wrds? Y/(N)   Y/(N)

Prelim. #s   Lt/(Rt)/Alt/Ctr   (Top)/Bottom   Ident wrds? Y/(N)   Y/(N)

Part	Exist? Y/N	Seq. #2	Separate? Y/N	Counted? Y/N	Pg. # Typed On? Y/N	
Frontispiece	Y/N		Y/N	Y/N	Y/N;	Rom/Ara.
Title page	(Y)N	1	(Y)N	(Y)N	Y/(N);	Rom/Ara.
Half-title	Y/N			Y/N	Y/(N);	Rom/Ara.
Dedication	(Y)N	2	(Y)N	(Y)N	Y/(N);	Rom/Ara.
Epigraph	Y/N			Y/N	Y/N;	Rom/Ara.

2

			Y/N; Rom/Ara.
Tbl of Cnts	(Y)N	(Y)N (Y)N (Y)N	(Y)N; (Rom)/Ara.
List of Ill	(Y)N 3	(Y)N (Y)N (Y)N	(Y)N; (Rom)/Ara.
List of Tbls	(Y)N 4	(Y)N (Y)N (Y)N	(Y)N; (Rom)/Ara.
Foreword	Y/N	Y/N Y/N Y/N	Y/N; Rom/Ara.
Preface	(Y)N 5	Y/(N) Y/N (Y)N	(Y)N; (Rom)/Ara.
Acknowl	(Y)N 5	Y/N Y/N Y/N	Y/N; Rom/Ara.
Biography	Y/N	Y/N Y/N Y/N	Y/N; Rom/Ara.
Abstract	Y/N	Y/N Y/N Y/N	Y/N; Rom/Ara.
Classif schem	(Y)N	Y/N Y/N (Y)N	Y/N; Rom/Ara.
Part ttl pg	(Y)N 9	Y/(N) (Y)N (Y)N	Y/(N); (Rom)/(Ara.)
Text	(Y)N 7	Y/(N) (Y)N (Y)N	(Y)N; Rom/(Ara.)
Chp ttl pgs	(Y)N 6	Y/N (Y)N (Y)N	(Y)N; Rom/Ara.
Each table	(Y)N 10	Y/N (Y)N (Y)N	(Y)N; Rom/(Ara.)
Each illus	(Y)N 13	Y/(N) (Y)N (Y)N	Y/N; Rom/Ara.
Caption list	Y/N	Y/N Y/N Y/N	Y/N; Rom/Ara.
Notes	(Y)N	Y/N (Y)N (Y)N	(Y)N; Rom/Ara.
Chp notes	(Y)N 8	Y/N (Y)N (Y)N	Y/N; Rom/Ara.
Ref notes	Y/N	Y/N Y/N Y/N	Y/N; Rom/(Ara.)
Ident refs	Y/N	Y/N Y/N Y/N	Y/N; Rom/Ara.
List of refs	Y/N	Y/N Y/N Y/N	Y/N; Rom/Ara.
Bibliography	(Y)N 11	(Y)N Y/N (Y)N	(Y)N; Rom/(Ara.)
Appendix	(Y)N 12	(Y)N (Y)N (Y)N	(Y)N; Rom/(Ara.)
Budget	Y/N	Y/N Y/N Y/N	Y/N; Rom/Ara.
Glossary	Y/N	Y/N Y/N Y/N	Y/N; Rom/Ara.
List of abbr	Y/N	Y/N Y/N Y/N	Y/N; Rom/Ara.
Index	Y/N	Y/N Y/N Y/N	Y/N; Rom/Ara.
Supplem Text	Y/N	Y/N Y/N Y/N	Y/N; Rom/Ara.

Text: empty lines, running head/pg. # to text _2_ Par. Ind. ___ Just. Y/N

Documentation: Author (date)/[#] (#) #/(superscript) *,**,#/#s a,b,c

Notes typed: Footnotes/(End of subunit)/Collected, end of doc./Not allowed

Designate by: *,#/(1,2) a,b   Superscript? Y/(N)   Spaces after? _2_

First line: (Flush left)/Para. Ind.   Period after #? (Y)N

Turnovers: (Flush left)/Block, hang under first letter

Style Sheet

Comments, examples: *Use numbers for specific notes when the body contains words. Use *, †, ‡, §, ||, # when the body contains numbers and letters. Example: table of matrices.*

Figures: Models? (Y)/N   #ed? (Y)/N, Rom/(Ara) #, capt: L/Ctr/Ind (5)/U-Line

Number: With "Figure" or "Fig."? (Y)/N   Caps/(Init)/Top/(Btm)   Per. after? Y/(N)

Caption: Caps/U-L/(Init)   Top/(Btm)   On line w/#? (Y)/N   Per. after? Y/(N)

   First line: Flush left/(Indent 5 spaces)

   Turnovers: Flush left/Centered/(Hanging Ind. 5 spaces)

   Comments, examples: *Put a period after the caption only when the legend immediately follows.*

Displayed equations: (Centered)/Indented ___ spaces from left margin

Equation Numbers: L/(R)/None/NA; In Brackets/(Parens)/Open

   Comments: *Number only the equations that are referred to in text.*

Readability analyses? Y/N   Word count? Y/N; Typed where? ___

Key words: Y/N   Total # of copies, including original: 1/2/3/4/5/6

Treatment of uncertain bibliographic data:

Other comments: *As Chapter 1 points out, this book follows a modified version of MSH to accommodate printing requirements. This style sheet is filled out strictly according to MSH requirements. It does not reflect the modifications.*

Style Sheet

Symbols: Handwritten/Type only/Rub-on   Accents: Handwritten/Type/Rub-on

Rules for numbers in text: (Hum.)/Tech./Other: ___ (Percent)/%

Headings: Empty lines above ___ below ___   Turnovers: Block/Indent 1 space

(1-level) Caps/(U-L)/Init. cap/#ed   Underline Y/N (C)/L/Para. leader

(2-level) Caps/(U-L)/Init. cap/#ed   Underline Y/(N) C/(L)/Para. leader

(3-level) Caps/(U-L)/Init. cap/#ed   Underline Y/(N) (C)/L/Para. leader

4-level   Caps/U-L/Init. cap/#ed   Underline Y/N C/L/Para. leader

Quotations: Brit/Amer   Block 5/7/#8 (L)/R/Both Indnt 1st line (C)/3/5 sp.
   "a few spaces"

Empty lines: Above 2 Below 2   Spacing: (Dbl)/Sngl/Other

Emphasis: []ed Inside quotes/(.) at end/In note

Comments:

Tables:

Number: Models? (Y)/N   #ed? (Y)/N, Rom/(Ara) #, ttl: Fl. Left/(Cntr)/U-Line

   W/"table"? (Y)/N   Caps/(U-L)/Init   On line with number? Y/(N)   Per. at end? Y/(N)   Spcs to ttl 1

Title: Caps/(U-L)/Init   Turnovers: Flush left/(Centered)/Hanging Ind. ___ spaces — *one line* (notes in body)

Bars: Above Y/(N)   Below (ttl) (1 or 2 lines)   Turnovers: (Ctr)/Lft

Cl. hds: Caps/(U-L)/Init (Ctr)/Lft   Turnovers: Flush left/(Indent 2 spaces)

Stubs: Caps/U-L/(Init)   Indent 2 spaces   Turnovers: Ind. ___ more sp.

Substb: Caps/U-L/(Init)   Turnovers: Ind. ___ more sp.

Notes: Which comes first: Source 1 General 2 Specific 3

   "SOURCE" and "NOTE" as labels? (Y)/N   Caps/(Initial cap only)

Specific: *,#/1,2,(a,b)   Superscript? (Y)/N   Spaces after? 1

First line: (Flush left)/Ind. ___ sp./Ind. to first letter of note

Turnovers: (Flush left)/Ind. ___ spaces

Tables in text: ___ spaces above and below

STYLE SHEET

Name _____ Address _____

Phones _____ Color of handwriting is: _____

Consultation desired? Y/N   Edit check: Spelling, Y/N   Punctuation, Y/N

Comma rules: Serial? (Y)/N   After short intro clauses? Y/N

Type of ms. _Scholarly Paper_   Style _AIP_   Draft/Final copy/Camera-Ready/OCR

Corrections: Eraser/Fluid/Tape/Cut-ins/Strikeovers   Hyphenation: Y/N

Paper wt., qual./Master (type) _Whik bond_   Size: Ltr/Legl/(ISO)

Ribbon: Carbon/Cloth/None   Self-corr OK? Y/N   Color: (Black)/Other: _____

Margins: Left "_wide_"   Right "_Wide_" Top "_wide_" Bottom "_wide_"   Boldface: (Y)/N

Pitch: Pica/Elite/Proport.   Style _____ Tabs _____

Underline: Words/Solid; For'n wrds? Y/N   Spelling: Webster/Oxford/Other

Spacing of text: Triple/(Double)/Single/One and a half/Other

Chp (Artcl) title   All caps/Up-Low/(Init cap)   Centered left to right/(flush left)

Chapter # Arabic/Roman/None   With/Above ttl/NA   _____ empty lines

Word "Chapter" before number?   Caps/Up-Low/NA/Other

Spaces: Top to # _____ # to title _____ Title to text _____

Running Hds: Lt/Rt/Alt/NA   Top/Bottom   Y/N   Title pgs? Y/N   Spaces to RH _____

Text page #s Lt/Rt/Alt/Ctr   Top/Bottom   Y/N   Title pgs? (Y)/N   Ident wrds? Y/N

Prelim. #s Lt/Rt/Alt/Ctr   Top/Bottom   Y/N   Title pgs? Y/N   Ident wrds? Y/N

Part	Exist?	Seq. #2	Separate? Y/N	Counted? Y/N	Pg. # Typed On? Y/N
Frontispiece	Y/N	Y/N	Y/N	Y/N	Y/N; Rom/Ara.
Title page	(Y)/N	(Y)/N 1	Y/(N)	(Y)/N	Y/N; Rom/(Ara).
Half-title	Y/N	Y/N	Y/N	Y/N	Y/N; Rom/Ara.
Dedication	Y/N	Y/N	Y/N	Y/N	Y/N; Rom/Ara.
Epigraph	Y/N	Y/N	Y/N	Y/N	Y/N; Rom/Ara.

Style Sheet

Part	Exist?	Seq.	Separate? Y/N	Counted? Y/N	Pg. # Typed On? Y/N
Tbl of Cnts	Y/N	Y/N	Y/N	Y/N	Y/N; Rom/Ara.
List of Ill	Y/N	Y/N	Y/N	Y/N	Y/N; Rom/Ara.
List of Tbls	Y/N	Y/N	Y/N	Y/N	Y/N; Rom/Ara.
Foreword	Y/N	Y/N	Y/N	Y/N	Y/N; Rom/Ara.
Preface	Y/N	Y/N	Y/(N)	Y/N	Y/N; Rom/Ara.
Acknowl	(Y)/N	(Y)/N 5	Y/N	Y/N	Y/N; Rom/Ara.
Biography	Y/N	Y/N	Y/N	Y/N	Y/N; Rom/Ara.
Abstract	(Y)/N	(Y)/N 2	Y/N	(Y)/N	Y/N; Rom/Ara.
Classif schem	(Y)/N	(Y)/N 3	Y/(N)	(Y)/N	Y/N; Rom/Ara.
Part ttl pg	Y/N	Y/N 4	Y/N	Y/N	Y/N; Rom/Ara.
Text	Y/N	Y/N	(Y)/N	(Y)/N	(Y)/N; Rom/(Ara).
Chp ttl pgs	Y/N	Y/N 7	Y/N	(Y)/N	(Y)/N; Rom/(Ara).
Each table	(Y)/N	(Y)/N 9	(Y)/N	(Y)/N	(Y)/N; Rom/(Ara).
Each illus	(Y)/N	(Y)/N 8	(Y)/N	(Y)/N	(Y)/N; Rom/(Ara).
Caption list	(Y)/N	(Y)/N	(Y)/N	Y/N	Y/N; Rom/Ara.
Notes	Y/N	Y/N	Y/N	Y/N	Y/N; Rom/Ara.
Chp notes	Y/N	(Y)/N	(Y)/N	Y/N	Y/N; Rom/Ara.
Ref notes	Y/N	(Y)/N	(Y)/N	Y/N	Y/N; Rom/Ara.
Ident refs	Y/N	Y/N	Y/N	Y/N	Y/N; Rom/Ara.
List of refs	(Y)/N	(Y)/N 6	(Y)/N	(Y)/N	(Y)/N; Rom/(Ara).
Bibliography	Y/N	Y/N	Y/N	Y/N	Y/N; Rom/Ara.
Appendix	Y/N	(Y)/N	Y/N	Y/N	Y/N; Rom/Ara.
Budget	Y/N	Y/N	Y/N	Y/N	Y/N; Rom/Ara.
Glossary	Y/N	Y/N	Y/N	Y/N	Y/N; Rom/Ara.
List of abbr	Y/N	Y/N	Y/N	Y/N	Y/N; Rom/Ara.
Index	Y/N	Y/N	Y/N	Y/N	Y/N; Rom/Ara.
Supplem Text	(Y)/N	(Y)/N 10	(Y)/N	(Y)/N	(Y)/N; Rom/(Ara).

Text: empty lines, running head/pg. # to text _____ Par. Ind. _____ Just. Y/N

Documentation: Author (date)/[#] (#) #(Superscript): *,**,#(Collected, end of doc.)/Not allowed

Notes typed: Footnotes/End of subunit/(Collected, end of doc.)   _Body_   _Title_

Designate by: *,#,1,2,(a,b)   Superscript? (Y)/N   Spaces after? (Y)/N 2

First line: Flush left/(Para. Ind.)   Period after #? (Y)/N

Turnovers: (Flush left)/Block, hang under first letter

Style Sheet

Comments, examples: *Double lines below title and body.*

Figures: Models? (Y)/N #ed? (Y)/N, Rom/(Ara) #, capt: L/Ctr (Ind 5)/U-Line
Number: With "Figure" or (Fig.?) (Y)/N (Caps)/Init Top/Btm Per. after? (Y)/N
Caption: Caps/U-(L)/Init Top/Btm On line w/#? (Y)/N Per. after? Y/N
First line: Flush left (Indent 5) spaces
Turnovers: (Flush left)/Centered/Hanging Ind. ___ spaces.

Comments, examples: *Do not type captions on illustrations. Do not hand letter.*

Displayed equations: (Centered)/Indented ___ spaces from left margin
Equation Numbers: L/(R)/None/NA; In Brackets/(Parens)/Open
Comments:

Readability analyses? Y/N Word count? Y/N Typed where? ___
Key words: Y/N Total # of copies, including original: 1/2/3/4/5/6
Treatment of uncertain bibliographic data:

Other comments: *Copyright release required. Use superscript letters on notes to title and authors' names. Use wider margins for abstract so it stands out from other text on page.*

Style Sheet

Symbols: Handwritten/(Type) only/Rub-on Accents: Handwritten/(Type)/Rub-on
Rules for numbers in text: Hum./(Tech)/Other: ___ Percent/(%)
Headings: Empty lines above 1 below 1 Turnovers: Block/Indent 1 space
as much as possible

1-level (Caps)/U-L/Init. cap (#ed) *Roman* Underline Y/(N) C/(L) Para. leader
2-level Caps/U-L/(Init.) cap (#ed) *A,B* Underline Y/(N) C/(L) Para. leader
3-level Caps/U-L/(Init.) cap (#ed) *Arabic* Underline Y/(N) C/(L) Para. leader
4-level Caps/U-L/(Init.) cap (#ed) *a,b* Underline (Y)/N C/(L) Para. leader

Quotations: Brit/Amer Block 5/7/10 L/R/Both Indnt 1st line 0/3/5 sp.
Empty lines: Above ___ Below ___ Spacing: Dbl/Sngl/Other ___
Emphasis: [ ]ed Inside quotes/( ) at end/In note
Comments: *No information*

Tables: Models? (Y)/N #ed? (Y)/N, (Rom)/Ara. #, ttl: (Fl. Left)/Cntr/U-Line 1
Number: W/"table"? (Y)/N (Caps)/U-L/Init Per. after? (Y)/N Spcs to ttl 1
Title: (Caps)/U-L/Init On line with number? (Y)/N Per. at end? (Y)/N
Turnovers: (Flush left)/Centered/Hanging Ind. ___ spaces.
Bars: Above #? Y/(N) Below: (ttl) (1 or 2) lines (Col. hds) (body) notes
one line
Cl. hds: Caps/U-L/(Init) Ctr/(Lft) Turnovers: Ctr/(Lft)
Stubs: (Caps)/U-L/Init Turnovers: Flush/Indent ___ spaces
Substb: Caps/U-L/(Init) Indent ___ spaces Turnovers: Ind. ___ more sp.
Notes: Which comes first: Source ___ General ___ Specific 1
"SOURCE" and "NOTE" as labels? Y/N Caps/Initial cap only
Specific: *,#/1,2/(a,b) Superscript? (Y)/N Spaces after? 1
First line: (Flush left) Ind. ___ sp./Ind. to first letter of note
Turnovers: (Flush left) Ind. ___ sp./Ind. to first letter of note
Tables in text: ___ spaces above and below

Style Sheet 1

STYLE SHEET

Name _____ Address _____

Phones _____ Color of handwriting is: _____

Consultation desired? Y/N   Edit check: Spelling, Y/N   Punctuation, Y/N

Comma rules: Serial? (Y)N   After short intro clauses? Y/N

Type of ms. _Scholarly article_   Style _Athens_ Draft/Final copy/Camera-Ready/OCR

Corrections: Eraser/Fluid/Tape/Cut-Ins/Strikeovers   Hyphenation: Y/N

Paper wt., qual./Master (type) _heavy duty_   Size: (Ltr)/Legl/ISO

Ribbon: Carbon/Cloth/None   Self-corr OK? Y/N   Color: Black/Other:

Margins: Left _2cm_ Right _2cm_ Top _2cm_ Bottom _2cm_   Boldface: Y/N

Pitch: Pica/Elite/Proport.   Style _____ Tabs _____

Underline: Words/Solid; For'n wrds? Y/N   Spelling: (Webster)/Oxford/Other

Spacing of text: Triple/(Double)/Single/One and a half/Other

Chp (Art)/title   All caps/Up-Low/Init cap   Centered left to right/flush left

Chapter # Arabic/Roman/None   With/Above ttl/NA ___ empty lines

Word "Chapter" before number?   Caps/Up-Low/NA/Other

Spaces: Top to # ___ # to title ___ Title to text

Running Hds: Lt/Rt/Alt/NA Top/Bottom

Text page #s Lt/(Rt)/Alt/Ctr Top/Bottom

Prelim. #s Lt/Rt/Alt/Ctr (Top)/Bottom

Part	Exist?	Seq. #2	Separate? Y/N	Counted? Y/N	Pg. # Typed On? Y/N
Frontispiece	Y/N		Y/N	Y/N	Y/N; Rom/Ara.
Title page	(Y)N	1	(Y)N	Y/N	Y/N; Rom/(Ara.)
Half-title	Y/N		Y/N	Y/N	Y/N; Rom/Ara.
Dedication	Y/N		Y/N	Y/N	Y/N; Rom/Ara.
Epigraph	Y/N		Y/N	Y/N	Y/N; Rom/Ara.

Style Sheet 2

Tbl of Cnts	Y/N	Y/N	Y/N	Y/N	Y/N; Rom/Ara.	
List of Ill	Y/N	Y/N	Y/N	Y/N	Y/N; Rom/Ara.	
List of Tbls	Y/N	Y/N	Y/N	Y/N	Y/N; Rom/Ara.	
Foreword	Y/N	Y/N	Y/N	Y/N	Y/N; Rom/Ara.	
Preface	Y/N	Y/N	Y/N	Y/N	Y/N; Rom/Ara.	
Acknowl	Y(N)	Y(N) 4	Y(N)	Y/N	Y/N; Rom/Ara.	
Biography	Y/N	Y/N	Y/N	Y/N	Y/N; Rom/Ara.	
Abstract	(Y)N	(Y)N 2	(Y)N	(Y)N	Rom/(Ara.)	
Classif schem	Y/N	Y/N	Y/N	Y/N	Y/N; Rom/Ara.	
Part ttl pg	Y/N	Y/N	Y/N	Y/N	Y/N; Rom/Ara.	
Text	(Y)N	(Y)N 3	(Y)N	(Y)N	Rom/(Ara.)	
Chp ttl pgs	Y/N	Y/N	Y/N	Y/N	Y/N; Rom/Ara.	
Each table	(Y)N	(Y)N 6	(Y)N	(Y)N	Rom/(Ara.)	
Each illus	Y(N)	(Y)N 8	(Y)N	(Y)N	Rom/(Ara.)	
Caption list	(Y)N	(Y)N 7	(Y)N	(Y)N	Rom/(Ara.)	
Notes	Y/N	Y/N	Y/N	Y/N	Y/N; Rom/Ara.	
Chp notes	Y/N	Y/N	Y/N	Y/N	Y/N; Rom/Ara.	
Ref notes	Y/N	Y/N	Y/N	Y/N	Y/N; Rom/Ara.	
Ident refs	Y/N	Y/N	Y/N	Y/N	Y/N; Rom/Ara.	
List of refs	(Y)N	(Y)N 5	(Y)N	(Y)N	Rom/(Ara.)	
Bibliography	Y/N	Y/N	Y/N	Y/N	Y/N; Rom/Ara.	
Appendix	Y/N	Y/N	Y/N	Y/N	Y/N; Rom/Ara.	
Budget	Y/N	Y/N	Y/N	Y/N	Y/N; Rom/Ara.	
Glossary	Y/N	Y/N	Y/N	Y/N	Y/N; Rom/Ara.	
List of abbr	Y/N	Y/N	Y/N	Y/N	Y/N; Rom/Ara.	
Index	Y/N	Y/N	Y/N	Y/N	Y/N; Rom/Ara.	
Supplem Text	Y/N	Y/N	Y/N	Y/N	Y/N; Rom/Ara.	

Text: empty lines, running head/pg. # to text ___ Par. Ind. ___ Just. Y/N

Documentation: (Author (date))[#] (#) (#)/superscript: *,**,#/#s/a,b,c

Notes typed: Footnotes/End of subunit/Collected, end of doc./Not allowed

Designate by: *,#/1,2/a,b   Superscript? Y/N   Spaces after?

First line: Flush left/Para. Ind.   Period after #? Y/N

Turnovers: Flush left/Block, hang under first letter

Style Sheet

Comments, examples:

Figures:
Number: Models? Y/N #ed? Y/N, Rom/Ara. #, capt: L/Ctr/Ind __ /U-Line
With "Figure" or "Fig."? Y/N Caps/Init Top/Btm Per. after? Y/N
Caption: Caps/U-L/Init Top/Btm On line w/#? Y/N Per. after? Y/N
First line: Flush left/Indent __ spaces
Turnovers: Flush left/Centered/Hanging Ind. __ spaces.

Comments, examples: *Type captions only. Illustrations should be professionally prepared.*

Displayed equations: Centered/Indented 5 spaces from left margin
Equation Numbers: L/R/None/NA; In Brackets/Parens/Open

Comments:

Readability analyses? Y/N Word count? Y/N; Typed where?
Key words: Y/N Total # of copies, including original: 1/2/3/4/5/6
Treatment of uncertain bibliographic data:

Other comments: *Do not number the abstract page when the abstract is solely for transmission to Chemical Abstracts. ACheme journals use more than one form of documentation.*

Style Sheet

Symbols: Handwritten/Type only Rub-on Accents: Handwritten/Type Rub-on
Rules for numbers in text: Hum./Tech./Other: _____ Percent/%
Headings: Empty lines above __ below __ Turnovers: Block/Indent 1 space

1-level Caps/U-L/Init. cap/#ed Underline Y/N C/L/Para. leader
2-level Caps/U-L/Init. cap/#ed Underline Y/N C/L/Para. leader
3-level Caps/U-L/Init. cap/#ed Underline Y/N C/L/Para. leader
4-level Caps/U-L/Init. cap/#ed Underline Y/N C/L/Para. leader

Quotations: Brit/Amer Block 5/7/10 L/R/Both Indnt 1st line 0/3/5 sp.
Empty lines: Above __ Below __ Spacing: Dbl/Sngl/Other
Emphasis: [ ]ed inside quotes/( ) at end/in note
Comments:

Tables:
Number: Models? Y/N #ed? Y/N, Rom/Ara. #, ttl: Fl. Left/Cntr/U-Line
W/"table"? Y/N Caps/U-L/Init On line with number? Y/N Per. after? Y/N Spcs to ttl 2
Title: Caps U-L/Init Turnovers: Flush left/Centered/Hanging Ind. __ spaces.
Bars: Above #? Y/N Below: ttl 1/or 2 lines Col. hds./body/notes
Cl. hds: Caps/U-L/Init Turnovers: ttl/Ctr/Lft
Stubs: Caps/U-L/Init Turnovers: Flush/Indent __ spaces
Substb: Caps/U-L/Init Turnovers: Ind. __ more sp.
Notes: Which comes first: Source __ General __ Specific __
"SOURCE" and "NOTE" as labels? Y/N Caps/Initial cap only
Specific: *,#/1,2/a,b Superscript? Y/N Spaces after? 1
First line: Flush left/Indent 5 spaces
Turnovers: Flush left/Ind. __ sp./Ind. to first letter of note
Tables in text: __ spaces above and below

STYLE SHEET (page 2)

Tbl of Cnts	Y/N	Y/N	Y/N	Y/N	Y/N	Rom/Ara.
List of Ill	Y/N	Y/N	Y/N	Y/N	Y/N	Rom/Ara.
List of Tbls	Y/N	Y/N	Y/N	Y/N	Y/N	Rom/Ara.
Foreword	Y/N	Y/N	Y/N	Y/N	Y/N	Rom/Ara.
Preface	Y/N	Y/N	Y/N	Y/N	Y/N	Rom/Ara.
Acknowl	Y/N	Y/N 6	Y/N	Y/N	Y/N	Rom/Ara.
Biography	Y/N	Y/N	Y/N	Y/N	Y/N	Rom/Ara.
Abstract	Y/N	Y/N 2	Y/N	Y/N	*Y/N	Rom/Ara.
Classif schem	Y/N	Y/N	Y/N	Y/N	Y/N	Rom/Ara.
Part ttl pg	Y/N	Y/N	Y/N	Y/N	Y/N	Rom/Ara.
Text	Y/N 3	Y/N	Y/N	Y/N	Y/N	Rom/Ara.
Chp ttl pgs	Y/N	Y/N	Y/N	Y/N	Y/N	Rom/Ara.
Each table	Y/N 8	Y/N	Y/N	Y/N	Y/N	Rom/Ara.
Each Illus	Y/N 10	Y/N	Y/N	Y/N	Y/N	Rom/Ara.
Caption list	Y/N 9	Y/N	Y/N	Y/N	Y/N	Rom/Ara.
Notes (Author/date notes)	Y/N 7	Y/N	Y/N	Y/N	Y/N	Rom/Ara.
Ref notes	Y/N 4	Y/N 6	Y/N	Y/N	Y/N	Rom/Ara.
Ident refs	Y/N	Y/N	Y/N	Y/N	Y/N	Rom/Ara.
List of refs	Y/N 5	Y/N	Y/N	Y/N	Y/N	Rom/Ara.
Bibliography	Y/N	Y/N	Y/N	Y/N	Y/N	Rom/Ara.
Appendix	Y/N	Y/N	Y/N	Y/N	Y/N	Rom/Ara.
Budget	Y/N	Y/N	Y/N	Y/N	Y/N	Rom/Ara.
Glossary	Y/N	Y/N	Y/N	Y/N	Y/N	Rom/Ara.
List of abbr	Y/N	Y/N	Y/N	Y/N	Y/N	Rom/Ara.
Index	Y/N	Y/N	Y/N	Y/N	Y/N	Rom/Ara.
Supplem Text	Y/N	Y/N	Y/N	Y/N	Y/N	Rom/Ara.

Text: empty lines, running head/pg. # to text 1   Par. Ind. 5   Just. Y/N

Documentation: (Author (date))   [#] (#) #/superscript: *,**,#/#s/a,b,c

Notes typed: Footnotes/(End of subunit)/Collected, end of doc./Not allowed

Designate by: *,#/1,2/a,b   Superscript? (Y)/N   Spaces after? Y/N

First line: Flush left/(Para. Ind.)   Period after first letter

Turnovers: (Flush left)/Block, hang under first letter   None

---

STYLE SHEET (page 1)

Name _____   Address _____

Phones _____   Color of handwriting is: _____

Consultation desired? Y/N   Edit check: Spelling, Y/N   Punctuation, Y/N

Comma rules: Serial? (Y)/N   After short intro clauses? Y/N

Type of ms. _Scholarly article_   Style _APA_   Draft/Final copy/Camera-Ready/OCR

Corrections: Eraser/Fluid/Tape/Cut-Ins/Strikeovers   Hyphenation: Y/N

Paper wt., qual./Master (type) _____   Size (Ltr)/Legl/ISO

Ribbon: Carbon/Cloth/None   Self-corr OK? Y/N   Color: (Black)/Other:

Margins: Left 1½"   Right 1"   Top 1-½"   Bottom 1-½"

Pitch: Pica/Elite/Proport.   Style _____   Tabs _____   Boldface: Y/N

Underline: Words/Solid; For'n wrds? Y/N   Spelling: (Webster)/Oxford/Other

Spacing of text: Triple/(Double)/Single/One and a half/Other

Chp (Artcl) title   All caps (Up-Low) Init cap   (Centered left to right)/flush left

Chapter # Arabic/Roman/None   With/Above ttl/NA   ____ empty lines

Word "Chapter" before number? _____   Caps/Up-Low/NA/Other

Spaces: Top to # _____   # to title _____   Title to text _____

Running Hds: Lt/Rt/Alt/NA   Top/Bottom   Title pgs? Y/N   Spaces to RH _____

Text page #s Lt/(Rt)/Alt/Ctr   (Top)/Bottom   Title pgs? Y/N   Ident wrds? (Y)/N

Prelim. #s Lt/Rt/Alt/Ctr   Top/Bottom   Title pgs? Y/N   Ident wrds? Y/N

Part	Exist?	Seq. #2	Separate? Y/N	Counted? Y/N	Pg. # Typed On? Y/N
Frontispiece	Y/N		Y/N	Y/N	Y/N; Rom/Ara.
Title page	(Y)/N (Y)N 1		(Y)/N	Y/(N)	Y/N; Rom/Ara.
Half-title	Y/N		Y/N	Y/N	Y/N; Rom/Ara.
Dedication	Y/N		Y/N	Y/N	Y/N; Rom/Ara.
Epigraph	Y/N		Y/N	Y/N	Y/N; Rom/Ara.

Style Sheet

Comments, examples:

Figures: Models? (Y)/N, Rom/(Ara.) #, capt: L/Ctr (Ind 5)/U-Line
Number: With "Figure" or "Fig."? (Y)/N Caps (Init) Top/Btm Per. after? (Y)/N
Caption: Caps/U-L (Init) Top/Btm On line w/#? (Y)/N Per. after? (Y)/N
First line: Flush left/Indent 5 spaces
Turnovers: Flush left/Centered/Hanging Ind. ___ spaces.

Comments, examples: *Captions go on caption list, not on the illustrations.*

Displayed equations: (Centered)/Indented ___ spaces from left margin
Equation Numbers: L/(R)/None/NA; In Brackets/(Parens)/Open
Comments:

Readability analyses? Y/N Word count? Y/N; Typed where?
Key words: Y/N Total # of copies, including original: 1/2/(3)/4/5/6
Treatment of uncertain bibliographic data:

Other comments: *Submit the original as one of the copies.*

Style Sheet

Symbols: Handwritten/Type only/Rub-on   Accents: Handwritten/Type/Rub-on

Rules for numbers in text: Hum./(Tech.)/Other: ___   Percent/(%)

Headings: Empty lines above 1 below 1   Turnovers: (Block)/Indent 1 space text *(Center if heading is centered)*

(1-level) Caps/(U-L)/Init. cap/#ed   Underline (Y)/N   (C)/L/Para. leader
(2-level) Caps/(U-L)/Init. cap/#ed   Underline (Y)/N   C/(L)/Para. leader
(3-level) Caps/(U-L)/Init. cap/#ed   Underline (Y)/N   C/L/(Para.) leader
4-level Caps/U-L/Init. cap/#ed   Underline Y/N   C/L/Para. leader

Quotations: Brit/(Amer.)   Block (S)/1/10 (L)/R/Both Indnt 1st line (Y)/3/5 sp.

Empty lines: Above 1 Below 1   Spacing: (Dbl)/Sngl/Other

Emphasis: □ed inside quotes/(.) at end/in note

Comments: *If two or more paragraphs, indent first line of second and subsequent paragraphs.*

Tables:

Number: Models? (Y)/N, Rom/(Ara.) #, ttl: Fl. Left/(Cntr)/U-Line
W/"table"? (Y)/N Caps/U-L (Init) On line with number? Y/(N) Spcs to ttl 1

Title: Caps/(U-L) (Init) On line with number? (Centered)/Hanging Ind. Per. after? Y/(N)
Turnovers: Flush left/(Centered)/Hanging Ind. ___ spaces.

Bars: Above #? Y/N Below: (ttl) (1)/or 2 lines/(Col. hds)/(body)/notes

Cl. hds: Caps/U-L (Init) Turnovers: (Ctr)/Lft

Stubs: Caps/U-L (Init) Turnovers: (Flush)/Indent ___ spaces

Substb: Caps/U-L (Init) Indent 2 spaces Turnovers: Ind. 2 more sp.

Notes: Which comes first: Source ___ General 1 Specific 2 Significance 3
"SOURCE" and "NOTE" as labels? (Y)/N Caps (Initial cap only)
Specific: *,#/1,2/(a,b) Superscript? (Y)/N Spaces after? ___
First line: (Flush left)/Indent ___ spaces
Turnovers: (Flush left)/Ind. ___ sp./Ind. to first letter of note *Not allowed*

Tables in text: ___ spaces above and below

S T Y L E   S H E E T

Name _____ Address _____

Phones _____ Color of handwriting is: _____

Consultation desired? Y/N Edit check: Spelling, Y/N Punctuation, Y/N

Comma rules: Serial? Y/N After short intro clauses? Y/N

Type of ms. *Scholarly article* Style *ASA (ASA)* Draft/Final copy/Camera-Ready/OCR

Corrections: Eraser/Fluid/Tape/Cut-Ins/Strikeovers Hyphenation: Y/N

Paper wt., qual./Master (type) *White* Size: (Ltr)/Legl/ISO

Ribbon: Carbon/Cloth/None Self-corr OK? Y/N Color: (Black)/Other: _____

Margins: Left 1/4" Right 1/4" Top 1" Bottom 1"

Pitch: Pica/Elite/Proport. Style _____ Tabs _____ Boldface: Y/N

Underline: Words/Solid; For'n wrds? Y/N Spelling: (Webster)/Oxford/Other

Spacing of text: Triple/(Double)/Single/One and a half/Other

Chp/(Artcl)/Title (All caps)/Up-Low/Init cap (Centered left to right)/flush left

Word "Chapter" before number? _____ With/Above ttl/NA ____ empty lines

Spaces: Top to ____ # to title ____ Title to text

Running Hds: Lt/(Rt)/Alt/NA Top/Bottom Title pgs? Y/N Spaces to RH

Text page #s Lt/(Rt)/Alt/Ctr (Top)/Bottom Title pgs? Y/(N) Ident wrds? Y/N

Prelim. #s Lt/Rt/Alt/Ctr Top/Bottom Title pgs? Y/N Ident wrds? Y/N

Part	Exist?	Seq. #?	Separate? Y/N	Counted? Y/N	Pg. # Typed On? Y/N
Frontispiece	Y/N		Y/N	Y/N	Y/N; Rom/Ara.
Title page	Y/(N) 1		(Y)/N	Y/(N)	Y/N; Rom/Ara.
Half-title	Y/N		Y/N	Y/N	Y/N; Rom/Ara.
Dedication	Y/N		Y/N	Y/N	Y/N; Rom/Ara.
Epigraph	Y/N		Y/N	Y/N	Y/N; Rom/Ara.

Tbl of Cnts	Y/N	Y/N	Y/N	Y/N; Rom/Ara.
List of Ill	Y/N	Y/N	Y/N	Y/N; Rom/Ara.
List of Tbls	Y/N	Y/N	Y/N	Y/N; Rom/Ara.
Foreword	Y/N	Y/N	Y/N	Y/N; Rom/Ara.
Preface	Y/N	Y/N	Y/N	Y/N; Rom/Ara.
Acknowl	(Y)/N	Y/(N)	Y/(N)	Y/N; Rom/Ara.
Biography	(Y)/N	Y/N	Y/N	Y/N; Rom/Ara.
Abstract	(Y)/N	(Y)/N	Y/(N)	Y/N; Rom/Ara.
Classif schem	Y/N	Y/N	Y/N	Y/N; Rom/(Ara.)
Part ttl pg	Y/N	Y/N	Y/N	Y/N; Rom/Ara.
Text	(Y)/N	(Y)/N	Y/N	(Y)/N; Rom/Ara.
Chp ttl pgs	Y/N	Y/N	Y/N	Y/N; Rom/Ara.
Each table	(Y)/N	(Y)/N	(Y)/N	(Y)/N; Rom/(Ara.)
Each illus	(Y)/N	(Y)/N	(Y)/N	(Y)/N; Rom/(Ara.)
Caption list	(Y)/N	Y/N	Y/N	Y/N; Rom/Ara.
Notes	(Y)/N	(Y)/N	Y/N	(Y)/N; Rom/Ara.
Chp notes	Y/N	Y/N	Y/N	Y/N; Rom/Ara.
Ref notes	Y/N	Y/N	Y/N	Y/N; Rom/Ara.
Ident refs	(Y)/N	(Y)/N	Y/N	(Y)/N; Rom/(Ara.)
List of refs	(Y)/N	(Y)/N	Y/N	(Y)/N; Rom/(Ara.)
Bibliography	Y/N	Y/N	Y/N	Y/N; Rom/Ara.
Appendix	Y/N	Y/N	Y/N	Y/N; Rom/Ara.
Budget	Y/N	Y/N	Y/N	Y/N; Rom/Ara.
Glossary	Y/N	Y/N	Y/N	Y/N; Rom/Ara.
List of abbr	Y/N	Y/N	Y/N	Y/N; Rom/Ara.
Index	Y/N	Y/N	Y/N	Y/N; Rom/Ara.
Supplem Text	Y/N	Y/N	Y/N	Y/N; Rom/Ara.

Text: empty lines, running head/pg. # to text 1 Par. Ind. 1 Just. Y/N

Documentation: (Author (date))[#] (#) #/superscript: *,**,#/s/a,b,c

Notes typed: Footnotes/End of subunit/(Collected, end of doc)/Not allowed *None*

Designate by: *,#/(1,2)/a,b Superscript? (Y)/N Spaces after? Y/(N)

First line: (Flush left)/Para. Ind. Period after #? Y/(N)

Turnovers: (Flush left)/Block, hang under first letter

Style Sheet

Comments, examples:

Figures:

Number: Models?(Y)/N #ed?(Y)/N, Rom/(Ara) #, capt:(L)/Ctr/Ind ___ /U-Line
With "(Figure)" or "Fig."? Y/(N) Caps(Init) Top/(Btm) Per. after? (Y)/N
Caption: Caps(U-L)/Init Top/(Btm) On line w/#? (Y)/N Per. after? Y/N
First line: (Flush left)/Indent ___ spaces
Turnovers: Flush left/Centered/(Hanging Ind. 11 spaces

Comments, examples:

Displayed equations: (Centered)/Indented ___ spaces from left margin
Equation Numbers: L/(R)/None/NA; In Brackets/(Parens)/Open
Comments:

Readability analyses? Y/N Word count? Y/N; Typed where?
Key words: Y/N Total # of copies, including original: 1/2/3/4/(5)/6
Treatment of uncertain bibliographic data:

Other comments: *Submit copies only. Retain original*

Style Sheet

Symbols: Handwritten/Type only/Rub-on   Accents: Handwritten/Type/Rub-on

Rules for numbers in text: Hum./Tech./Other: ___   Percent/%

Headings: Empty lines above ___ below ___ Turnovers: Block/Indent 1 space

(1-level) (Caps)/U-L/Init. cap/#ed   Underline Y/(N) C/(I)/Para. leader
(2-level) Caps/(U-L)/Init. cap/#ed   Underline (Y)/N C/(I)/Para. leader
(3-level) Caps/U-L/(Init). cap/#ed   Underline (Y)/N C/L/(Para.) leader
4-level Caps/U-L/Init. cap/#ed   Underline Y/N C/L/Para. leader

Quotations: Brit/(Amer)   Block (5)/7/10 (L)/R/Both Indnt 1st line 0/3/(5) sp.
Empty lines: Above 2 Below 2   Spacing: (Dbl)/Sngl/Other
Emphasis: []ed Inside quotes/(() at end)/in note
Comments:

Tables:

Number: Models?(Y)/N #ed?(Y)/N, Rom/(Ara) #, ttl:(Fl. Left)/Cntr/U-Line
W/"table"? (Y)/N Caps/(U-L)/Init Per. after?(Y)/N Spcs to ttl 2
Title: Caps/(U-L)/Init On line with number? (Y)/N Per. at end? Y/(N)
Turnovers: Flush left/Centered/(Hanging Ind. 10 spaces.
Bars: Above #? Y/(N) Below: (ttl)(1 or (2) lines) (Col. hds) (Body) notes one/line
Cl. hds: Caps/(U-L)/Init (Ctr)/Lft Turnovers: Flush/(Indent 2 spaces
Stubs: Caps/U-L/(Init) Indent 2 spaces Turnovers: Ind. ___ more sp.
Substb: Caps/U-L/(Init) Indent 2 spaces
Notes: Which comes first: Source 1 General 2 Specific 3
"SOURCE" and "NOTE" as labels? (Y)/N Caps/Initial cap only
Specific: *,#/1,2/(a,b) Superscript? (Y)/N Spaces after? 1
First line: (Flush left)/Indent 2 spaces
Turnovers: (Flush left)/Ind. ___ sp./Ind. to first letter of note   *Not allowed*
Tables in text: ___ spaces above and below

Bibliography

Belnap, N. D. 1978. BINDEX: A book indexing system. _Scholarly Publishing_ 9 (January):167-170.

This article describes a computer program, written in FORTRAN, that can index text not prepared on a word processing system. Those who want a copy of the program can get it by sending Belnap a blank magnetic tape.

Bestor, D. 1981. Starting out as a freelance editor. _Scholarly Publishing_ 13 (October):55-69.

Using as a basis findings from a questionnaire survey of veteran editors, Bestor gives practical advice for aspiring freelance editors on training, finding clients, setting rates, specializing, and other topics.

Chickering, R. B. and Hartman, S. 1980. _How to register a copyright and protect your creative work._ New York: Charles Scribner's Sons.

This book summarizes details of the 1978 copyright law.

Clements, W. and Waite, R. G. 1979. _Guide for beginning technical editors._ Livermore, California: Lawrence Livermore Laboratory.

This booklet, written primarily for technical editors, contains technical typing details that would help typists who offer editorial services.

Cross, R. C. 1980. _Indexing books._ Cambridge, Mass.: The Word Guild.

This excellent book, written by an experienced indexer, covers all aspects of preparing indexes.

Datapro Research Corporation. 1977. Current word processing systems, A10-200-101, the current office. Delran, N. J.: Datapro Research Corporation.

This short report on word processing describes the general features of

equipment, applications, advantages, tradeoffs, the marketplace, the out-
look for the future, planning considerations, and salient features.

Day, R. A. 1979. _How to write and publish a scientific paper_. Philadelphia,
Pa.: ISI Press.

This small, well-written book describes characteristics of successful scientific writing in biology and chemistry. It would be helpful to editors,
typists, and writers who specialize in these areas.

De Sola, R. 1977. _Abbreviations dictionary_. 5th ed. Rev. New York: Else-
vier.

This international fifth edition of a 20-year classic supplies more than
160,000 entries and an extraordinary collection of appendixes.

Domitrovic, R. 1977. _How to prepare a style guide_. Washington, D.C.: Society for Technical Communication.

This short pamphlet, available for a small fee from the society, tells editors, typists, and writers how to plan a style guide and what to include in
it.

Eckersley-Johnson, A. L. and Soukhanov, A. H. 1976. _Webster's secretarial_
handbook. Springfield, Mass.: G. & C. Merriam.

This book, written with some references to word processing, would be of
help to typists working in offices. Also contains hints on how to organize
paper files.

Firman Technical Publications. n.d. _Designing technical manuals_. Pembroke,
Mass.: Firman Technical Publications.

This booklet, available from Firman at 95 Church Street, Pembroke, MA.,
02359, explains the creative use of word processing in document production.

Flesch, R. F. 1974. _The art of readable writing_. New York: Harper & Row.

S.T.A.R., a computerized readability analysis program, is based on the
readability measures described in this book.

Garfield, E. 1978. Style in cited references. _Current Contents_ (March
13):5-12.

Garfield decries the variety of bibliographic formats that afflict the work
of writers, editors, and typists.

Ceneral Motors. n.d. S.T.A.R. Detroit: General Motors Public Relations
Staff.

This booklet describes the BASIC language computer program that General Motors wrote to help its staff write readable instructions for mechanics. It
is available free from GM Public Relations Staff, 3044 W. Grand Blvd.,
Detroit, Michigan, 48202. Ask also for the sample program.

Glenn, P. n.d. How to start and run a home typing business. Huntington
Beach, California: PIGI Publishing.

This book, written by a successful free-lance typist and and founder of the
Independent Professional Typists Network, supplies lots of useful information on topics that range from supplies to money, advertising, and customer relations. Glenn can be reached at 924 Main Street, Huntington
Beach, CA 92648.

Gunning, R. 1968. The technique of clear writing. Rev. ed. New York:
McGraw-Hill.

Gunning, a former journalist, gives many useful suggestions for writing
readable prose.

Horn, R. E. 1975. Information Mapping. Datamation (January):85-88.

Horn explains the information-mapping technique for writing computer documentation.

Hughes, B., Coordinating Author. 1979. Typing Manual. Alexandria, Virginia:
Editorial Experts, Inc.

Prepared as a company manual by Editorial Experts, this document contains
many tips that experienced typists would find helpful, especially when they
type documents in GPO style.

Jerome, J. 1980. The poet's handbook. Cincinnati: Writer's Digest.

This book provides technical details of poetry production. Would interest
mainly poet/writers and typists who serve poets.

John, R. C. 1976. Improve your technical writing. Management Accounting
(September):49-52.

John's is one of several good articles on use of plain language.

Laird, E. S. 1973. Data processing secretary's complete handbook. West

Nyack, N.Y.: Parker Publishing.

This book discusses details of typing computer-related materials.

Laird, E. S.   1967.   Engineering Secretary's complete handbook. Englewood
Cliffs, N.J.: Prentice-Hall.

This book covers the specialized details of typing engineering documents.

Landreman, D.   1966.   Technical writing style manual.   Columbus, Ohio: Ohio
Academy of Science.

This manual, designed for use by high school students, would be useful to
typists who frequently type student papers.

McCabe, H. M. and Popham, E. L.   1977.   Word processing: A systems approach to
the office.   New York: Harcourt Brace Jovanovich, Inc.

This book explains in detail the development of word processing. Especially helpful are sections on job organization and several case studies.

McGraw-Hill Book Company.   n.d.   Guidelines for equal treatment of the sexes
in McGraw-Hill Book Company publications.   New York: McGraw-Hill Public Information and Publicity Department.

This publication, available from McGraw-Hill's publicity department (1221
Avenue of the Americas, New York, N.Y., 10020), shows many ways to avoid
sexist language.

McLaughlin, G. H.   1969.   SMOG grading--a new readability formula.   Journal of
Reading (12):639-646.

This article tells how to use the simplest of the readability formulas.

Maloney, M. and Rubenstein, P. M. 1980.   Writing for the media.   Englewood
Cliffs, N. J.: Prentice-Hall.

This book provides the technical details of producing radio and television
shows, educational and promotional films, and filmstrips.

Marra, J. L. 1981. For writers: Understanding the art of layout. Technical
Communication 28 (3):11-13, 40.

Marra, describing an intern program that put writers in the artists' seat,
describes the basic principles of layout as unity, balance, sequence, and
proportion.

Matthies, L. H. 1977. The task outline. <u>The Technical Writing Teacher</u> IV (Spring, 3):107-109.

This article, a companion to Matthies' 1963 article, tells how to write a task outline.

————. 1963. Preparing a playscript procedure. <u>The Systemation News-letter</u>, No. 115. Available from Systemation, Inc., Box 730, Colorado Springs, Colorado, 80901.

Playscripts are a useful way to give instructions on complicated proced-ures. This article tells how to write them.

Menzel, D. H., Jones, H. M., and Boyd, L. G. 1961. <u>Writing a technical paper</u>. New York: McGraw-Hill.

This little classic would be helpful to editors, writers, and typists who specialize in the physical and natural sciences.

Miller, C. and Swift, K. 1980. <u>The handbook of nonsexist writing</u>. New York: Lippincott & Crowell.

This excellent little book offers many ways to avoid sexist writing.

Mullins, C. J. 1977. <u>A guide to writing and publishing in the social and behavioral sciences</u>. New York: Wiley-Interscience.

This book would be useful mainly to editors, writers, and typists who spe-cialize in the social and behavioral sciences. Table 7.1 contains data on the style of scholarly journals in the social and behavioral sciences.

———. 1980. <u>The complete writing guide to preparing reports, proposals, memos, etc.</u> Englewood Cliffs, N. J.: Prentice-Hall.

This book, on systematization of the writing process, gives useful advice on formatting principles and creative use of word processing.

O'Connor, M. 1980. <u>Model guidelines for the preparation of camera-ready typescripts by authors/typists: Suggestions from an IFSEA-Ciba Foundation Workshop</u>. London: Ciba Foundation.

This manuscript describes in detail authors' responsibility for preparing camera-ready copy.

O'Neill, C. L. and Ruder, A. 1979. 2d. ed. The complete guide to editorial free-lancing. New York: Dodd-Mead.

This book provides advice on everything from finding work to keeping records. Readers should be warned that the tax information is not current.

Pate, E. and Spengler, B. 1980. Handbook for typists. Dubuque, Iowa: Kendall-Hunt.

This 8 1/2-by-11 book gives operational and technical information on the selectric typewriter. It also contains formats for letters, envelopes, and business forms. The booklet would help business education students, novice typists, and others who need technical information on business typing details. All techniques are directed to typists without word processing.

Root, W. 1979. Writing the script. New York: Holt, Rinehart, & Winston.

This book, directed at scriptwriters, would be most useful to scriptwriters and their typists.

Sandman, L. 1980. A guide to greeting card writing. Cincinnati: Writer's Digest Books.

This book, which explains the details of writing and marketing greeting card verses, would be useful mainly to writers and typists who specialize in greeting cards.

Smith, P. 1980. Simplified proofreading. Arlington, Virginia: National Composition Association.

This booklet on proofreading will help anyone who needs to learn the skill. For beginners, the book offers many practice exercises.

Society for Technical Communication. 1976. Typing guide for mathematical expressions. Washington, D.C.: Society for Technical Communication.

This booklet is an excellent guide for typists who want to achieve technical accuracy and professional quality in their typewritten documents. The STC's address is 815 Fifteenth Street. NW, Washington, D.C. 20005.

Stultz, R. A. 1981. The word processing handbook. Englewood Cliffs, N. J.: Prentice-Hall.

This book, written for managers, provides a great deal of technical information on word processing. Of special help to typists and writers who are purchasing word processors.

Sussman, M. B. 1978. <u>Author's guide to journals in sociology and related fields</u>. New York: Haworth.

This book contains data on the styles preferred by scholarly journals in the social and behavioral sciences.

Turabian, K. L. 1976. <u>Student's guide for writing college papers</u>. 3rd ed. Chicago: University of Chicago Press.

This classic has guided many students in writing class papers. It would help typists whose main clientele is students.

Van Duyn, J. 1975. <u>Practical systems and procedures manual</u>. Reston, Virginia: Reston.

This book describes many useful techniques for preparing instructions.

Waterhouse, S. A. 1979. <u>Word Processing Fundamentals</u>. New York: Harper & Row.

One of the better textbooks on word processing, this book provides a very useful introduction to word processing.

GRAMMAR AND USAGE

Bernstein, T. M. 1958. <u>Watch your language</u>. New York: Atheneum.

This book tells how to avoid common errors in usage. Entertainingly written.

------. 1965. <u>The careful writer: A modern guide to English usage</u>. New York: Atheneum.

This highly readable classic deals with many common errors in usage.

Follet, W. 1966. <u>Modern American usage</u>. New York: Hill & Wang.

Follet's is one of several books on usage. Editors, typists, and writers need at least one such book in their offices.

Fowler, H. W. 1965. <u>A dictionary of modern English usage</u>. 2d ed. Rev. by Sir Ernest Gowers. Oxford: Oxford University Press.

Fowler's is a classic guide to English usage.

Jordan, L., ed. 1976. <u>The New York Times manual of style and usage</u>. New York: Times Books.

This book is one of several guides to proper English usage. Topics are arranged alphabetically.

Morris, W. and M. 1975. <u>Harper dictionary of contemporary usage</u>. New York: Harper & Row.

This guide to language usage is distinguished by its reliance on a panel of experts who give their opinions on each topic raised by the authors.

Olsen, U. G. 1978. <u>Preparing the manuscript</u>. 9th ed. Boston: The Writer.

This small book, written before the blossoming of word processing, discusses tool and materials, typing mechanics, checking and correcting, and submitting a manuscript for publication. Additional sections discuss indexing, copyright regulations, author's rights, and permissions. Strong emphasis on the author's point of view.

Perrin, P. G. 1972. <u>Writer's guide and index to English</u>. Rev. ed. by Wilma R. Ebbitt. Glenview, Illinois: Scott, Foresman.

This book, which contains a highly useful salmon-colored index, is one of several good texts on grammar and writing.

1933. <u>The Oxford English dictionary</u>. Oxford: At the Clarendon Press.

The Oxford dictionary is the primary reference on correct British usage.

Strunk, W. and White, E. B. 1959. <u>The elements of style</u>. New York: Macmillan.

Many experts maintain that this excellent little classic says everything there is to be said about writing style.

Walpole, J. 1980. <u>A writer's guide: Easy ground rules for successful written English</u>. Englewood Cliffs, N. J.: Prentice-Hall.

This small book, designed to aid adults who need help with their writing, provides basic grammatical guidelines.

Annual. <u>Webster's new collegiate dictionary</u>. Springfield, Mass.: G. & C. Merriam.

The <u>Collegiate</u> is a reasonably complete and affordable dictionary.

1961. <u>Webster's third new international dictionary of the English language,
unabridged</u>. Springfield, Mass.: G. & C. Merriam.

The <u>Third</u> is considered by many to have the most nearly correct information
on American usage.

STYLE GUIDES

Major Styles

American Chemical Society. 1978. <u>Handbook for authors of papers in American
Chemical Society publications</u>. Washington, D. C.: American Chemical
Society. [1]

This 121-page book provides information on ACS books and journals, manuscript preparation, an editorial review.

American Mathematical Society. 1978. <u>A manual for authors of mathematical
papers</u>. Providence, R. I.: American Mathematical Society. [2]

This 20-page booklet explains organizing a paper, style requirements, type
and format requirements for equations, and publication policies of the AMS.

American Medical Association. 1981. Instructions for authors. <u>Journal of
the American Medical Association</u> 245 (6):560; Barclay, W. R., Southgate, M.
T., and Mayo, R. W. 1981. <u>Manual for authors & editors: Editorial style &
manuscript preparation</u>. 7th ed. Los Altos, Calif.: Lange Medical Publications. [3]

This brief style sheet and excellent book tell how to prepare manuscripts
for American Medical Association journals.

American Psychological Association. 1974. <u>Publication manual of the American
Psychological Association</u>. 2d ed. Washington, D. C.: American Psychological Association. [4]

This excellent manual sets the standards for more than 200 journals in and
outside psychology. It contains information on organization, clarity,
grammar, construction of tables and illustrations, style, and journal
procedures.

American Society for Testing and Materials. 1973. <u>ASTM style manual</u>.

Philadelphia: ASTM. See also American Society for Testing and Materials.
n.d. Instructions to authors of papers for ASTM journals. Philadelphia:
ASTM. [5]

This 35-page booklet and 4-page flyer contain information on writing a
paper, preparing a manuscript, and following ASTM style.

American Sociological Association. Notice to contributors. Inside front
cover of every issue of the American Sociological Review. [6]

These brief, sketchy guidelines describe only a few of the stylistic details that writers and typists need to know.

Council of Biology Editors Style Manual Committee. 1978. CBE style manual.
4th ed. Arlington, Virginia: Council of Biology Editors. [7]

This excellent, 265-page manual covers all aspects of preparing and publishing manuscripts in the biological sciences.

Craig, R. J. and Yeatts, H. W. 1976. The complete guide for writing technical articles. Norcross, Georgia: American Institute of Industrial Engineers. [8]

This 25-page booklet (8 1/2 by 11 format) tells why and how to write a
technical article and how to treat the mechanics. It also lists publications and addresses.

Hathwell, D. and Metzner, A. W. K. 1978. Style manual for guidance in the
preparation of papers for journals published by the American Institute of
Physics and its member societies. 3d ed. American Institute of Physics.
New York: American Institute of Physics. [9]

This excellent 56-page booklet (in 8 1/2 by 11 format) summarizes information for journal contributors and describes preparation of a scientific
paper, general style, and treatment of figures and mathematical
expressions. It has several useful appendixes.

Modern Language Association. 1977. MLA handbook. New York: MLA. [10]

This 163-page style manual covers most topics in manuscript preparation and
provides a model manuscript. It is of interest mainly to editors, writers,
and typists in the humanities.

Turabian, K. L. 1973. A manual for writers of term papers, theses, and dissertations. 4th ed. Chicago: University of Chicago Press. [11]

This 216-page book contains a wealth of information about writing and documenting research papers; includes detailed information on treatment of citations.

United States Government Printing Office. 1973. _United States Government Printing Office Style Manual_. Rev. ed. January 1973. Washington, D.C.: U.S. Government Printing Office. [12]

This thick book emphasizes printing requirements more than typing requirements. It gives many lists of GPO's preferred spellings.

University of Chicago Press. 1979. _A manual of style_. 12th ed., rev. Chicago: University of Chicago Press. [13]

This book contains information on writing, manuscript typing, editing, indexing, and many other topics related to publishing. It is a style guide for many publications. A revised guide is due in June 1982.

Minor Styles

American Anthropologist. 1977. Style guide and information for authors. _American Anthropologist_ 79 (4):774-779.

These guidelines, followed by many publications in anthropology, describe a style that is much like the style of the American Sociological Association.

American Journal of Orthopsychiatry. 1981. Information for contributors. _American Journal of Orthopsychiatry_ 51 (1).

These brief guidelines describe a style much like that of the American Mathematical Society.

American Journal of Sociology. 1981. Information for contributors. _American Journal of Sociology_ 87 (1):vii-viii.

These brief guidelines describe a style much like that of the _Manual of Style_'s natural science style--the style used in this book.

American National Standards Institute. 1977. _American national standard for bibliographic references_. New York: American National Standards Institute.

These guidelines are followed, in part, by some of the major styles.

Journal of the American Statistical Association. 1977. _JASA_ style guide for authors. _Journal of the American Statistical Association_ 72 (359, September):696-702.

These detailed guidelines are primarily of interest to editors, writers, and typists in statistical and mathematical fields.

Index Medicus. 1981. Change of Index Medicus citation format. Index Medicus (August):xvii.

These brief guidelines describe a style much like that of the AMA. It follows American National Standards Institute (ANSI) standards.

International Steering Committee. n.d. Uniform requirements for manuscripts submitted to biomedical journals.

This 11-page booklet, available from the American Medical Association, describes a style very similar to that of the AMA.

Linguistic Society of America. n.d. LSA style sheet. Arlington, Virginia: Linguistic Society of America.

These brief guidelines describe a style much like that of the Manual of Style's natural science style.

Sage Publications. n.d. Guide for preparation of mathematical and quantitative material. Beverly Hills, California: Sage Publications.

These brief (3-page) guidelines leave out many essential topics. They are of interest mainly to editors, writers, and typist who specialize in professional social science manuscripts.

Social Forces. n.d. Instructions to authors. Chapel Hill, N.C.: Social Forces.

These brief instructions describe a style much like that of the American Sociological Association.

Standing Committee on Publications of the British Psychological Society. 1971. Suggestions to authors. Rev. ed. London: Standing Committee on Publications of the British Psychological Society.

This 19-page booklet covers a style of interest mainly to editors, writers, and typists of manuscripts in psychology intended for British publication.

Index